A Virgin Conceived

A Virgin Conceived

Mary and Classical Representations of Virginity

MARY F. FOSKETT

INDIANA
University Press
Bloomington & Indianapolis

This book is a publication of

Indiana University Press
601 North Morton Street
Bloomington, Indiana 47404-3797 USA

http://iupress.indiana.edu

Telephone orders 800-842-6796
Fax orders 812-855-7931
Orders by email iuporder@indiana.edu

© 2002 by Mary F. Foskett

The paper used in this publication meets
the minimum requirements of American
National Standard for Information
Sciences—Permanence of Paper for
Printed Library Materials, ANSI
Z39.48-1984.

Manufactured in the United States of
America

Library of Congress Cataloging-in-Publication Data

Foskett, Mary F., date
A virgin conceived : Mary and classical representations of virginity / Mary F. Foskett.
    p. cm.
Includes bibliographical references and index.
    ISBN 0-253-34055-1 (alk. paper)
    1. Mary, Blessed Virgin, Saint—Virginity—History of doctrines—Early church,
ca. 30–600. 2. Virginity—Religious aspects—History of doctrines. 3. Bible. N.T.
Luke—Criticism, interpretation, etc. 4. Bible. N.T. Acts—Criticism, interpretation,
etc. 5. Protevangelium Jacobi—Criticism, interpretation, etc.   I. Title.
    BT625 .F67 2002
    232.91'3—dc21

                                                                            2001004784

1 2 3 4 5   07 06 05 04 03 02

CONTENTS

Preface

This study proposes a fresh look at the Virgin Mary by asking not what the Virgin means, but what virginity connotes for and adds to the portrayal of Mary in two early Christian narratives, namely Luke-Acts and the Protevangelium of James. By placing these texts in the context of ancient discourse about virginity and virgins, I have aimed to expose the multivalence of virginity in antiquity as well as ways in which the characterization of Mary resonates with particular images and meanings associated with female sexual status. Although not all of my conclusions about the characterization of Mary are original to this study, the path to them represents a new way of inquiring into the language that has given shape to centuries of Marian reflection.

I owe many thanks to the staff of Indiana University Press for taking on this project. I am especially grateful for the suggestions, criticisms, and support of the senior and assistant sponsoring editors, Robert Sloan and Kendra Boileau Stokes, without whom this book would not have been published. Thanks, too, to the copy editor, Carol Kennedy, for her excellent and careful work.

As this book is a revision of the doctoral dissertation that I completed in 1997, I am indebted to Gail O'Day, Vernon Robbins, Carl Holladay, and most especially Luke Johnson, my teachers, mentors, and friends in New Testament studies at Emory University. While they bear no responsibility for the book's inevitable shortcomings, the best that this study has to offer is due in large part to the time, energy, criticism, and support that they each contributed to it.

I owe special thanks, too, to Alexandra Brown, Mary Pendergraft, and Carol LaHurd, friends and colleagues who read sections of the manuscript and offered critical insights and suggestions. I also want to gratefully acknowledge the assistance that Jeannette Quick and Brad Tharpe, students at the Wake Forest University Divinity School, provided me as I prepared the manuscript for publication.

Finally, I dedicate this book to my husband, Scott Hudgins, with deepest thanks.

A Virgin Conceived

Which Virgin? What Virginity?

One

Since the earliest decades of Christianity, interpreters and adherents of the tradition have pondered the virginity of Mary, the mother of Jesus. In recent scholarship, biblical interpreters and theologians alike have examined the significance of Mary's virginity. Although biblical scholars have given extensive consideration to what the Gospels of Matthew and Luke seem to suggest about Jesus when underscoring the virginity of his mother, much less attention has been given to how such narrative detail figures in the portrayal of Mary herself, let alone how it has helped shape Mary's place in Christian tradition.[1] While the christological relevance of Mary's sexual status is an undoubtedly important dimension of both texts, we need not assume that christocentric concern exhausts the rhetorical significance of Mary's virginity. Instead, we may examine what virginity can mean for how readers envision Mary.

As Jaroslav Pelikan has observed, scriptural study has dominated but not entirely controlled theological contemplation of the Virgin.[2] In contemporary theological circles, feminist interpreters especially have explored the symbolic meaning of Mary's sexual status.[3] Consensus, however, has proven elusive. Some feminist readers have associated Mary's virginity with a misogyny that reifies male power over women, subordinates female sexuality and creativity to a virginal ideal, and perpetuates the notion of femininity as passive receptivity. Others have found in Mary's virginity a positive expression of female autonomy and power. Thus feminist reflection demonstrates both the positive and the negative connotations that Mary's sexual status can evoke.

As fruitful and provocative as previous studies have been, none has focused primarily on the significance and meaning of virginity in the ancient narratives that provide the basis for Christian veneration of Mary. The roots of the traditions and celebrations associated with the virginity of Mary are, for the most part, connected with narrative details located in Luke's Gospel and the second-century extracanonical composition the Protevangelium of James (hereafter also identified as PJ). Although scholars have addressed the development of virginity as a Christian ideal in late antiquity, much more can be said of the early texts that served as a foundation for later Christian understandings of Mary and female sexuality.[4]

The Virgin(s) of Early Christian Imagination

Modern interpreters of Luke-Acts and the Protevangelium of James have long regarded allusions to Mary's virginity as significant in both narratives.[5] Lucan scholars have most often pondered the virginity of Mary in the context of asking whether or not Luke's story implies the virginal conception of Jesus (Lk 1.26–38). Interpreters of PJ have noted both the narrative's emphatic portrayal of Mary's sexual status and the theme of purity that permeates Mary's story. In Luke's writing, Mary is in primary focus only in the first two chapters of the Gospel and then again at the opening of Luke's sequel, Acts. In contrast to its canonical predecessor, the second-century Protevangelium retains Mary as its central protagonist and narrates her biography, rather than that of her son.

Despite the prominence that virginity enjoys in both canonical and extracanonical portrayals of Mary, critical differences in the way that each narrative refers to her virginity quickly emerge. In the Lucan account, Mary's sexual status is mentioned twice, but in only a single scene (Lk 1.26–38). She implicitly relinquishes her virginity when she weds Joseph. In PJ, Mary's virginity is repeatedly underscored, and her sexual status remains unchanged even after she marries Joseph and gives birth to Jesus. Her virginity yields to nothing and no one. Thus the well-known designation *virgin birth* properly refers to PJ, not to the more familiar Gospel of Luke.[6] Whereas Luke focuses on the extraordinary nature of Mary's pregnancy, the apocryphal text casts Mary's virginity itself as cause for wonder and praise. In short, each text's contextualization and emphasis of Mary's sexual status differs from the other's. With respect to these two early Christian texts, it is clearly insufficient to speak of *the* Virgin Mary. Instead we must ask, which Virgin? And of what virginity do we speak?

Although each figure is identified as a *parthenos,* from their respective narrative contexts the Lucan and apocryphal Mary emerge as distinctly different *parthenoi.* Thus it is immediately clear that the term *parthenos* is capable not only of functioning in different narrative contexts but of giving rise to a number of images and meanings. The multiplicity of these images is notable. Whereas New Testament interpreters have long wrestled with the ambiguity of *parthenos* (whether it more properly denotes a "virgin" or a young woman) we may now address its multivalence by seeking and exploring not a single or "better" meaning, but a constellation of images and expectations that *parthenos* connotes. Therefore the aim of this study is to examine the significance of virginity for readers' constructions of Mary by identifying both what virginity implies and what it contributes to the characterization of Mary in Luke-Acts and PJ. The concern of this project is not the historical Mary, but rather the literary figure who emerges from these early Christian texts. It is in this sense that virginity can be seen not only as a vehicle for christology but as a Marian character indicator, a textual sign that lends shape specifically to Mary's portrayal.

In both narratives, references to virginity help readers envision the character "Mary." Understood as a construct and effect of reading, a character is an impression that, once formed in the process of reading, attains a degree of autonomy that outlasts the reading process itself. As one narrative critic suggests:

> To say that "character" is a construct that is developed during the reading process means, on the one hand, that character as an effect of reading can be reduced to textuality. . . . On the other hand, character as an effect of the reading process can "transcend" the text.[7]

In the history of interpretation, Mary has often been afforded such textual transcendence and analyzed as an autonomous and reified religious symbol. However, because this investigation is concerned with the process that precedes consideration of Mary as an extratextual icon, my focus is on the narrative construction of Mary, a "paradigm of attributive propositions" that emerges in the very act of reading to lend the reader "the illusion of individuality or even personality."[8] Specifically, it is the significance of related character indicators, *parthenos* and *parthenia* (virginity), for the construction of Mary in Luke-Acts and PJ with which this study is most interested.

Constructing the Virgin Mary

In order to proceed to a discussion of Mary's narrative portrayal, attention must be given to the nature of characterization. We may well ask, how does the character Mary emerge from a narrative text to reside in the imagination of a reader?[9] Does the text simply set the image of Mary before the reader, or does the reader conjure her character in a more active manner? These are questions with which literary theorists and biblical critics alike are concerned. As Petri Merenlahti queries, "the mystery of biblical characters is the mystery of the mustard seed: how

does so much come out of so little? How do figures who are
sketched with only a few harsh strokes manage to give an impression of individuality and personhood?"[10] In the absence of a
dominant theory of character, critics have tended to work induc-
tively, analyzing the data they discover in the process of reading.[11] For example, Baruch Hochman and Seymour Chatman
focus on the occurrence of character traits to examine the dynamics of characterization.[12] John Darr, a biblical scholar, studies Lucan characterization by analyzing the data that accumu-
lates in a linear reading of the third Gospel.[13] In her monograph
on the portrayal of Mary in early Christian literature, Beverly
Roberts Gaventa subjects a variety of narratives to a list of questions about each text's depiction of the character.[14]

With modern literary theorists failing to produce a dominant theory of characterization, one may wonder whether ancient critics fared any better. Given the paucity of extant narrative theory, it is ancient rhetorical theory that appears to have
addressed most the topic of characterization. The observations
and recommendations of ancient rhetoricians demonstrate that
here, too, theories of characterization were largely inductive and
dependent upon both conventional values and practices. For example, in situations that called for epideictic rhetoric, writers
were advised to use modes of speech and *topoi* that reflected and
reinforced accepted social values, cultural scripts, and ethical
norms.[15] Indeed, writers identified and recommended *topoi* similar to those one sees at work in Luke-Acts and PJ. Although the
two compositions are clearly narratives and not speeches, each
engages the rhetorical devices and strategies recommended by
ancient rhetoricians.[16]

Despite Scholes and Kellogg's famous dictum that the characters of ancient literature are "invariably 'flat,' 'static,' and quite
'opaque,'" biblical interpreters have demonstrated the complexity
of characterization in biblical texts.[17] David Gowler, Robert Alter, and others have observed the relative dynamism and intri-
cacy of ancient, including biblical, characters.[18] As has been
noted in studies that have tended to draw heavily on the reader-
oriented theory of Wolfgang Iser and Meier Sternberg, readers
construct images of characters as they assimilate the various

clues that narratives provide about them.[19] These textual clues function as "character indicators," that is, as data that readers bring together and assess in order to construct the impression of a character. Although such information is provided by narrative elements such as plot and setting, as well as by the speech, actions, and traits attributed to specific characters, it is the work of the reader that realizes characterization. Alone, a text is only a framework for meaning, replete with formal patterns marked nevertheless by "blanks" and "gaps of indeterminacy."[20] It is the reader who performs the "variety of cognitive acts within a temporal (sequential) framework" necessary to render perceived patterns of signification meaningful.[21] Accordingly, interpretation is grounded not in isolated textual elements, but in the "configurative meanings" that readers construct.[22]

Because readers always make use of information external to a given text in order to actualize it, a literary work functions as a synthesis of both textual and extratextual data. Often without realizing it, readers regularly engage material absent from a text in order to assign meaning to the data they retrieve and to negotiate any narrative gaps that arise over the course of reading. It is precisely this dimension of reading, the dynamic interaction of text and reader, that allows us to move beyond the impasse created by interpreters who aim to cast Mary in definitive and sometimes contrasting terms. Because "the potential text is infinitely richer than any of its individual realizations," no single pattern of reading and no particular construction of Mary should be taken as inherently normative.[23] The notion of character-as-construction serves to draw attention away from the misguided goal of arriving at a single apprehension of Mary and allows us to focus instead on those textual and extratextual cues with which readers work to create an impression of her. Therefore, rather than seeking a normative image of Mary, I aim to explore a particular dimension of Mary's portrayal, her sexual status, and its significance in different literary contexts. This is a road not previously taken by interpreters of Mary's virginity.

The notion that "every text is a product of various cultural discourses" undergirds my presupposition that when we read ancient texts in the context of the cultural discourses from which they emerged and with which they were originally engaged, we gain specific insights into the literature.[24] Not a new idea, this perspective has been brought to bear repeatedly on New Testament interpretation. For example, Abraham Malherbe pioneered interpretation of the Pauline corpus in light of Greco-Roman epistolary traditions and the symbolic world of ancient popular philosophy.[25] In Gospel studies, characterization has been examined from a similar perspective. Because characters stand in relation to both a given text and "characteristics not immediately signaled in the text, but familiar from other texts and from life," a reader's repertoire of cultural images and meanings exercises a significant role in character construction.[26] In Gospel studies, David Gowler has employed socio-rhetorical criticism to analyze Luke's portrayal of the Pharisees, and Darr has highlighted the work of a reader who "weaves together text and extratext" to produce the effect of Lucan characterization.[27] Similarly, interpreters of the Protevangelium have noted the motifs and language that the narrative shares with both Jewish and Greco-Roman literature.[28] Reading Luke-Acts and PJ in terms of the larger cultural matrix in which they were generated is consistent with much recent New Testament interpretation.

My interest in examining the ways in which Mary's portrayal as a virgin resonates with, exploits, reinscribes, or subverts cultural notions of virginity shares some of the concerns of New Historicist biblical interpretation.[29] Like critics working in New Historicism, I proceed on the assumption that rather than simply reflecting a particular historical-cultural context, Luke-Acts and PJ function as participants in a larger cultural discourse wherein "text and culture are understood to be in a mutually productive relation to one another."[30] In other words, this study is interested in both how our early Christian texts represent virginity and how they "use" cultural constructions of virginity to advance the characterization of Mary. As evidenced in chapters 2 and 3, consideration of cultural notions of virginity contemporary with Luke-Acts and the Protevangelium of James constitutes an essential component of this project. There I identify as extratextually relevant a broad spectrum of material that would have been readily accessible to persons of the late first- to middle second-century Mediterranean world, namely, the literature of the early Roman empire. Keeping in mind the symbiotic relationship between text and cultural norms, in chapters 4 and 5 I bring this material to bear on textual cues in Luke and PJ that pertain to Mary's virginity. My purpose is to reconstruct neither ancient readers nor their experience of reading, but the connotations and images implied by Mary's sexual status when Luke-Acts and PJ are read alongside other ancient texts.

Thus three primary objectives direct the methodology and design of this investigation: (1) establishment of the multivalence of *parthenia* in literature of the first- and second-century Mediterranean world; (2) establishment of the ambivalence of ancient narrative representations of *parthenia;* and (3) identification of images of *parthenia* that resonate with and mutually reinforce the portrayals of Mary in Luke-Acts and the Protevangelium. The construction of a literary character forms one part of this study. Attention to the "cultural intertexture" of texts serves as another.[31] Finally, by bringing the multivalence of *parthenia* in literature contemporary with our two narratives to bear on the portrayal of Mary, I invite readers to consider the different ways in which two Christian texts advance the construction of Mary as a virgin and render her virginity meaningful.

Foundations of the Investigation

While this project takes a new approach to a familiar question, it depends upon and is greatly indebted to previous readings of Luke-Acts and PJ. Although scholarly interpretation of Luke-Acts far exceeds that devoted to PJ, both narratives have been objects of rigorous investigation. The following overview of pertinent aspects of earlier scholarship underscores the issues and questions that have generated my consideration of Mary and her virginity. Previous textual and literary analyses, as well as modern interpretations of Mary in Luke-Acts and PJ, provide the foundation for the present study.

LITERARY FOUNDATIONS

Luke-Acts

Whether it is characterized as the preview, overture, prologue, or introduction to the Gospel, the narrative and rhetorical significance of Luke 1–2 (the so-called infancy narrative) is now generally recognized.[32] Not only have scholars assumed the integrity of the opening chapters of the Gospel, they have found within the infancy narrative key themes that function programmatically throughout the larger story.[33] With the rise of narrative and rhetorical criticism, biblical interpreters have assimilated a variety of literary strategies into their reading of Luke-Acts and shed new light on the significance of the Gospel's opening chapters.[34] Previously suspected of having little bearing on the rest of the narrative, Luke 1–2 is now seen as critical for understanding the Gospel. Today the burden of proof rests with those interpreters who would argue against the integrity of the infancy narrative.

Arguments for the unity of Luke-Acts also undergird my analysis of Mary's characterization.[35] Only in a narrative that can reasonably be read as a unity can we examine figures *as* characters, that is, as literary constructs "that are named, that are endowed with traits, and that 'ask' us to envision them, for a moment at least on the model of people."[36] Although Mary functions as a dominant figure in the infancy narrative and only a minor player in the remainder of Luke-Acts, the narrative nevertheless creates the effect of a single literary personality. It is in this sense that I refer to Mary as a discrete Lucan character.

The Protevangelium of James

Efforts to establish the text and literary unity of the Protevangelium of James have dominated scholarship on this early Christian document.[37] While a definitive edition of PJ has not yet been published, several critical texts have appeared.[38] The present project depends largely upon Ronald F. Hock's recent edition of PJ.[39] As is the case with Luke-Acts, this study follows the work of recent interpreters in presupposing the unity of PJ.[40] Like Hock and Gaventa, who have not only assumed the literary unity of PJ, but also read and analyzed the text as a coherent narrative, I read the text as a single story that presents the figure of Mary as a single character.[41]

IMAGES OF MARY IN LUKE-ACTS: LOOKING BACK AND LOOKING AHEAD

Lucan interpretation is rife with discussions of Mary. Consideration of the nature and range of the various images associated with Mary provides an important context for this investigation, for they attest to the complexity of Luke's narrative and provide a framework for examining the significance of Mary's sexual status.

The Mother of Jesus

Since at least the middle of the second century, the figure of Mary as the virgin mother of Jesus has been the cause for pious wonderment and the locus of heated debate. Countering charges that Mary's pregnancy was illegitimate and all too profane, early patristic writers strove to defend both the honor of Mary's virginal maternity and the legitimacy of Jesus.[42] As doctrine concerning the extraordinary nature of Mary's maternity exercised an increasingly important role in the formation of a catholic christology, the figures of both Mary and Jesus stood at the center of the great christological debates of the fifth and sixth centuries. It was precisely because they refused to honor Mary as *theotokos*, the "mother of God," that Nestorius and the Antiochene church came under condemnation.[43]

Mary's maternal identity is the most christologically relevant dimension of her character. Yet the meaning and significance of her role as mother are not always easy to discern. At times, her maternal persona appears to be quite complex. In the scenes that recount the events surrounding Jesus' birth (Lk 2.1–7, 8–20), Mary is set apart from other characters. As Gaventa observes,

> The story provides scant glorification of Mary, since its focus everywhere is the baby rather than the mother. And yet at several points Luke distinguishes Mary and her response from others who are also present. . . . These brief notices serve several func-

tions in the narrative, one of which is to capture the very normal attachment of mother to child.[44]

While all who hear the shepherds' account of their encounter with an angel in the fields are amazed (2.17–18), Luke distinguishes Mary by commenting upon her response in particular. Having listened to the shepherds, she alone keeps their words in her heart (2.19). Yet even as such description at first appears to align Mary and her son, subsequent references serve instead to distance them. Luke's portrayal of Mary as a mother who ponders, but fails to understand, the events around her is rather cryptic (2.33, 50). Is Mary a figure of wisdom and insight? Or is she an unwitting player in a story of which she is only partly aware?[45] Gaventa underscores the narrative tension created by Mary's seeming ignorance.[46] Heikki Räisänen sees Mary not only as the mother of Jesus but as a member of the eschatalogical family.[47] That Mary is the mother of Luke's protagonist is clear; the implications of her role, however, are not.

As it is Mary who receives Simeon's prophecy that her own soul will be pierced by a sword (Lk 2.35), Mary's maternity has frequently been associated with suffering. Seen in this light, the same woman who had been gifted with divine favor suffers the tragic loss of her firstborn to death by crucifixion. Despite the popularity of viewing Mary as the prototypical suffering mother, Raymond E. Brown and Joseph A. Fitzmyer both dismiss the image, for, unlike the Fourth Gospel, the Lucan narrative fails to place Mary at the foot of the cross.[48] Gaventa, however, allows for this interpretation of Luke's portrayal of Mary and observes how the air of foreboding that Simeon's oracle infuses into the narrative lends Mary's character a certain roundness.[49] Whether cast in terms of suffering or not, Mary's role as the mother of Jesus is rich and complex.

Ideal Disciple

While Mary's maternal role is never altogether dismissed by any interpreters, some have questioned whether maternity is indeed the most significant dimension of her characterization. For although Mary's identity as the mother of Jesus certainly distinguishes her, her portrayal is also laden with the images and themes of discipleship. Identifying the virgin's faithfulness as the very reason why God selected her to give birth to Jesus in the first place, some interpreters see in Mary Luke's prototypical disciple.[50] Fitzmyer holds that it is because she embodies the ideal of Christian discipleship that Mary is suited for the role of Jesus' mother.[51] She is blessed precisely because she is one who believes the Word of the Lord (cf. Lk 1.45). According to this reading, it is Mary's faithfulness that most distinguishes her.

Lucan passages that allude to Mary's faith either explicitly (Lk 1.45) or implicitly (Lk 8.21, 11.27–28) reinforce the faithfulness associated with her in the annunciation scene.[52] Interpreters see in Mary's response to the angel's message (1.38), her activity following the birth of Jesus (2.19, 21–24, 33), and her reaction to Jesus in the Temple (2.45–51) repeated evidence of her patience and commitment. Long before the appearance of the twelve, the image of Mary as exemplar of faith is etched into Luke's narrative landscape.

For some, Mary's presence at Pentecost (Acts 1.14) confirms her status as a disciple.[53] Gathered with the faithful in Jerusalem, Mary witnesses and receives the sending of the Holy Spirit. Indeed, she is the only figure whom Luke places at the opening of both the Gospel and Acts. It is she alone who welcomes the initiating activity of the Spirit both before and after Jesus' earthly appearance.

Biblical Symbol

Reading the infancy narrative in the context of the Jewish scriptures whose influence is evidenced in the Septuagintal syntax and style of Luke's opening chapters, a number of scholars have noted the biblical images that resonate throughout Luke's presentation of Mary and have debated whether and to what degree Mary embodies particular Septuagintal themes and images. The symbols most often associated with the Lucan Mary, each a subject of debate, are those of the Daughter of Zion, the Ark of the Covenant, and the Tabernacle.[54] The Marian significance attributed to each image rests largely upon lexical data. In some cases, interpreters depend upon patterns of meaning and language that Luke and the Septuagint share. In others, readers depend upon little more than the occurrence of a single commonly held verb to suggest that Mary represents a biblical symbol. Although the latter readings suffer from being somewhat atomistic, they highlight nonetheless the intertextual dimension of Luke's narrative and remind us that a variety of images can figure in the portrayal of a single character. Most pertinent to this study, intertextual insights open the door to investigating the portrayal of Mary in light of literature other than the Septuagint. For as significant as the Septuagint may have been for Luke, it was surely not the only text on either his literary horizon or that of his readers.

Servant of the Lord

In a manner of reading that represents a fusion of the approaches noted above, Mary's narrative role has been considered in terms of both biblical themes and motifs that are distinctive to Luke's Gospel. Attentive to the Lucan emphasis on Mary's faithfulness as well as the importance that biblical tradition places upon religious fidelity, some interpreters have chosen to underscore Mary's role as servant of the Lord. When she is compared with well-known biblical figures, the virgin's place among her literary foremothers and forefathers emerges. Like Abraham, Isaac, Jacob, Moses, Joshua, David, Hannah, and the prophets, Mary demonstrates an unconditional willingness to serve the Lord. When she declares, "Let it be to me according to your word" (Lk 1.38), Mary becomes a model servant, prefiguring all those in the narrative who carry on the scriptural tradition of obedient service to God (cf. Lk 2.29; Acts 4.29).[55]

Luke not only perpetuates the biblical ideal of servanthood, he elevates it by developing its eschatological significance and casting Jesus as its exemplar (cf. Acts 2.18, 3.13). Having established Jesus as a model servant in the Gospel, Luke portrays the disciples in Acts as prophet-servants. But as the exemplar of servanthood in the Gospel's opening chapter, it is Mary, not Jesus, who introduces Luke's interpretation of the servant tradition.[56] Luke uses her to establish continuity between Israel's servant traditions and the ministry of Jesus. Thus it is Mary who first serves as the pivotal figure in God's unfolding plan.

In her discussion of the identification of Mary as *doule* (slave), Jane Schaberg emphasizes the sexual exploitation to which female slaves in the ancient world are known to have been subjected. As she considers the resonance of such imagery with Mary's predicament in Luke, Schaberg begins to expose the sometimes rich, sometimes disturbing complexity of the images that coalesce around the character.[57] Although her reading is more provocative than it is conclusive, it is helpful in raising the question of how Mary's sexual status interacts with other character indicators.

Prophet and Spokeswoman for the Poor

Ever since the artistry of the speeches in Luke-Acts first came to the attention of biblical scholars, Luke 1.46–55 ("the Magnificat") has been the subject of much inquiry.[58] As the first speech in Luke-Acts and the only such form ascribed to Mary, its importance for understanding the Lucan portrayal of Mary cannot be overestimated. The Magnificat plays a significant role in two popular images of the Lucan Mary. Since the canticle is rendered in a cycle of aorist verbs and refers to the future fulfillment of God's plan as if it has already occurred, it is often seen as an instance of prophetic speech.[59] Although the narrative stops short of explicitly identifying Mary as a prophet per se (cf. 1.67), it ascribes to her speech that nevertheless casts her in such a light.[60] The Magnificat demonstrates that not only is Mary cognizant of God's plan, she is moved to declare it openly.

The characterization, if not the designation, of Mary as prophet finds important support in the prophetic role that the Holy Spirit occupies throughout Luke-Acts.[61] As the Spirit of prophecy, it is the Holy Spirit who directly inspires the prophetic utterance of all the canticles in Luke 1–2. When Gabriel declares that the same Spirit will come upon Mary (Lk 1.35), the virgin is implicitly ushered into the prophetic dimension of Luke's story.[62] Turid Karlsen Seim suggests that the very message of the Holy Spirit coming upon Mary (Lk 1.35) functions as a consciously rendered parallel to Jesus' words to his disciples in Luke 24.49 and Acts 1.8.[63] Whether or not such a parallel was intended by the author, like John (Lk 1.76), the prophets before him, and Jesus yet to come, Mary is clearly an object of and witness to the Spirit's activity. Like the prophets before her, she declares the justice and salvation of God. And in speaking prophetically, Mary prefigures those male characters whose own bold speech in Luke and Acts makes known the *boule tou theou*, or plan of God (cf. Lk 1.67–79; Acts 2.14–36, 3.11–26, 7.2–53).

Not only does Mary speak prophetically, she voices particular concern for the poor and oppressed. Among interpreters who have concentrated on the historical and theological significance of the hymn, Brown contends that the Magnificat, like all the canticles in the Lucan infancy narrative, originated in a Jewish-Christian eschatologically oriented community similar to that of the so-called Jewish Anawim. He argues that though

> this title meaning the "Poor Ones" may have originally desig-
> nated the physically poor (and frequently still included them), it
> came to refer more widely to those who could not trust in their
> own strength but had to rely in utter confidence upon God: the
> lowly, the poor, the sick, the downtrodden, the widows and or-
> phans.[64]

After noting how the canticle supports the Lucan theme of eschatological reversal, Brown goes on to suggest that Luke borrowed the Magnificat from an earlier source and attributed it to Mary.[65] Whether the hymn was borrowed or, perhaps even more probably, penned by Luke himself, it functions to cast Mary as a representative of the oppressed. She proclaims hope and redemption to those who, poor in either standing or means, look to the God of Israel for their salvation.

Reading from an ideological rather than historical perspective, other interpreters have also identified Mary as the representative of a suffering and marginalized people.[66] According to liberationist interpretation, Mary's speech is a powerful testimony to God's preferential option for the poor and oppressed. She embodies both the promise and the fulfillment of the redemption of her people Israel. Just as she introduces the ideal of

A Virgin Conceived ⤳ 16

servanthood, so does Mary give voice to the liberative themes that recur in the preaching of both John (Lk 3.10–14) and Jesus (Lk 4.18–19).

Parthenos

In the midst of multiple understandings of Mary, one is hard pressed to find discussions that do not mention, at some level, Luke's portrayal of her as a *parthenos* (Lk 1.27). New Testament interpreters have long addressed the problematic ambiguity of the term *parthenos,* an issue that has vexed Christian interpreters since at least the mid-second century.[67] Both the Septuagint's *parthenos* and the roughly corresponding Hebrew *betulah* of the Masoretic Text can refer to either sexual status, age, or both. The terms are therefore alternatively translated as "virgin" or "young woman."[68] Scholarly consideration of *parthenos* not only has demonstrated the futility of making a hard and fast decision as to its proper translation, it has confirmed the importance of attending to the literary context in which the term appears.

Thus Lucan interpreters have debated whether the context of Luke 1.27 better affords the translation of *parthenos* as "virgin" or "young woman." While Luke 1.27 by itself allows for either rendering, Mary's question in Luke 1.34 tips the interpretive scale toward the translation "virgin." It is precisely because of her sexual inexperience that she asks Gabriel, "How can this be, since I know no man?"[69] Although the notion that Mary is here a virgin (Lk 1.26–38) meets little resistance, much debate has ensued over whether the angel's message implies a virginal conception. Indeed, discussions of Mary's virginity almost inevitably turn into explications of Jesus' conception.

In an overwhelming majority of interpretations of Luke 1–2, it is christological interest in Jesus' conception that dominates consideration of Mary's sexual status.[70] Arguing that the Lucan annunciation was incompatible with the notion of a virginal conception of Jesus, Fitzmyer once suggested that the angel's promise, rendered in the future tense, *syllempse* ("you shall conceive"), not only failed to preclude a natural conception but implied a natural and legitimate pregnancy that was to commence after Joseph and Mary's wedding.[71] Whereas Fitzmyer later altered his position, Schaberg, too, has proposed a less than supernatural explanation for Mary's pregnancy. Casting an altogether different light on the notion that Jesus was conceived by natural means, Schaberg argues that Luke drew on an ancient tradition of Jesus' illegitimacy and offered a theologically significant interpretation of Mary's pregnancy.[72] According to Schaberg's reading, the annunciation foreshadows both the (unnarrated) sexual violation of the virgin and her subsequent redemption. It is the promise of consolation and restoration, not conception, that Mary hears in the angel's assurance: "The Holy Spirit will come upon you and the power of the Most High will overshadow you" (Lk 1.35). The *tapeinosis* (lowliness, disgrace) to which she later refers (Lk 1.48) is her own sexual humiliation. As Schaberg reasons, the wonder of Mary's pregnancy rests not in its origin, but in its redemption.

In contrast to these readings, numerous scholars have cited the structure of step parallelism in Luke 1–2, the narrative logic of Mary's question in Luke 1.34, and the narrator's comment in Luke 3.23 that Jesus was the supposed son of Joseph (*hos enomizeto*) as cumulative evidence that the narrative does indeed point to a virginal conception.[73] According to this majority interpretation, Mary's question serves to underscore the supernatural origin of her conception, a phenomenon that surpasses even the miraculous pregnancy of Elizabeth, her aged kinswoman.[74] The structure and content of the final form of the infancy narrative imply the virginal conception of Jesus.

The abundance of commentary on this issue only underscores the degree to which attention to Mary's sexual status has often had little to do with Luke's portrayal of Mary and everything to do with the Lucan Jesus. Brown writes, "Indeed, the virginal conception of Jesus is affirmed, but it is set forth in order to explain something about him, not primarily about Mary."[75] While Brown is surely correct in seeing that Mary's sexual status figures in the characterization of Jesus, his claim need not eclipse the significance of virginity for the portrayal of Mary. In Luke 1–2, Mary's character is presented on the model of a young Jewish virgin. By immediately presenting her sexual status, the narrative identifies virginity as a key dimension of

Mary's portrayal. It is an early textual cue that conveys essential information about her. When we read that Mary is a *parthenos* (Lk 1.27), we may well ask what such direct description might connote. What does virginity add to the portrayal of Mary? How does it shape the images with which she is associated? The paradox of virgin maternity not withstanding, we may yet investigate how Mary's sexual status informs her own characterization.

Scholars searching for non-Christian origins of the infancy account also exhibit a primary interest in Lucan christology, particularly its historical development and cultural milieu. For instance, rather than generally surveying ancient discourse about virgins, they limit their investigations to a quest for parallels in Jewish and Hellenistic infancy stories of cult heroes. The male hero with which such accounts are concerned serves as the starting point for comparison.[76] The claim that Luke's account avoids the *hieros gamos* (sacred marriage) of pagan myth is driven more by concern for Lucan christology than by interest in the portrayal of Mary.[77] The significance of ancient traditions concerning *parthenia* need no longer be limited to this single dimension of Luke's story.

Lucan interpretation has prepared the way for examining the multiple images and meanings that virginity, in general, and Mary's virginity, in particular, might connote. Understanding the possible implications of Mary's sexual status may help clarify issues raised by previous studies. For instance, against those who look to Mary's virginity to posit the Lucan identification of her as the Daughter of Zion, Brown and others have argued that "(t)he connection of Mary as 'virgin' to Mary as 'Daughter of Zion' is dubious, since almost all the OT references to the virgin Zion or virgin Israel are uncomplimentary, portraying her in a state of oppression, waywardness, and lust."[78] Contra Brown, Schaberg agrees that the Lucan Mary is cast in only a positive light but then suggests that the image of the virgin as a victim of sexual oppression (cf. Lam 5.11) is precisely what Luke has in mind.[79] The validity of each of these suggestions depends in part on what readers can surmise about the significance and implications of Mary's identity as *parthenos*.

Consideration of her prophetic role also calls for a closer look at what Mary's sexual status might connote. Although the relationship between Mary's prophetic identity and her sexual status remained unexamined by Brown, he nevertheless allowed for the possibility of an inherent connection between prophecy and virginity. In a single footnote in his mammoth study of the infancy narratives, he observes: "We may speculate whether in Luke's view the celibate status had something to do with the ability to prophesy. The four daughters of Philip who prophesy are unmarried."[80] Historian Peter Brown also posits a possible connection between virginity and prophecy in Luke 1.34–35 and Acts 21.9.[81] More recently, Seim has gone farther and suggested that Mary's virginity should be viewed "in light of her prophetic capacity."[82]

Reconsidering Virginity

An overview of the way in which the Lucan Mary has been understood by modern interpreters reveals that the figure of Mary resists a single identification. Instead, her portrayal is multifaceted, emerging in a complex configuration of images, themes, and comparisons with other characters. Even as interpreters focus upon particular dimensions of Mary's character, each image conjures other images and comparisons, so that none exists in isolation.

While scholars have been careful to note ways in which various dimensions of Luke's portrayal of Mary emerge, comparatively little attention has been given to the significance of Mary's virginity apart from its contributions to Lucan christology. Although the language and style of Luke-Acts have been plumbed for clues to Mary's significance in the narrative, the designation *parthenos* has been largely overlooked as a Marian character indicator. Therefore after detailing in chapters 2 and 3 the range of connotations that *parthenos* and *parthenia* elicit in literature of the first and second centuries, I show in chapter 4 how Luke's narrative exploits particular images of virginity and suppresses others to advance Mary's portrayal as a prophet and servant of God. Quite apart from how it demonstrates the remarkable nature of Mary's conception of Jesus, virginity serves

to help cast Jesus' mother as an extraordinary figure in the plan
of God.

IMAGES OF MARY IN THE PROTEVANGELIUM OF JAMES

Like Luke-Acts, the Protevangelium of James draws upon the
language and style of the Septuagint and situates Mary's story
in the context of ancient Judaism.[83] Despite long-standing recognition of PJ's contribution to the development of Marian piety
and tradition, scholars have devoted surprisingly little detailed
attention to the way in which PJ characterizes Mary. Only the
recent studies of Hock and Gaventa take into account the rhetorical details of Mary's portrayal.[84] In modern interpretation of
PJ, two dimensions of Mary's portrayal have most received attention: the images of Mary as a virgin and of Mary as the pure
virgin of the Lord. Each is integral to this study.

Virgin In Partu and Post Partum

As interpreters of the Protevangelium have observed, this apocryphal text not only underscores Mary's virginity, it establishes
her *virginitas ante partum* (literally, before giving birth, but including conception and pregnancy), *in partu* (while giving birth
to Jesus), and *post partum* (after Jesus' birth). In its vivid description of a *post partum* gynecological exam, PJ testifies that despite
having given birth to Jesus, Mary is yet a *parthenos*. Hers is
clearly an extraordinary virginity.

As the confirmation of Mary's virginity functions as the
climax of the story, Emile Amann identifies it as the "idée capi-
tale" of the Protevangelium.[85] What occurs as a single, but significant, character trait in the third Gospel appears as the central
theme of this narrative. Debate over the translation of *parthenos*
is conspicuously absent from modern discussion of PJ because
here the meaning of *parthenos* is decidedly unambiguous. It
clearly designates Mary as a *virgo intacta*.

As historical criticism has dominated scholarly discussion
of PJ, the narrative's importance in the development of early
Christian tradition has served as the primary focus of inquiry. A
majority of interpreters argue that PJ functions apologetically to
uphold both Mary's virginity and, more importantly, the vir-

ginal conception and honorable origins of Jesus.[86] Hock, however, suggests that PJ is an encomiastic history functioning to praise Mary. Rather than an apology offered in defense of the legitimacy of Jesus, PJ is an extended homage to his mother.[87] Hock maintains that although apologetic elements permeate the narrative, they do "not explain the gospel as a whole, and even passages that do admit an apologetic reading permit another one."[88] In chapter 5, we examine more fully the rhetorical significance of Mary's virginity.

The Pure Virgin of the Lord

Both Hock and Gaventa identify the theme of purity as the center around which PJ's plot unfolds.[89] According to their readings, the narrative's primary concern is the establishment and preservation of Mary's purity. So pronounced is PJ's interest in purity that Gaventa claims Mary can almost be mistaken as a mere function of the theme. [90]

It is in the midst of this sustained interest in purity that the character Mary is introduced and developed. From the very beginning of her story, purity and virginity are placed in close juxtaposition. Together they are used to establish the boundaries of her environment and the limits of her activity. From her own miraculous origin to the birth of her son, Jesus, she remains set apart, dedicated to the Lord. Even as a young child, Mary keeps the exclusive company of the "pure virgins of the Lord." At the age of three, she is safely housed in the temple, itself a symbol of purity and holiness, where she remains until the age of twelve.[91] When she reaches sexual maturity and the threshold of adulthood, she too assumes the designation *parthenos,* only to be quickly removed from the temple and placed under the care of a guardian.

Although interpreters have recognized the thematic function of purity in PJ, the significance of *parthenia* as the primary expression of such purity has remained in need of further investigation. Thus chapter 5 examines how the portrayal of Mary as a virgin resonates with images of virginity outlined in chapters 2 and 3. Just as the Gospel of Luke makes selective use of particular connotations associated with female sexual status in order to advance the characterization of Mary, so does the Protevangelium capitalize on and promote certain cultural presuppositions about virginity to tell the story of a *parthenos* so extraordinary that she becomes for Christians in later antiquity the exemplar of an idealized female sexuality.

Bodies and Selves

Two

The repertoire of ancient images and meanings that readers may bring to their construction of the Virgin Mary depends largely upon what can be adduced from ancient literary sources about the significance and meaning of *parthenos* and *parthenia*. Thus it is not the imagined mindset of past readers but rather ancient cultural images associated with the language of virginity that serve as the object of inquiry. This chapter explores the contexts in which virginity was discussed and what virginity connoted in Greco-Roman, Jewish, and Christian literature of the first two centuries of the common era.

The vast amount of literature in the ancient world that addresses sexual morals, conduct, and health betrays a pervasive concern for that aspect of self and society that today we identify as sexuality. Historians have posited several conceptual frameworks for understanding the significance of this widely varied discourse. As Michael Satlow demonstrates, certain trends distinguish recent study of sexuality in the ancient world.[1] Since the late 1970s, historians of ancient Judaism, early Christianity, and imperial Rome have taken increasing note of the ways in which discourse on sexuality reflects larger social dynamics. Among these, Michel Foucault's history of sexuality provides an interpretive framework that has proven helpful to subsequent studies.[2] Observing how the literature of the first and second centuries reveals "the existence, strength, and intensification of . . . themes of sexual austerity," Foucault demonstrates the transformation of classical Greek notions concerned with the "care of the self."[3] He argues that Greco-Roman literature, with its intensification and valorization of one's relation to oneself, lends witness to a "culture of the self" that was distinguished by a "greater apprehension concerning the sexual pleasures . . . a more intense problematization of *aphrodisia*."[4] Thus he describes an ancient sexual ethic that neither denigrated nor elevated sexuality, but rather located sexual activity within a comprehensive regimen more preoccupied with diet than sex. This relativization of sexuality in the early Empire counters popular stereotypes of a culture characterized by rampant excess and debauchery. A construct as sober as it is sensual, sexuality emerges here as one of several means of developing and maintaining agency, honor, and accountability.

The overall application of Foucault's argument can, of course, benefit from further refining.[5] Kate Cooper adds critical nuance to his reading by observing how ancient anxiety about sexual desire was rooted in a more general, and largely androcentric, concern for the social good. As Cooper sees it, antiquity's conceptualization of the self was inextricably linked to that of the larger society. She writes, "though excessive indulgence in pleasure was perceived as a threat to the common good, so was its excessive repudiation."[6] Cooper rightly notes that the exercise of pleasure could be either limited or promoted in service to society.

A word needs to be said about the literary sources I engage in this chapter. Just as androcentric texts should not be construed as reliable reflections of actual woman's life and experience, neither should ancient literary sources such as medical writings, philosophical literature, and dream handbooks be taken as evidence of widespread sexual practice. While they may certainly convey the idealized preoccupations of the privileged, we cannot simply assume the adoption of whatever sexual ethics they prescribe, nor can we infer mass adherence to those ethics and practices that such literature implicitly aims to supplant. On the other hand, the material examined in this chapter does reflect, at the very least, ideals held and promoted by ancient literate culture. It is within this culture that *parthenia* and *parthenos* prove to be subjects of concern, and it is the range of idealized, if not always coherent, images of each that I examine here.

Parthenos and *Parthenia:* Issues in Definition

Before we explore the cultural connotations associated with *parthenia* and *parthenos,* we must first review the wider semantic range of these terms as well as the working definitions of each employed by this chapter. By "working definitions," I mean understandings of these terms that will allow us to approach the extant primary material under consideration in a manner that remains focused but not rigid. Because this study is concerned with establishing the complex of cultural images associated with *parthenos* and *parthenia,* it is important to begin with general concepts that lend themselves to examination within a range of literary contexts.

As indicated in chapter 1, biblical interpreters have long wrestled with the ambiguity of *parthenos.*[7] Classicists, too, have sought to resolve the question whether *parthenos* refers only to age and marital status or to sexual status as well. Greek does not always distinguish between marital status and sexual status. Terms can connote either one or the other, or both at the same time. The question is compounded by the common occurrence of *gyne* (woman, wife) and *aner* (man, husband), both of which refer to gender and marital status.

A consensus understanding of *parthenos* affirms its sociological reference to a female who has not yet achieved the marital status of a *gyne*.[8] There is less agreement on the precise distinction between *kore* (girl) and *parthenos*. Without at all denying the possibility of semantic overlap between the two terms, I have chosen to focus on the meaning and significance of *parthenos*, the term that occurs in Luke-Acts and PJ. Since images of virginity are sometimes shared by different linguistic cultures, occasional references to the Latin *virgo* and the Hebrew *betulah* appear when necessary.

Among those interpreters who have sought to define *parthenos*, Giulia Sissa offers an extended discussion of the relationship between *parthenos* and *parthenia*. First she makes note of the equivocation evidenced by classicists who speak of *parthenoi* in terms of age and marital status, that is, as nubile, not-yet-married, young females, but allude to the loss of *parthenia* as a distinctly sexual event. Then Sissa underscores the implicit relationship between the two terms.[9] She observes:

> Whereas the word *parthenos* tends to arouse skepticism in non-religious interpreters and to call for cautious handling, it is not easy to capture the meaning of the abstract noun *parthenia* with a purely sociological definition. It is something subject to seizure (*lambanein*), a treasure that one guards (*phylassein*), a value that must be respected (*terein*). . . . When Pindar in his eighth *Isthmian Ode* attributed to Themis the wish that the daughter of Nereus, the future mother of Achilles, "conquered by love of a hero, loosen the charming tether of her virginity," it is not easy to understand the point of the image if virginity refers to nothing more than an age group.[10]

Sissa argues that if taking a bride's *parthenia* connotes more than just stealing her youth, then *parthenos* likewise implies more than merely age or marital status. She observes that classical Greek literature assumes the sexual, if hidden, status of a *parthenos*, but nevertheless contains numerous accounts of *parthenoi* being tested for their *parthenia*. Sissa recalls how in his account of *parthenoi* competing at a festival in honor of a Libyan goddess, Herodotus notes that, though nubile and unmarried, those who died in competition were deemed *pseudoparthenoi*.[11] Clearly age and marital status alone fail to ensure sexual status.

Sissa's study demonstrates that *parthenia* becomes most significant when it is lost. Unless there is particular reason to believe otherwise, the *parthenia* of a *parthenos* is regularly assumed. She argues that "sexuality and virginity were compatible only if sexual activity remained secret."[12] If the sexual life of a *parthenos* remained clandestine, she would retain her sexual status. Not surprisingly, the surest evidence of virginity lost was pregnancy. Sissa considers the designations *parthenios* and *parthenias* ("son of a virgin" and "daughter of a virgin") in light of ancient stories about *parthenoi* giving birth to children. Evidence more damning than any test for *parthenia*, children of *parthenoi* were public testimonies to their mothers' forbidden sexuality. Sissa argues that far from pointing to the prevalence of "virgin births," or calling into question the very notion of virginity, the terms *parthenios* and *parthenias* sarcastically underscore how children were "sometimes the only sign of a fraud that had otherwise gone unnoticed."[13]

Thus Sissa cautions, "Even if these texts do not come close to clarifying the essential nature of the *parthenos,* they tell us to be wary of defining the virgin solely in terms of the outward sign of youth."[14] It is the tension between *parthenia* assumed and *parthenoi* disgraced that underlies the ambiguity of the *parthenos* defined. Nubile and not-yet-married, sexual status nevertheless remained integral to the identity of those called *parthenoi.* Therefore this investigation presupposes that, unless explicitly indicated to the contrary, *parthenos* implies *parthenia. Parthenos* signals a "virgin."

Mapping the Cultural Connotations of *Parthenia* and *Parthenos*

Despite the range of sources, discussions concerning the figure of the *parthenos* and the topic of *parthenia* tend to coalesce around particular issues and connotations. The following review of these discussions aims to represent various modes of discourse and what they connote when they refer to *parthenia* and *parthenos.*

In her study of the book of Judges, Mieke Bal underscores

the liminality inherent in the social and sexual status of the Hebrew *betulah*. No longer a young child, and not yet a married woman, the *betulah* stands poised at the threshold of adult womanhood. Awaiting her transition from the legal jurisdiction of her father to that of a husband, she faces not only the future obligations of a wife and mother but the vulnerability and danger that failure threatens.[15]

Sissa's and Bal's discussions of the *parthenos,* and Foucault's interpretation of the "culture of the self," sound common notes of anxiety. As she awaits the transition to becoming a *gyne,* the *parthenos* is a figure of testing and a reason for suspicion. Sexuality itself, according to Foucault, can be cause for concern. It can either express and engender the harmony of the body and soul, or it can threaten to destroy the balance between the two. Like Bal's *betulah,* the *parthenos* is a liminal figure, moving from childhood to adulthood. In a culture of the self, she is on her way to becoming a mature social and moral agent.

As a female body, the virgin also signifies a condition of physical liminality. For as Thomas Laqueur has observed, a prominent medical model posited the human body as a "one-sex body," defining the female as an incomplete male.[16] Beginning with Aristotle and continuing with Soranus and Galen, both writing in the second century C.E., the human body was seen as the expression of a "purported telos of perfection," whereby one could conclude that "just as mankind is the most perfect of all animals, so within mankind the man is more perfect than the woman, and the reason for his perfection is his excess of heat, for heat is Nature's primary instrument."[17] Viewed in this light, the female body appears perpetually and futilely poised at the threshold of completeness, of idealized maleness. As such, it suffers distinctive physical processes, ailments, and risks.[18] Moreover, within the schema of chronic deficiency, the body of the *parthenos* negotiates the transition from ripeness to fertility. She is moving toward becoming a *gyne,* when she will be expected to produce a child.

Given her social, moral, and physical liminality, it is no wonder that the *parthenos* serves as the subject of multiple modes of ancient discourse. She is a topic of medical, moral, religious, legal, and historical discussions, as well as the focus of several ancient narratives. The *parthenos* is cause for both celebration and concern, signaling ripeness on the one hand and incompleteness on the other. Within various modes of discourse, discussion can shift and blur, accenting here the *parthenos* as an active, thinking subject, and there the *parthenos* as a body, a landscape visited by both the divine and profane. Neither conceptualization precludes the other. What has thus far seemed ambiguous may better be construed as multivalent. The *parthenos* is both a liminal subject and a liminal body.

Ancient notions of *parthenia* and *parthenos* fall into two major, nonexclusive categories. In the first place, a good deal of discussion tends to focus on the body of the *parthenos*. Across a spectrum of modes of discourse, one can identify understandings of the virginal body that posit the *parthenos* as the site of particular kinds of health and disease, as well as the site of sacred encounter or profane disrupture. In some discussions, the *parthenos* functions as an object of exchange, signaling both the social contracts that exist between other persons of agency and the imposition of new social obligations. In each of these construals, the virgin's body exists in a precarious state, poised on the brink of continual threat from within and without. Such focus on the body of the *parthenos* is evidenced in medical, moral, legal, and religious discourse, among others.

In the second place, discussion tends to focus on the figure of the *parthenos* as an acting subject. The virgin is presented as the potential subject of either integrity or duplicity. As an ethical subject, she must negotiate the line between the two. While some discussions especially emphasize either the body or the agency of the virgin, others assume both images of the *parthenos*.

The Virgin Body

THE VIRGIN BODY AS THE SITE OF HEALTH AND DISEASE

The Female Body

Ancient medical discussion of the virgin is predicated upon medical views of the female body that were in vogue during the early centuries of the imperial period. Despite variations in detail, medical literature of the ancient Mediterranean world generally views the female as either an incomplete male or as "other."[19]

For example, Aristotle notes that male and female are distinguished not in terms of the whole, but in terms of the parts, namely, the male penis and the female uterus. The definitive distinction between male and female lies not in their anatomical differences, but in the former's unique capacity to generate life. The seed-producing male functions as the active, efficient cause of generation, while the female functions as the passive, material cause, providing matter that male semen can infuse with movement and definition.[20] Aristotle's distinction was:

> as powerful and plain as that between life and death. To Aristotle being male *meant* the capacity to supply the sensitive soul without which "it is impossible for face, hand, flesh, or any other part to exist." Without the sensitive soul the body was no better than a corpse or part of a corpse (*Gen. an.* 2.5.741a8–16). The dead is made quick by the spark, by the incorporeal *sperma* (seed), of the genitor. One sex was able to concoct food to its highest, life-engendering stage, into true sperma; the other was not.[21]

Thus semen, composed of bodily fluids and *pneuma,* became idealized as the life-giving substance in procreation. While other physicians posited the production of female as well as male semen, the priority of the male form posited by Aristotle dominated medical theory.[22] Even those who argued for the existence of female semen noted the inferiority of such seed.[23]

Construed as the material substance that nourished the body's vessels and vital organs, it was *pneuma* that provided the vital spirit necessary for generation.[24] Yet it was also the very emission of semen, in both men and women, that brought on the exhaustion that followed sexual intercourse. Loss of semen signaled generative potential on the one hand, and loss of power, energy, and vitality, on the other, making sexual activity a risky enterprise.

Ancient images of the female in gynecological discourse are especially informative. Lacquer finds in this material confirmation of the notion that women's bodies bear direct, if inferior, correspondence to those of men. He cites as examples Aristotle,

Galen, and Soranus, the first of whom asserts that the female possesses all of the organs that the male possesses, plus a uterus. Yet even the uterus, "always double just as the testes are always two in the male," corresponds to male anatomy.[25] Aristotle even suggests that women have an internal penis-like tube (*kaulos*) through which semen travels.[26]

Galen and Soranus likewise view female genitalia in male terms. Galen especially details the correspondence between male and female. The female sexual organs are simply those of the male, only repositioned. The cervix and vagina correspond to the penis, the uterus to the scrotum, the ovaries to the testes.[27] Soranus, too, posits a female physiology that resembles that of the male—with an inner part of the female anatomy wrapping around the *kaulos* of the uterus "like the prepuce in males around the glans," and the *kaulos* "elongating like the male genital" during intercourse.[28] In opposition to the Hippocratic notion of a wandering womb, Soranus, along with Galen and Aristotle, also holds to a fixed womb.[29] The conditions and particulars of female anatomy arise from a common physiology that men and women share.

Such a state of affairs is due, in part, to the distance from which male physicians "studied" the female body. Drawing upon comments in the medical writings, Aline Rousselle notes,

> Greek and Roman women were not willing to be examined by men and Soranus said he was writing essentially for midwives who were able to have access to female patients. Women's bodies were shrouded in such secrecy that Galen learned more from dissecting female monkeys, insofar as their organs were the same as human ones, than all the men of ancient times learned through their sexual contacts with their own wives.[30]

These physicians leaned heavily upon logical reasoning, combined with whatever oral tradition may have been shared by women and midwives, to theorize women's bodies. The female body of the medical writers was constructed by and in relation to men.

Various interpreters of ancient medical literature have observed a second kind of correspondence in the female form, that between the upper and lower parts of the body.[31] The repeated occurrence of terms used to describe corresponding parts of the upper and lower female body points to the physiological symmetry that physicians attribute to women. For instance, the part of the body that ingests food, is attached to lips that open and close, and is connected to the neck, is called the *stoma*. Medical writers speak of the uterus, too, as a *stoma*. It also is connected to a "lower neck" and attached to a set of lips. Thus semen deposited in the lower neck of the womb is taken up "with the aid of breath, as with the mouth or nostrils."[32]

That the correspondence between a woman's head and her sexual organs is more than a clever trope is evidenced in at least one physician's suggestion that female singers especially suffer from amenorrhea.[33] As Laqueur observes, "(W)hat we would take to be only metaphoric connections between organs were viewed as having causal consequences in the body, as being real. Here the association is one between the throat or neck through which air flows and the neck of the womb through which the menses passes; activity in one detracts from activity in the other."[34] The Hippocratics cite, without elaboration, the change in a woman's neck and voice that follows first intercourse.[35] Thus in Aristotle, Soranus, and the Hippocratic corpus, prescriptions for sexual activity sometimes depend upon similarities between the upper and lower *stoma:* both become moist when active, both function better when activity is motivated by appetite.[36] Galen, too, describes in detail the lower orifice: "Just as the uvula is for the protection of the pharynx, in the same way what is called the 'nymph' protects the womb, covering and protecting from the cold the opening of the cervix, which comes out into the vagina."[37]

In a detailed consideration of Greek images and terms for pregnancy (*en gastri lambanein, syllambanein, echein*), Sissa argues that despite medical knowledge of the anatomical and functional distinctions between the stomach and the womb, language blurring such differences nevertheless persists in gynecological discussion. She considers the implications of such a cultural commonplace, "Whatever the linguistic status of *gaster,* the word's polysemy superimposed or at any rate associated two specific images: to ingest and digest through the upper orifice, to be penetrated and caused to conceive a child through the lower."[38] Thus the correspondence between *stomata* permeated both metaphorical and literal references to the female body.

The Virgin Body

Medical texts discuss the physiology of the *parthenos* in terms identical to those used in reference to the bodies of other women.[39] The *parthenos,* however, is often seen as susceptible to risks and diseases directly related to her lack of sexual experience. Gynecological discourse, with its interest in the reproductive health of women, weighs the potential drawbacks and benefits of *parthenia.* Here Soranus stands out as a proponent of virginal health. At least one interpreter credits him with "trying to disentangle female health from reproductive functions, extending now to the female body that which was available at the time of the (Hippocratic) *Corpus* to the male body—the possibility of considering personal health and survival independent of reproduction."[40] Soranus argues that "one must not suppose the uterus to be essential to life" and that virginity is healthful because it prevents loss of seed. Indeed, he goes so far as to detail reasons why both menstruation and pregnancy are *not* conducive to optimal health.[41]

Not surprisingly, as Dale Martin argues, "the care and keeping of virgins constituted a subcategory of debate within . . . concerns about passionate women."[42] Prescriptions for sexual health were sometimes tempered by the popular image of the *parthenos* dangerously aflame with sexual desire. Rufus, like Soranus, discussed the dangers of pregnancy and encouraged the delay of first intercourse. In addition, he recommended a regimen designed to prevent young virgins from reaching the peak of their sexual desire too early. Rufus encouraged the exercise of *sophrosyne* (self-control) from the onset of puberty, "the 'precarious' time (*sphaleros*)."[43] Thus medical prescription could both challenge and reinforce larger cultural constructions of female sexuality.

Models of female sexual anatomy were both confirmed and debated in discussions of the risks and benefits of virginity. On the one hand, Soranus affirmed the healthfulness of even lifetime virginity. On the other, the Hippocratics and even Rufus argued the necessity of sexual intercourse for good health. Differences in their recommendations correspond to differing models of the female sexual organs. At issue in discussions of first intercourse is the question of a sealed uterus or vagina. Did the commencement of normal menstruation require the unsealing that accompanies first intercourse? Was women's health dependent upon male intervention?

In the Hippocratic writings, menstruation, intercourse, and pregnancy not only are healthful, they are integrally related. Because the female is cooler than the male, she retains moisture and an excess of bodily fluids. Menstruation and pregnancy are ways in which the body uses and rids itself of this surplus. Thus Hippocratic medicine traces women's diseases to an inability to menstruate and bear children and posits intercourse as one well-known remedy for a virgin's life-threatening retention of blood. With a popular image of the uterus being that of an inverted jug in need of unsealing (*kredemnon lysai*), Hanson observes, "'Unsealing the wine jug' is expressed in the same terms as 'violating the young girl' and 'penetrating the city walls,' for all three actions share a conspicuous visual similarity, whereby a rounded and sealed-off inner space is opened up and made available to the man who penetrates the protective barrier."[44] Hence it is the unsealed jug that flows to release blood and also receives semen.

Yet the exact images that the medical writers intended to convey remain cloudy. The question remains whether the vagina, in particular, was sealed by a hymen or not. Sissa argues that the Greek writers posited the hymen (membrane) only as an anomaly, a pathological condition. For the Hippocratics note that "if the woman does not receive the semen even though menstruation occurs regularly, the problem is that the membrane is in front."[45]

Soranus argues explicitly against a seemingly popular (but unattributed) Roman belief in the existence of a membrane that seals the vagina.[46] Furthermore, he suggests that furrows of blood vessels become dilated with defloration, so that "when the furrows are spread apart in defloration, these vessels burst and cause pain and the blood which is usually excreted follows."[47]

Soranus's argument against the normal occurrence of a vaginal hymen assumes the pain-free menstrual flow of virgin women.[48] Contra Roman opinion, Soranus argues that menstruation and reproductive health are not contingent upon first intercourse. Defying both Greek and Roman medical wisdom, he contends that virginity is not dangerous.

While interpreters use his *Gynecology* to argue for varying images of female anatomy, consensus holds that Soranus believed virginity beneficial to women's health.[49] As we have seen, the Hippocratics posited several dangers associated with prolonged virginity and recommended intercourse to promote the regular flow of the menses and prevent a dangerous buildup of fluid in the uterus. First intercourse was prescribed for prepubescent girls experiencing symptoms associated with the retention of menstrual blood.[50] Intercourse was also recommended for any woman whose uterus was suspected of a pathological loss of moisture that could lead to either the cessation of menstruation or a hysterical displacement of the womb, both of which could result in death.[51] While later writers such as Galen and Rufus departed from Hippocratic gynecology, they nevertheless continued to associate intercourse with the maintenance of women's health. Galen, citing the ill effects of female continence in general, argues that the retention of either blood or semen is potentially dangerous for women.[52] Rufus, addressing the subject of virgins in particular, argues that prolonged virginity could lead to a number of diseases.[53]

Not surprisingly, Soranus resists casting intercourse as curative. Throughout Book 3 of the *Gynecology,* he argues for alternative means of treating the female body. Citing the great dangers posed by early childbearing, Soranus not only advocates the delay of first intercourse and marriage, he even promotes complete abstinence, noting that women "who, on account of regulations and service to the gods, have renounced intercourse and those who have been kept in virginity as ordained by law are less susceptible to disease."[54]

As Martin observes directly and Foucault assumes, a consensus of ancient medical wisdom associates the danger of sexual desire with women in general, and with virgins especially.[55]

Even Soranus argues, "since virgins who have not been brought up wisely and lack education arouse in themselves premature desires, one must, therefore, not trust the appetites."[56] For some, the buildup of hot desire is as dangerous as the retention of blood. Both put the naturally more moist and cool female body at risk. Once sustained, the heat of passion, semen, and blood requires release. Given such a physiology of desire, it is not surprising that female sexual desire remains a preoccupation of medical writers and their prescriptions. Bodily "climate control" is at a premium for women, who, *as women,* "are assumed to be markedly more open to erotic emotion than men and sexually insatiable once aroused."[57] When semen stored signals vitality and semen lost connotes cost, eroticism poses a multiple threat. Virgins are seen at once as endangered and dangerous.

THE VIRGIN BODY AS THE SITE OF SACRED ENCOUNTER
Prophecy

Distinctions between prophecy and *manteia* (divination) notwithstanding, it is safe to follow George Luck's observation that "in general, *prophetes* is a person who speaks for a god, or through whom a god speaks and reveals his plans."[58] Throughout the early Empire, prophecy functioned as a phenomenon that was central to a variety of religious practices.[59] Whereas Plutarch and Cicero speak of the decline of oracles, Pausanias testifies to their continued popularity.[60] According to Cicero, not only did philosophers debate the legitimacy of prophecy, but some, like the Stoics, defended both natural and artificial modes of prophecy.[61] Ancient Jewish texts, though diminishing or even demonizing divination, elevate prophecy. The Book of Deuteronomy upholds the prophet Moses as "the only legitimate channel of communication between Yahweh and the people."[62] Early Christian regard for prophecy has been skillfully demonstrated by David E. Aune.[63]

Interpreters of the first and second centuries have noted a relationship between sexual continence and prophecy. As Peter Brown observes, Jewish, pagan, and Christian witnesses attest to the belief that "abstinence from sexual activity, and especially virginity, made the human body a more appropriate vehicle to receive divine inspiration. Possession was an intimate and dramatically physical experience. It involved a flooding of the body with an alien, divine Spirit."[64] Thus Philo's Moses, the prophet of prophets, remains continent in order "to hold himself always in readiness to receive oracular messages."[65]

Although Brown cites Irenaeus's discussion of the "false (and blatantly sexual) heat induced by magic in false prophetesses" in order to contend that such prophetic phenomena excluded the "rush of vital spirits . . . traditionally associated with intercourse," literary evidence suggests that some in the ancient world did see a strong parallel between the two experiences.[66] Citing Plutarch (*Mor.* 5.404E, 405C), Martin notes that "one can hardly read accounts of the physiology of prophecy, especially descriptions of prophecy enacted by a male god on a female seer, without detecting the sexual connotations of the language."[67] It is to this aspect of ancient prophecy that we now turn. For although prophecy was limited neither to women nor to those who practiced sexual continence, there is a strand of discourse that relates prophecy particularly to female sexual status, and most notably, to virginity.

Lucan's violent and sexually charged account of the oracle at Delphi illustrates the point. It is significant because it recounts a story of the Delphic oracle, which was the subject of several treatises authored by Plutarch, and perhaps the most prominent oracle of the early Empire.[68] While one cannot demonstrate that Delphi is either typical of ancient prophetic phenomena or even historical, its fame underscores its importance as a leading cultural image of such occurrence. The scene revolves around a virgin seer forced upon the oracular tripod by Apollo:

> Scared at last, the *virgo* took refuge by the tripods. . . . At last Apollo mastered the breast of the Delphian priestess; as fully as ever in the past, he forced his way into her body, driving out her former thoughts, and bidding her human nature to come forth and leave her heart at his disposal. Frantic as she careens about the cave, with her neck under possession . . . she boils over with fierce fire, while enduring the wrath of Phoebus . . . first the wild frenzy overflowed through her foaming lips; she groaned and ut-

> tered loud inarticulate cries with panting breath, next a dismal
> wailing filled the vast cave; and at last, when she was mastered,
> came the sound of articulate speech . . . then Apollo closed up
> her throat.[69]

Lucan uses sexual imagery to describe an event that, by definition, cannot be a sexual act. Pausanias claimed that Delphic
divination was always performed by a female.[70] The figure in
Lucan's account is not only female but a virgin, who, caught
by the "neck" and "mastered" by Apollo, is gripped by an alien
power.

Although the details of Lucan's account may tend toward
hyperbole, Aune argues that it is "virtually certain that the
popular view of the Pythia was that she was divinely possessed
when she uttered the oracles of Apollo."[71] Indeed, aspects of
Lucan's description accord with that of Plutarch. As Aune notes,
"Plutarch does refer to the Pythia as 'regaining her composure'
after descending from the tripod (*Amatorius* 759b), a reference
which seems to presuppose a prior state of excitation, and in *De
Pyth. orac* 404e he describes the Pythia as unable to keep silent."[72] In divination, the spirit comes upon the body (*soma*) of
the seer and enters her *psyche,* the very material of the prophetic
art.[73] Just as medical writers identify optimal bodily conditions
for sexual intercourse, so does Plutarch insist that particular conditions of the female's body and soul either inhibit or facilitate
reception of the god. The seer is to "surrender herself to the control of the god" only when she is unhindered by bodily and psy-
chic distractions. Otherwise, she risks great harm to herself.[74]
As a negative example, Plutarch recounts the story of a woman
who died after she participated in an oracular episode unwill-
ingly.[75] He concludes that it is because of such risks that the
chastity of the priestess is well guarded (*synousias hagnon to
soma*). Sexual continence is maintained for the sake of the oracle
and the seer.

Thus both prophecy and sexual activity reflect ancient
economies of the body. Martin suggests that "the physiology of
prophecy could be analyzed by analogy with the physiology
of sex, because prophecy was thought of as the penetration of
the body of the priestess by the god or some other, perhaps in-

animate, invading force."[76] The penetrating force of the prophetic *pneuma* was analogous to that of the *pneuma* bearing sperm.[77] Moreover, the prophetic availability of women "was a physiological fact, anchored in the very nature of female flesh."[78] Women, whose flesh was cooler, moister, and more porous than that of men, were considered more penetrable. Therefore debate about the decline of oracles centered not on whether some form of possession was actually involved, but on the nature of the one who possessed the female seer.[79]

It is important to note the attention given to the sexual status of the Pythian priestess who mounts the tripod in order to receive the spirit of the deity and the exhalations rising from the earth. Some allude to the sexual continence of the seer who mounts the tripod, while others underscore her virginity. Diodorus of Sicily records that "in ancient times virgins (*parthenoi*) delivered the oracles because virgins have their natural innocence intact (*tes physeos adiaphthorou*) and are in the same case as Artemis; for indeed virgins were alleged to be well suited to guard the secrecy of disclosures made by oracles."[80] However, he goes on to note that after one such virgin was carried away and violated by a male visitor enamored of her beauty, the Delphians instituted a law that only older women of at least fifty, dressed in the attire of a virgin, would be allowed to prophesy. Plutarch tells how the seer is to be one without technical skill, faculty, or experience, having been raised by peasants. She comes like a bride to her husband's house, unhindered by knowledge or experience, "a pure, virgin soul" (*kai parthenos hos alethos ten psychen*) who communes with the god.[81]

How is it that one like Artemis is best suited to maintain the secrets of the oracle? Metaphor and physiology surely blur in Diodorus's statement about a virgin's intact *physis*.[82] Examining the significance of the seer's sexual status, Sissa contends that "the ignorance of perfect *parthenia*" precedes and follows, and we might add seals, the prophetic event.[83] The unhindered virginal body is empty and free both to open its mouth and, once released from the trancelike grip of the spirit, to close its throat in silence. Having been penetrated in an altered state by a god and not a man, the virgin bears neither lasting memory nor mark

of the encounter. According to Sissa, a combination of emptiness, openness, and ignorance distinguishes the prophetic body
of the *parthenos*. Although her argument rests, in part, on a particular Greek notion of a hymenless female, one need only recall
ancient models of female anatomy and the image of the oracular
tripod to see the provocative symmetry of an upper mouth that
opens to speak for, and a lower orifice that opens to receive, the
spirit of a male god.

In contrast to the *parthenos*, the pregnant *gyne* signifies closure: "In women who are pregnant, the mouth of the uterus
closes."[84] Because sexual reproduction opposes emptiness, sexual
intercourse signals the possibility of closure. Female fertility
and sexual activity are not generally associated with prophecy.
When Diodorus remarks that the Delphians replaced the virginal priestesses with older women, he notes that the women
were beyond the age of childbearing and regular sexual activity.
The Delphians' choice may reflect something similar to what
Peter Brown identifies as an early Christian assumption that
"the abandonment of intercourse followed the normal rhythms
of life: it was usually associated with widowhood and with the
onset of old age."[85] It may also confirm Sissa's notion that in the
closedness and silence of sexual inactivity, the *parthenos* and
widow are functional equivalents.[86]

While it would be misleading to contend that either virginity or sexual renunciation was seen as essential to prophecy in
the ancient Empire, literary evidence does suggest that *parthenia*
supplied the seer with a certain advantage. Communion with the
divine was facilitated by a virginal body. Although prophecy was
seen as analogous to, but not synonymous with, sexual union, it
was a highly charged physical phenomenon. Indeed, it was by
implying that the encounters at Delphi were truly sexual that
later Christian argumentation sought to discredit the Pythian
oracle.[87]

Priesthood

While the Pythian seers were identified as priestesses, not all
priestesses were associated with prophetic utterance. Many were

described more in terms of their priestly duties and privileges, where, as in the case of prophecy, virginity sometimes bore special significance. Among the cults of the early Empire, the Vestal Virgins stand as the premier example of a virginal priesthood. It was the duty of these women to reside at Vesta's temple, maintaining both their vows of virginity and the perpetual fire in the temple hearth.

Mary Beard once advocated an anthropological reading of the Vestals that identified the cult as the corporate embodiment of sexual ambiguity and a "model of primitive strangeness." More recently, however, she has criticized her former interpretation as a "denial of reading."[88] Giving greater attention to "the character, point and focus of the texts so expertly dissected," Beard now observes that

> the overwhelming preoccupation of the ancient writers is the punishment of the Vestals, the Vestals who broke their oath of chastity, or those suspected of having done so. . . . The Vestals, in other words, can be seen not merely as a parade of anomaly, but as a focus of the negotiation around the category of virginity.[89]

Indeed, ancient discussion of the Vestals does revolve around the issue identified by Beard. Dionysius of Halicarnassus recounts the origins of the Vestal institution, but focuses on those instances in which virgins were accused of betraying their vows of *parthenia*.[90] When the priestess Aemilia prays to Vesta for help in proving her innocence, "I have performed the sacred offices to thee in a holy and proper manner, keeping a pure mind (*psychen echousa katharan*) and a chaste body (*soma hagnon*)," she underscores the sanctity of her virgin body and its function as a site of priestly activity.[91]

Plutarch and Dionysius both attempt to explain the significance of the priestesses' sexual status, but neither claims complete comprehension. Since the Vestal hearth is sometimes overseen by "women past the age of marriage," Plutarch correlates the chastity of virginity with the purity of fire, and virginity's unfruitfulness with fire's barrenness.[92] Similarly, when Dionysius recounts how Numa determined that the guarding of the holy things should be committed to *parthenoi*, he observes that the uncorrupt (*amiantos*) fire and the undefiled (*aphthartos*) virgin are well-matched. The bodily condition of the priestess mirrors that of the sacred hearth. While she is not united with the fire, as is a prophetess with the spirit of a god, she does commune with the sacred presence.

We may understand better the significance of Vestal virginity when we observe the "negotiation of the boundary between virginity and non-virginity" evidenced in the declamations of the elder Seneca that address the virgin priesthood.[93] Lending witness to Roman understanding of what specifically constitutes sacred virginity, the declamations clearly assume that virginity is something that can be taken away ("*Nemo . . . mihi virginitatem eripuit*," *Controv.* 1.2.1). As a bodily condition, it connotes chastity. Thus one speaker argues vehemently that "(n)o one can be convicted of unchastity unless her body has been violated" (*Controv.* 6.8). Without physical evidence to the contrary, chastity is assumed.

Yet the declamations also include disputation over this very point. The question of whether virginity, in and of itself, is sufficient evidence of chastity persists throughout Seneca's text. Is the body an adequate witness to the chastity that a priestess should exhibit? Or must the virgin produce additional evidence of her chastity? As one argument goes, "This is enough for a bride—but not enough for a priestess" (*Controv.* 1.2.8). The arguments detailed by Seneca cause the reader to wonder if, in the context of the priesthood, being a virgin connotes *more* than virginity.

Consider the case of the *virgo* who claims that although she was once captured by pirates and sold into prostitution, she nevertheless managed to maintain her chastity. Because the virgin seeks a priesthood, discussion of her case is based upon the following law: "A priestess must be chaste and of chaste (parents), pure and of pure (parents)" (*Controv.* 1.2; cf. 1.2.13). Arguments for and against the woman alternate in focus. Some concentrate on the woman's body, while others argue for or against the quality of her character. In some instances the woman's chastity is discussed solely in terms of her virginity. In other instances, the notion of chastity is expanded and generalized. Hence the woman is faulted for having been "at least *kissed* by all those who believed (her) chaste" (1.2.1), and for having had "every part of her body . . . inspected—and handled" (1.2.3). Arguments for and against the woman's purity also exhibit nuance. In some arguments, purity refers to the nature of the woman's intention, reputation, and experience. In others, purity clearly refers to her body. Remarking upon one particular argument against the woman, the Elder Seneca observes that it is posed "in reference not to her motivation but to her body" (*non ad animum hoc referens sed ad corpus, Controv.* 1.2.16). The true virgin must be proven worthy in body and intention. Throughout the discussion, the boundaries between virginity, chastity, and purity become increasingly indistinguishable. While various arguments emphasize particular terms, in the context of priesthood each term appears to connote the others.

In a case that suggests that its central figure is a Vestal Virgin, the facts are thus: "A woman condemned for unchastity appealed to Vesta before being thrown from the rock. She was thrown down, and survived. She is sought to pay the penalty again" (*Controv.* 1.3). Porcius Latro offers the following against her: "Shall a woman go to worship the divinity guaranteeing the rule of Rome who has been made unchaste if not by an act of lust, at least by the hand of the executioner? . . . If nothing else, you have stood where the unchaste stand" (1.3.1). In this case, unchastity is presumed, despite the woman's sexual status. Furthermore, it is rooted not in the woman's body, but in her reputation, her public standing. The semantic blurring of chastity, virginity, and purity, as they relate to the priesthood, lies at the foundation of the law concerning admission into the priesthood. Seneca records how the law "enquires into a woman's ancestors, her body, her life" (*Controv.* 1.2.11). From another source we learn that the Vestal Virgins, in particular, were permitted neither questionable parentage nor bodily defect.[94] Such inquiry, as well as the arguments adduced in Seneca's account, demonstrate that a priestess must not only evidence but embody virginity, chastity, and purity. Together they form the tripartite requisite of women seeking the priesthood.

THE VIRGIN BODY AS THE SITE OF SOCIAL CONSTRUCTION
The Virgin Body and the Economics of Marriage

In both Jewish and Greco-Roman discourse, the virgin is often viewed as a female awaiting marriage. The virgin, nubile and ripe, stands in a liminal state. Roman valuation of marriage is reflected in Augustus's legislation concerning marriage and family. Following his *lex Julia de maritandis ordinibus*, heavier taxes were incurred by unmarried citizen men and women, while incentives and awards were expended on those who married and bore children.[95] Moreover, adultery became punishable by exile, death, or confiscation of property. Although the impact of the *lex Julia* was somewhat modified by the more relaxed *lex Papia Poppaea* of 9 C.E., both legislations reflect a high Roman regard for marriage.

Whether such laws were strictly enforced is difficult to determine. However, as has been noted,

> All women's lives were affected profoundly in various ways by the social ideology being articulated in laws and dynastic imagery by the emperor. From the "best" of women to the "worst," the terms were set and debated within the frame of family and reproduction even when women's lives at every social level frequently moved out of the frame.[96]

Evidence of sexual transgression notwithstanding, the presence of a Roman ideology favoring marriage and family cannot be doubted.[97]

As we have already seen, much of Soranus's discussion of *parthenia* revolves around the medical risks posed by the Roman practice of early marriage. His arguments for the healthfulness of *parthenia* and the postponement of marriage reflect two sides of a single coin. Soranus contends that it is early intercourse and childbearing, owing to early marriage, that specifically endangers the health of young women. His promotion of women's health apart from marriage and reproduction brings into bold relief the extent to which marriage was generally considered not only desirable but necessary for the health of marriageable young virgins.

Roman cultic practices mirrored the expected life course of the female. As Ross Shepard Kraemer notes,

> At puberty, elite young girls dedicated their childhood togas to Fortuna Virginalis, and began instead to wear the *stola,* which publicly differentiated respectable women from prostitutes, who wore togas. At marriage, these same women were transferred to the protection of *Fortuna Primigenia.* . . . [A] significant number of religious cults for Roman matrons were instituted with the explicit intention of instilling and reinforcing male aristocratic expectations of women's appropriate behavior. The worship of Pudicitia Patricia, Pudicitia Plebeia, Venus Verticordia, and Venus Obsequens, among others, are presented as obsessively concerned with women's sexual chastity and marital fidelity.[98]

Roman religion guided virgins through the transition to marriage and reinforced the fidelity and virtue of *matronae.*

That virgins were to be wed, rather than simply to be used for sexual pleasure, is clear in Roman legal discourse. Following the *lex Julia,* sexual crimes other than adultery were grouped under the category of *stuprum.* The *Digest* states that "*stuprum* is committed by someone who keeps a freewoman for the sake of sexual relations not marriage, unless indeed she is a concubine . . . *stuprum* is committed with a widow, a virgin, or a boy."[99]

It is in Judaism, especially, that we find such a favorable estimation of marriage that virginity as a prolonged bodily state receives little notice. This is not to suggest that virginity itself was devalued, but rather that virginity was most often viewed as a temporary state in preparation for marriage, an even greater good. One of the tragic consequences of Jepthah's vow is that his daughter dies as a virgin, one who will never wed nor realize her reproductive potential (Jdg 11.37–40).

Judaism's high regard for marriage and its positive valuation of sexuality has been explored by numerous interpreters.[100] Discussion of biblical tradition has often focused on the Genesis creation accounts.[101] Especially significant when considering ancient Jewish views of virginity is rabbinic understanding of sexuality.[102] Daniel Boyarin has recently argued that whereas dominant Hellenistic understanding viewed the human person as a soul housed in a body, rabbinic Judaism defined the human person as an animated body. While Boyarin's thesis somewhat overstates the case, he successfully demonstrates that rabbinic Judaism considered sexuality beneficial and integral to human experience. Virginity was seen as a temporary condition that preceded proper conjugal relations. Thus the Mishnah, our earliest extant rabbinic text, and one derived from the latter part of the period with which this study is concerned, offers no positive valuation of virginity sustained beyond the customary marriageable age. As Boyarin observes, rabbinic Judaism "so strongly approved the married life, including the life of the sexual body, that there was virtually no escape from marriage within that culture—either for men or women."[103]

This is not to say that sexuality and virginity prove wholly unproblematic in rabbinic discourse. Rather, sex remains necessarily subject to regulation and control. As has been noted, concern for sexual discipline characterizes much ancient discourse on the body and sexuality. Peter Brown summarizes the rabbinic view, "As the rabbis chose to present it, sexuality was an enduring adjunct of the personality. Though potentially unruly, it was amenable to restraint."[104]

Lest one mistake such concern as a rabbinic innovation, Eilberg-Schwartz offers the reminder that "the body has always been a central preoccupation within Judaism. Despite any sharp antithesis between body and soul, and despite the importance of procreation, certain bodily processes are regarded as problematic."[105] The problematized body is a regulated body, an entity that necessitates the construction of social and cultic regimens, prescriptions, and boundaries. No wonder then that purity, cleanness, and wholeness are but a few of the carnal topics with which the Book of Leviticus is concerned. In his reading of Genesis, Eilberg-Schwartz's attention is drawn not to the generally positive valence attributed to the body, but rather to the "fundamental tension between being made in God's image and being obliged to reproduce. . . . Pressed between these conflicting impulses, the body became a cultural elaboration."[106]

Marriage and requisite female virginity provide a matrix for such elaboration. Numerous passages in both the Jewish Scriptures and the Mishnah attest to the importance of the pre-marital female body. In the idealized world of these literary texts (the degree to which they reflect actual practice is unclear), females who leave their father's house in order to marry are to approach the marriage bed as virgins. Not only does the bride-price depend upon the bride's virginity (M. Ket. 1.2; 5.2), but the very validity of a marriage can rest upon the truth of her virginal status (Deut 22.13–21; M. Ket. 1.6).[107] According to the Mishnah tractate *Ketubbot*, the bride-price for virgins is double the amount for non-virgins.[108] The significance of the virgin's higher monetary value is confirmed in the opening discussion of marriage law—the newly married husband can take legal action if he finds that his wife is not a virgin (M. Ket. 1.1.; cf. Deut 22.13–21).

In an argument similar to Sissa's discussion of virginity among pagan women, Judith Romney Wegner observes that the Mishnah posits virginity as something that is culturally assumed. Virginity is only problematized when a situation arises in which it can be assumed that a virgin has been sexually violated:

> Curiously, the sages judge virginity not by direct examination of the girl herself, but by external cultural criteria. "Virgin" means any girl or woman *conventionally* presumed innocent of sexual activity. These fall into two groups: first, girls who have never been married, including those once betrothed but divorced by their fiancés before consummation of the marriage (M. Ket. 1.2B); second, girls rescued before the age of three from an environment that had exposed them to sexual abuse (M. Ket. 1.2D). The latter qualify as virgins because the sages believe a hymen ruptured before the age of three will spontaneously regenerate. . . . Nonvirgins form the mirror image of these groups of virgins. Thus girls divorced after presumed consummation count as nonvirgins even if they somehow remain intact (M. Ket. 1.4A).[109]

Cultural convention establishes and perpetuates the assignment of sexual status. As Wegner states, "Everyone 'knows' that female slaves, female captives, and girls raised by gentiles have been subjected to sexual abuse—even those under the age of three."[110] Exceptions to the rule are rare. Wegner cites the example of M. Ket. 1.3, in which the details of *how* a female's virginity is "lost" figure significantly. In the case of a female who has been "injured by a piece of wood," the majority view diminishes the bride-price, but R. Meir recommends retaining it in full as for a virgin. When the question, "Who is the virgin?" is raised, M. Nid. 1.4 answers, "Any girl who never in her life saw a drop of blood, even though she is married."[111] The reference to blood, interpreted later in the Tosefta, remains ambiguous here. Does it refer to hymeneal blood or menstrual blood, or both? Or might it refer to another kind of bleeding? Whatever the case, both of these texts rely on physical criteria to determine who may rightly be called a *betulah*. Such references, however, are few. In the overwhelming majority of discussions, cultural convention determines who is, and who is not, a virgin.

Prescriptions concerning bride-price reveal that virgin females were afforded a higher value than females who were presumed to be sexually experienced. They also provide us with a glimpse of how the Mishnah often understands the place of minor daughters. According to M. Nid. 5.7 and M. Qid. 2.1, a father can claim the fruit of his minor daughter's labor, annul her vows, and arrange her marriage. Upon reaching the age of twelve and one-half, however, a daughter no longer remains subject to her father's dominion (M. Nid. 5.7). She either passes into the jurisdiction of her betrothed (or spouse) or gains legal autonomy. Given the norm of marriage that permeates the Mishnah, the latter case was likely expected to remain in the minority. Ideally, minor daughters were both constrained by patriarchal authority and attributed sexual and reproductive power. As Wegner observes,

> the young girl possesses one salient characteristic: She is a sexual chattel. Nearly all references to the girlchild under twelve (*qetannah*) or the pubescent girl between twelve and twelve and one-half years (*naarah*)—unlike references to minor sons—speak directly or indirectly of her sexuality, with particular emphasis on her virginity.[112]

Several interpreters have identified ways in which control of
female sexuality, especially that of the minor daughter, permeates rabbinic sexual rhetoric. Rather than controlling their
daughters' behavior per se, fathers bore responsibility for guarding their reproductive potential.[113] Except in cases involving virgins beyond the age of twelve and one-half (cf. M. Ket. 1.6),
fathers, not daughters, are the parties charged with virginity
suits. Legal precedent for such cases occurs in Deuteronomy
22.13–21, 29 (cf. Sir 42.9–14).

In at least one instance, the Mishnah details the moment
that a female passes from the domain of her father to that of her
spouse (M. Ket. 4.5). When concern for control is extensive,
liminality is not welcome.[114] Wegner cites M. Ket. 4.5 when she
identifies as the principal social difference between males and
females the fact that the latter "rarely attains the autonomy that
routinely accrues to her brother on reaching the age of thir-
teen."[115] Instead, she is carefully ushered from one male jurisdiction to another. In the idealized economics of marriage, the virgin body is monitored, evaluated, and transferred. It is a valuable
commodity in a carefully regulated marketplace.

In a different text altogether, a well-known Jewish writer
addresses the issue of whether or not virgins should marry:
"Now concerning virgins" (*peri de ton parthenon*, 1 Cor 7.25).
Throughout his discussion, Paul attends to his male audience in
second- and third-person address, but refrains from addressing
the female *parthenoi*. Rather, he talks about them, directing his
comments to the men to whom they are presumably betrothed
(*ten eautou parthenon*, 1 Cor 7.36–38). While Paul addresses the
wife (1 Cor 7.16a), the husband (1 Cor 7.16b), the married
(1 Cor 7.10), and even the unmarried and the widow (*lego de tois
agamois kai tais cherais*, 1 Cor 7.8), it is only the *parthenos* to
whom he offers no direct word. Like the framers of the Mishnah, in matters of marriage and sexuality, Paul regards the virgin through the lens of male jurisdiction.

At least two interpreters see a coupling of concerns in 1 Corinthians 7.[116] Focusing on the occurrence of *hyperakmos* ("past
puberty") in 1 Corinthians 7.36, Martin examines the notion of

being "over the limit." He recalls Soranus's discussion of virgins who are *hyperakmos* as well as his suggestion that puberty is the ideal age for marriage and defloration. Together with the well-attested assumption that sexual desire increases dangerously with sexual development, these cultural notions of virginity lead Martin to conclude that 1 Corinthians 7.36 is primarily concerned with the behavior of the betrothed male toward the virgin who is *hyperakmos*, that is, in the precarious position of being both beyond puberty and full of desire.[117] He suggests that the presumed vulnerability and unreliability of the *parthenoi* leads Paul to avoid addressing them directly. The men must act on behalf of the young women. Martin's interpretation deftly synthesizes ancient notions of marriage and sexuality in general, and virginity in particular.

Rape/Seduction of the Virgin Body

Closely related to the notion of being subject to male authority is the presumption that virgins live under the threat of rape and seduction. Jewish texts that depict virgins kept indoors and out of the view of sexually dangerous men (2 Macc 3.19; 3 Macc 1.18) lend evidence to the idealization of the well-guarded virgin. Deuteronomy 22.25–27 considers the case of the betrothed virgin who is raped in the open country, and the Mishnah considers the rape that takes place at a spring (M. Ket. 1.10). Even to be gazed upon invites trouble (Job 31.1; Sir 9.5). The cultural assumption of the virgin's vulnerability is matched only by the expectation that the power of the virgin body to induce sexual desire is beyond anyone's control. Thus the groans of a eunuch embracing a virgin serve as a fitting image of a person tragically unable to partake of life's pleasures (Sir 30.20).

The notion of keeping virgins out of the public eye is not exclusive to Jewish literature. As we will see in chapter 3, Greco-Roman novels portray virgins protected from both seeing men and being seen by them. Christian writers, too, are familiar with the tradition of thwarting the virgin gaze. One of Tertullian's best-known treatises defends the custom of veiling virgins both in the public arena and during Christian worship. His arguments attest to how widespread the custom was: "Throughout

Greece, and certain of its barbaric provinces, the majority of Churches keep their virgins covered" (*On the Veiling of Virgins* 2; cf. 13). Indeed, for Tertullian, unveiling a virgin is so grave an offense that it is synonymous with rape. He writes, "Every public exposure of an honorable virgin is (to her) a suffering of rape; and yet the suffering of carnal violence is the less (evil), because it comes of natural office" (3).

Here Tertullian allows for a "natural" component of rape. Nature itself is the source of sexual desire and consciousness. In keeping with the ancient association of sexual maturation and unruly desire, he explains that a virgin requires veiling not in early childhood, but

> from the time when she begins to be self-conscious, and to awake to the sense of her own nature, and to emerge from the *virgin's* (sense), and to experience that novel (sensation) which belongs to the succeeding age . . . a *virgin* ceases to be a *virgin* from the time that it becomes possible for her *not* to be one. (11)

Through the effects of Time and Nature, the virgin ceases to be a virgin when she is sexually and physically ripe. She becomes, instead, a woman. Yet she is still unmarried and still addressed as a virgin. In a subtle reinterpretation of virginity as something that counts only when a woman resists its natural demise, Tertullian exhorts:

> I pray you, be you mother, or sister, or *virgin*-daughter—let me address you according to the names proper to your years—veil your head: if a mother, for your sons' sakes; if a sister, for your brethren's sakes; if a daughter for your father's sakes. . . . Wear the full garb of *woman*, to preserve the standing of *virgin*. (16)

The virgin must remain veiled. As she remains hidden from the public's intensely sexual gaze, so is the public protected from the undeniable power of her sexuality.

In Greco-Roman tradition, *parthenoi* are objects of both divine and human desire. Beverly Ann Bow shows that sexual interaction between deities and mortals is not uncommon in Greco-Roman myth and demonstrates how the women in such stories are victims of divine deceit.[118] Ovid's account of Jove's rape of Callisto is especially pertinent, for in order to trick Callisto, the god disguises himself as the virgin goddess Diana.[119] The cruelty of his deception is only deepened by his mockery of virginity.

The father who dreads the disgrace of a minor daughter's rape or seduction fears economic loss as well as shame. Therefore Exodus 22.15–16 entitles a father to collect the equivalent of a virgin's bride-price from his daughter's seducer. If he chooses, he may also demand that the man marry his daughter. Likewise, if a man rapes an unbetrothed virgin, he must marry the woman and pay her father fifty shekels of silver. He is also denied the option of ever divorcing her (Deut 22.28–29). The Mishnah awards monetary damages to a father for the seduction or rape of his minor daughter (M. Ket. 4.1). Moreover, it exceeds scriptural directives (Ex 22.16; Deut 22.29) by comparing the violated daughter to a slave girl whose value has been diminished and demanding compensation for the father's disgrace (M. Ket. 3.7). As Wegner observes, monetary damages are rendered only for those females who are culturally assumed to be virgins. Those who violate a proselyte, former captive, or slave who was either converted, ransomed, or freed after the age of three years and one day incur no penalty (M. Ket. 3.2). In light of these conventions, it is no wonder that Sirach 42.9–10b attests to the paternal anxiety associated with raising a daughter: "A daughter is a secret anxiety to her father, and worry over her robs him of sleep; when she is young, for fear she may not marry, or if married, for fear she may be disliked; while a virgin, for fear she may be seduced and become pregnant in her father's house."

Cases involving betrothed virgins clarify the difference between seduction and rape. If sexual intercourse occurs between a man and a betrothed virgin in the city, the situation is treated as adultery. Both parties may be subject to stoning, the man because he violated his neighbor's wife, the woman because she did not cry out for help (Deut 22.23–24). If a sexual encounter occurs in the country, the betrothed virgin, unable to cry out for help, is not liable. The case is regarded as a rape, and only the perpetrator can be punished with death (Deut 22.25–27). Satlow observes how the Mishnah qualifies this Deuteronomic prescription:

Deut 22.23, which deals with the betrothed girl, uses the phrase
. . . "a girl, virgin, betrothed." Regardless of how this phrase may
have been meant, the rabbis seize upon the term, *na ara,* a girl or
maiden, which in even early rabbinic law has a very precise and
narrow meaning: a woman who is between 12 years and a day
old and 12 years and six months old. The force of this interpretation is to limit the applicability of the biblical law.[120]

Thus M. Sanh. 7.9 states not only that the girl must satisfy all
three conditions but that she must also be in the house of her
father in order for her seducer to be liable. Here again, male concerns dominate. Violation of the father's house elevates the seriousness of the crime.

In Roman law as well, violation of a father's house figures
prominently in sexual offenses. The jurisdiction and the legal responsibility of the *paterfamilias* over both sons and daughters is
well attested.[121] Only upon the legal surrender or death of one's
father did children become independent (*sui iuris*).[122] By the time
of Augustus, when *manus* (literally, "hand") marriage that placed
wives under their husbands' power had become far less common
than in previous eras, married men and women would remain
under a father's power (*patria potestas*). Thus the *lex Julia* gave a
father the authority to punish his daughter if he found her com-
mitting adultery in either his household or that of his son-in-
law.[123] In light of such comprehensive paternal authority, seduction of a Roman virgin was seen as a violation of a father's honor,
an infringement upon his household, and a threat to his lineage.

In cases where children were left fatherless, they would be
assigned a legal guardian, or tutor. Boys remained under tutelage
until the age of fourteen. But girls, under guardianship (*tutela
impuberis*) until the age of twelve, passed into a form of adult
tutelage (*tutelage mulieris*) thereafter. Although guardianship
became less strict with the *lex Julia* and *lex Papia Poppaea,* even
adult women would receive a tutor upon the death of a father.[124]
The authority of the *paterfamilias* was so respected that later the
intentions of a deceased father remained binding, even over those
of a guardian.[125] Marriages conducted against a deceased father's
wishes were denied legal status, and later came to be compared
to the crime of rape.[126]

If a twice-cited statement in the Elder Seneca's *Controversiae* reflects actual case law, Roman response to rape resembled Jewish legal codes. Rape was punishable in two ways. The first imposed on the offender monetary loss and compulsory marriage to his victim. The second cost the offender his life: "A girl who has been raped may choose either marriage to her ravisher without a dowry or his death."[127] In contrast to Jewish law, authority to determine the fate of an offender was exercised by the victim. If she decided to marry the offender, he would be denied her dowry. Rather than paying a fine to either his victim or her father, he would forfeit the customary monetary benefit obtained in marriage.

As illustrative as are such cases, the significance of male interests in the construction of rape is perhaps most evidenced in Jewish and Greco-Roman non-legal discourse. Roman literature reveals an ideology of rape and seduction that counters that which surfaces in the legal codes. For instance, not only does Ovid present rape as an erotic strategy, but ancient practices of erotic magic and bridal theft, or abduction marriage, show how sexual violence against women was sometimes seen as a legitimate means of securing a marriage partner.[128] Each of these examples demonstrates how the definition of rape and the determination of sexual assault were guided by androcentric interests.

In other cases, sexual assault was portrayed as a social strategy for preserving male honor. Livy shows how rape was used as an expression of tyranny, and biblical texts depict fathers offering their daughters for violent sexual abuse. In order to protect his male houseguests, Lot offers his daughters, two women "who have not known a man," to be sexually abused by the men of Sodom (Gen 19.8). Similarly, an old man in Gibeah protects his male guest by offering his virgin daughter and his guest's concubine to be raped by the men of the city (Judg 19.24). Both stories illustrate the expediency of sacrificing one's virgin daughters for the sake of a male guest. The sexual violence, although horrific, is portrayed less as rape and more as a necessary strategy exercised by an honorable host.[129]

In contrast, Shechem's violation of Dinah, the daughter of Jacob (Gen 34.2) is regarded as a rape. Yet as Dinah's brothers cry out, "Should our sister be treated as a whore (*porne*)?" (Gen 34.31), this story, too, focuses on male honor and interests. Even David's sexual abuse of Bathsheba (2 Sam 11.1–12.15) and Amnon's assault on Tamar (2 Sam 13.1–22) are cast as key moments in the violation and distortion of male honor and power. Not surprisingly, the impotence of David's rule in the final days of his kingship is expressed by his failure to use a beautiful young virgin for his sexual pleasure (1 Kings 1.1–4). It is male interests that often determine whether a wronged virgin is seen as a victim of sexual violence, a necessary sacrifice, or an object lesson about male dishonor.

The Virgin Body as the Body Politic

Many readers have noted the way in which the human body is an important trope in ancient discourse. As Wayne Meeks suggests, "There is hardly a political metaphor more well worn than the representation of the commonwealth as a body."[130] In numerous Jewish, Christian, and Greco-Roman texts that employ such imagery, the body politic as virgin is a familiar trope.

Whereas the well-known metaphors of adulterous wife and harlot are frequently used to illustrate Israel's infidelity to the Lord God, the image of Israel as virgin can bear both positive and negative connotations. Ezekiel casts Israel not as a virgin daughter, per se, but as a ward who has been placed in the care of the deity. When she exhibits signs of sexual maturation, the Lord enters into covenant with her:

> Your breasts became firm and your hair sprouted. You were still naked and bare when I passed by you and saw that your time for love had arrived. So I spread My robe over you and covered your nakedness and I entered into a covenant with you by oath—declares the Lord God; thus you became Mine. (Ezek 16.8)[131]

Howard Eilberg-Schwartz takes note of the sexual overtones that permeate the passage. Although he notes that "(t)he Ezekiel passage is as close as we get to a graphic image of God having sexual intercourse," he reminds us that "the divine body is behind the look and not the object of it."[132] Indeed, Eilberg-Schwartz discovers a consistent pattern in the Scriptures: "when the gaze is focused on bodies and beauty, it is typically the male who is doing the looking, the female who is the object of the gaze."[133] As the political body who commands the Lord's attention, Israel is female. She is the object of the divine gaze.

Throughout the Jewish Scriptures, Israel is repeatedly referred to as "virgin daughter Zion," and "virgin Israel." Both titles underscore the relationship between Israel and her Lord—Israel is God's virgin daughter, the one on whom God lays claim. The Lord hears Israel's prayers and acts to protect his daughter, and avenge her enemies (Isa 37.22; 2 Kings 19.21). When Israel returns from exile, the Lord lays claim upon the people with the following promise: "I will be the God of all the families of Israel, and they shall be my people. . . . Again I will build you, and you shall be built, O virgin Israel!" (Jer 31.1, 4). Israel is to the Lord as a virgin daughter is to her father.

Therefore Israel is expected to return God's fidelity. When she is seduced by idolatry, her willful behavior is cause for the Lord's anger and despair. Israel's God is left to lament the shameful ways of his "virgin daughter" (Jer 18.13, 31.21). For her rebellion, she is crushed by the Lord (Lam 1.15; 2.10, 13), and she falls, as if dead (Amos 5.2). God's claim upon the body politic is as complete as that of a father on his virgin daughter. She is his to discipline as well as his to protect.

The distinctiveness of the deity's relationship with Israel is illustrated by the contrasting application of the appellation "virgin daughter" to other nations. Babylon (Jer 46.11) and Egypt (Isa 47.1) are identified as virgin daughters only when they are humiliated by the God of Israel. At no time does God act as the guardian of "virgin" nations other than Israel. The metaphor of the father-daughter relationship is applied to gentile nations only in instances that call for disciplinary action. Thus Babylon and Egypt embody only the negative images of a virgin daughter—one who is untrustworthy, deceptive, and shameful. But God regards virgin Israel with both authority and care.

While Israel's relationship with its deity is expressed by the virgin-daughter metaphor, Rome's relationship with Vesta manifests itself in the priestly office of the Vestal Virgins. According to Dionysius of Halicarnassus, the extinction of the sacred fire attended by the virgin priestesses not only signals the unchastity of one of the Vestals, it also functions as a *semeion,* or sign, that portends the city's destruction.[134] The story of Aemilia indicates, too, that the city shares in an unchaste priestess's guilt. Aemilia prays to Vesta, "if I have been guilty of any impious deed, let my punishment expiate the guilt of the city."[135] Thus the figure of the Vestal somehow embodies Rome's standing before the deity. As Ariadne Staples observes, "a Vesta's virginity represented life and death, stability and chaos for the Roman state."[136]

Noting that the only documented instances of ritual interment between the first Punic War and the end of the Republic occurred during periods of political upheaval and the destruction of the Roman military, Staples identifies the dual service that the Vestals provided for the body politic. The women either symbolized the well-being of Rome or served as an opportunity for the people to regain hope and honor if all was not well:

> The Vestal Virgin and the Vestal who had lost her virginity were both, and in equal measure, vital for the welfare of the polity. The sexuality of the Vestal was inseparable from the welfare of the state. If the state was in trouble the spectacle of the burial of an unchaste Vestal would restore hope for its recovery. If the state was peaceful and prosperous the Vestals were clearly chaste.[137]

It comes as no surprise, then, that when a young girl between the ages of six and ten was taken as a Vestal, she became Rome's. Aulus Gellius reports that "(t)he word 'taken' is used, so it seems, because the Pontifex Maximus literally takes her by the hand and leads her away from the parent in whose power she is, as though she had been captured in war."[138] In keeping with her new identity, whenever a Vestal died, her estate passed neither to kin nor to any other designee, but to the public treasury.[139]

Reference to the human body as a metaphor for the church is well attested in the New Testament. Paul, who makes ample use of the trope, likens the church, a "chaste virgin" (*parthenos hagne*), to the virgin Eve who was deceived by the serpent (2 Cor 11.2–3). Here again, *parthenos* is multivalent, implying at once a sense of purity, vulnerablity, and weakness. The church is valued by Christ, yet like all virgins, she remains one who is easily seduced.

The figure of the virgin serves as an ecclesiastical metaphor in *The Shepherd of Hermas,* as well. In a spectacular vision, Hermas sees a *parthenos* approaching him, "adorned as if coming forth from the bridal chamber," and immediately recognizes her as the church.[140] Dressed as a bride, she exemplifies the faithful virgin betrothed to Christ (cf. 2 Cor 11.2; Rev 21.2, 9) and explains to Hermas the nature of double-mindedness (Vis 4.2.4–6). Having proven her fidelity and singleness of heart, the church exemplifies the ideal virgin bride.

Virginal triumph over temptation is cause for praise. Revelation 14.4 exalts the 144,000 redeemed whose purity is manifested in their virginity. In this singular instance in the New Testament canon where the faithful are presented as triumphant, invulnerable virgins, the figures are *male,* ones "who have not defiled themselves with women, for they are virgins (*parthenoi gar eisin*) . . . and in their mouth no lie was found, for they are spotless" (Rev 14.4ab, 5). That the moral vulnerability so commonly associated with female virginity yields here to the unqualified morality of male virgins suggests again that the multivalence of *parthenia* is rooted in ancient constructions of gender.

The Virgin as Subject

As the preceding discussion demonstrates, ancient discourse frequently considers the virgin in terms of her body. Because she is a sexually ripe but inexperienced female, her body is associated with varying degrees of health or sickness, increased sexual desire, emptiness and openness, holiness, monetary and reproductive worth, vulnerability, and weakness. Across a plurality of contexts, the virgin body remains a highly charged image. Yet ancient discourse also portrays the virgin as a subject, a person endowed with agency. As virginity signals sexual vulnerability, it also signals moral culpability. The virgin is as much an ethical, spiritual, and moral agent as she is a bodily presence.

Seneca's declamations reveal that a virgin priestess's body is not the only aspect of her person that comes under scrutiny.

Concern about personal experience and exposure to the more base dimensions of life surfaces in the case against a (supposed) virgin seeking the priesthood. When Pompeius Silo condemns her disreputable history, he warns, "Turn away your ears, you others seeking the priesthood, while I narrate the rest."[141] Virginity is retained, in part, by ignorance. To be virginal is to be "unknowing" and single-hearted in intent. As Clement of Alexandria writes, the speech that befits the Christian is "virgin speech, tender and free of fraud."[142]

Just as the virgin body is often viewed in terms of a dangerous increase of desire, the threat of moral dissolution hovers over the virgin subject. Therefore her moral standing is most secure after the fact, when she has successfully negotiated the proper transition from *parthenos* to *gyne*. Until that point, she signals physical, social, and moral liminality.

Virginity as a Means and a Sign

Because the virgin's sexual status functions as both a means to and a sign of her moral, spiritual, and social disposition, she can be associated with both virtue (*arete*) and its deficiency. Each category that follows implies the possibility of its opposite. Just as virginity can signify honor and purity, so can its demise or betrayal degenerate into dishonor and impurity. The virgin stands continually poised on the brink of moral excellence and moral decay. In a culture that values virtue and often distrusts sexuality, the virgin is a figure infused with moral significance.

Virginity as Singleness of Heart

Although ancient Jewish discourse tends to hold human sexuality in favorable esteem, certain traditions uphold the option of "sexual renunciation as a means to singleness of heart."[143] In *The Contemplative Life*, Philo praises the Therapeutae for their virtuous manner of life. Of their shared meals, he writes,

> The feast is shared by women also, most of them aged virgins, who have kept their chastity not under compulsion, like some of the Greek priestesses, but of their own free will in their ardent yearning for wisdom. Eager to have her for their life mate they have spurned the pleasures of the body and desire no mortal off-

spring but those immortal children which only the soul that is dear to God can bring to the birth unaided because the Father has sown in her spiritual rays enabling her to behold the verities of wisdom.[144]

The women's sexual status expresses the singleness of their spiritual commitment. Hungering only after wisdom, their souls give birth to virtue. Here Philo indirectly employs the image of a virginal conception (cf. *On the Cherubim*, 12–15, where God is the husband of *parthenia*) to suggest that the seeds of immortal virtue are sown in those who possess the singleness of heart that virginity evidences.

At one point in his First Letter to the Corinthians, Paul addresses celibate members of the community. Whether or not it is "well for a man not to touch a woman" (1 Cor 7.1), Paul urges his audience to take up marriage rather than fall into *porneia*. Likewise, he cautions married persons not to deprive one another sexually "except by agreement for a time, so that you may be free for fasting and prayer" (1 Cor 7.5). He reasons that such periods of celibacy are necessary, "lest Satan should tempt you through your lack of self-control" (1 Cor 7.5). The need for virtuous self-control (*enkrateia*) against the flame of passion (cf. 1 Cor 7.9) undergirds Paul's teaching. While celibacy facilitates fasting and prayer, it also opens the door to sexual immorality. Therefore Paul tries to guide his audience to a middle way, one that allows for periods of celibacy as well as conjugal intercourse. In short, celibacy and marriage are both placed in service to virtue.

That virginity, in particular, can express singleness of heart is clear in Paul's exhortation to the unmarried and widowed (1 Cor 7.25–40). The unmarried man (*agamos*) and the virgin (*parthenos*) are both free of anxieties about "the things of the world," namely, how to please a spouse. Instead, they care only for "the things of the Lord, how to please the Lord" (1 Cor 7.32–34). They are undivided, able to devote themselves entirely to the "things of the Lord" (cf. 1 Cor 7.37). Clearly, singleness of heart, a privilege of the unmarried and the virgin, is forfeited in marriage. Thus whereas Paul allows for marriage, he does so in a way that presents the institution as neither an ideal nor a norm, but as a prophylactic measure. Marriage is pervasively presented as normative in other Jewish texts, but appears as contingent in Paul's letter to the Corinthians. It functions as an effective means of containing sexual desire that could otherwise prove dangerous.

Virginity as Honor

The possibility of marriage deferred or denied conjures two distinct modes of virginity—virginity retained for a duration and virginity preserved for perpetuity. The first implies sexuality reserved for a particular man (a husband), the second implies sexuality shared with no man. Virginity yielding only to marriage, the dominant ideal for females in antiquity, presumed a virgin's honor. The virgin practiced a temporary and virtuous continence that was to lead to a virtuous marriage. The virgin and the wife, both praised for their chastity, were to reserve their sexuality for a husband. For the virgin whose social status was inextricably tied to male kin, her sexual status afforded both her and her family honor. The higher bride-price commanded by the Jewish *betulah* was a monetary expression of honor.

The association of virginity and honor undergirds the biblical case of the husband who charges his bride with sexual fraud. If his accusation that his wife was not a virgin when she married is proven false, the man incurs a fine. Because he slandered the woman, "bringing an evil name upon a virgin of Israel" (Deut 22.19), he must compensate his father-in-law for the dishonor brought upon his household. Likewise, in the inverse case of females assumed to be non-virgins, the very lack of honor ascribed to them confirms the relationship between honor and sexual status. Just as the Mishnah assumes that female slaves, captives, and girls raised by gentiles have been sexually violated, so does it fail to ascribe them any honor. In the case of a minor daughter who has been raped or seduced, the victim is compared to a slave girl whose worth has been diminished (M. Ket. 3.7).

Greco-Roman sources, too, associate virginity with honor.

Such honor is expressed most appropriately by a virgin's sense of shame.[145] Ovid's sibyl credits her sense of shame as that which enabled her to resist Phoebus's advances. She tells Aeneas,

> I am no goddess, nor is any mortal worthy of the honour of the sacred incense. But, lest you mistake in ignorance, eternal, endless life was offered me, had my virgin modesty consented to Phoebus' love. . . . I spurned Phoebus' gift and am still un-wedded.[146]

Shame enabled the virgin to retain both her honor and her virginity.

In a similar vein, the honor of the so-called virgin of Seneca's controversies is brought into question by one of her detractors. By hinting that the woman has no shame, he assails both her honor and her virginity: "At the sale no-one wanted to make a bid when it was known she had been a pirate's slave. They found nothing virginal in that face, that self-possession, that boldness that feared not even an armed man." When a second detractor adds, "Do not fear girl. You are chaste. But give yourself that sort of credit to a husband, not a temple. You were called a whore," he demonstrates that honor, not chastity, is at issue.[147] A true virgin, especially one seeking the priesthood, is not only chaste, she is also honorable.

As has been noted, much was made of transgressing Vestals who brought shame not only upon themselves but upon all of Rome. Vestals who failed tests of their virginity incurred dishonor worthy of death. By contrast, those who remained faithful to their vows achieved great public honor. They were assigned special seats in the theater, and when they appeared in public, they were preceded by lictors carrying fasces.[148]

Although Greco-Roman sources detail the punishments incurred by women caught in adultery, relatively little mention is made of non-priestly females who relinquished their virginity prior to marriage. Perhaps the Roman custom of marrying elite females at an early age rendered such circumstances improbable. Of such virgins, Peter Brown writes:

> Too labile a creature to be allowed the periods of sexual freedom granted to young men, and tolerated even in husbands, her family

> must guard her carefully. . . . The girl's loss of virginity was, simply, a bad omen for her future conduct. A girl who had already enjoyed furtive love affairs might do the same when married. She was not a "well brought up" girl.[149]

Loss of honor was the price paid by a virgin who allowed herself to be seduced.

As we have already seen, various modes of discourse detail how virginity could be tested and honor retracted. The "tokens of virginity" to which Deuteronomy 22.13–21 alludes were subject to physical verification. Vestals were tested for their virginity.[150] In some cases, they were formally tried and punished for unchastity.[151] Sissa details various virginity tests to which *parthenoi* were subjected. What such rituals reveal about ancient anatomy remains debatable; that virginity could be an object of testing, however, is certain.

Our discussion of the virgin body explored various economic, legal, social, and cultic responses to the clandestine loss of virginity. Suffice it to note here that while such responses reflect cultural re-evaluation of the female body, they also ascribe to the no-longer-virgin a degree of culpability. Whereas the violated virgin could be regarded as a victim, the sexually active "virgin" was treated as a deceitful and dishonorable woman. Deuteronomy 22.13–21 likens the false virgin to a harlot.

Virginity as Power

Absolute virginity is associated not with the average female in antiquity, but with mythical or sacred women. It denotes a certain undeniable power that the virgin embodies. Hers is an extraordinary continence. As an adult, she stands independent of the culturally established roles of wife and mother. The absolute virgin, whose sexual status signals not so much emptiness or singleness of heart, but self-containment and singularity, is always powerful and sometimes dangerous.

Such virgins figure prominently in the visions recounted in *The Shepherd of Hermas*. Here the central concern is the problem of "double-mindedness." For it is not those who cleave "to the double-minded and empty" (*tois dipsychois kai kenois,* Mand.

11.13), but all who "purify their hearts from the vain desires of the world" who "shall live to God" (Mand. 12.5). The double-minded are persons rooted in an emptiness devoid of any real power (*dynamis*). They are easily swayed, corrupted, and deceived by the empty teachings of false prophets (Mand. 11. 1–7). Thus Hermas is exhorted to "believe yourself in the Spirit which comes from God and has power, but have no faith in the spirit which is from the earth and empty, because there is no power in it, for it comes from the devil" (Mand. 11.17) and to "take now the power which comes from above" (Mand. 11.20).

In the dualistic world of *The Shepherd*, persons must choose between desire that is good and desire that is bad, power that is empty and corrupt and that which is power-full. The two ways cannot be reconciled. The ninth Similitude presents the opposition of these two ways in a detailed parable, recapitulating and refining an earlier identification of seven virtues with seven female figures who each possess power (Vis. 2.8). Here, we meet two opposing sets of figures—twelve *parthenoi* and twelve *gynaikes*.

The twelve women, beautiful and clothed in black, represent twelve vices, the strongest of which are *apistia* (unbelief), *akrasia* (impurity), *apeitheia* (disobedience), and *apate* (deceit). The twelve virgins are twelve *pneumata*, or virtues, the strongest of which are *pistis* (faith), *enkrateia* (continence), *dynamis* (power), and *makrothymia* (endurance). Those who would enter the kingdom can do so only if they, like the Son, bear the names and *dynamis* of these virgins (Sim. 9.13.3–4). Virtue identifies the nature of the virgins' power. Thus repentance occurs when persons "put away the lusts (*epithymiai*) of these women, and return to the *parthenoi* and walk in their power (*dynamis*) and in their deeds" (Sim. 9.14.1). The two ways represent an opposition of powers. One way is marked by the seductive pull of emptying, sensual desire; the other by the powerful raiment of virginity.

The alignment of sexual status and spiritual power is further illustrated during Hermas's overnight stay with the twelve virgins (Sim. 9.11.3). Waiting for the shepherd's reappearance, Hermas is given charge of the virgins, with whom he is to sleep "as a brother and not as a husband" (Sim. 9.11.3). As a prelude to prayer rather than impropriety, they kiss and play and embrace. Upon his return, the shepherd rewards Hermas's continence with further teaching. Disciplined sexuality is both a means to further revelation and a sign of spiritual comprehension.

Finally, in the last vision, the angel informs Hermas that the virgins were sent to him for a purpose. For without them, "it is not possible that these commandments be kept" (Sim. 10.3.1). It is they who provide the power to abide by the commandments. Yet if Hermas is to retain them in his house, he must keep his household pure (*katharos*): "Only do you make your house pure, for in a pure house they will willingly dwell, for they are pure and chaste and industrious and all have favor with the Lord" (Sim. 10.3.2). The power of the virgins is made manifest only in an environment of purity. Their presence is necessary, but conditional. Whereas their company signals promise, so does their absence constitute failure.

In the arena of pagan religion, the goddesses Athena and Artemis exemplify the power that distinguishes the absolute virgin. Because she remains a virgin perpetually, Athena is free from the sexual drives associated with the bodies of mortal virgins. Far from the unrefined, uncontrolled virgin of popular understanding, she is most often a figure of reason who functions as the patron goddess of war, wisdom, and artisans. Unfettered by the demands of marriage and reproduction, Athena is able to move outside the strictures assigned women. She is autonomous —indeed, "she is what she is, fully apart from whether she even belongs to a man or not."[152] Yet she is also the guardian of marriage and children. Thus Athena plays an integral role in all that upon which civilization depends—politics, wisdom, arts and crafts, and reproduction.

> Athena is the goddess most identified with the work of civilization, the work that makes us human, the works that express our humanity. . . . Athena's virginity, her lack of susceptibility to Aphrodite's wiles, rightly understood, stems from her commitment to cultural activity.[153]

It is Athena's virginal status, her autonomy, that enables her to move in arenas associated with both male and female productivity. Yet, as Christine Downing observes, the goddess's autonomy does not exclude her from culture; rather it enables her to generate and support culture. She "is not a goddess of procreation, but of creation."[154] Athena's is a civilizing power.

The powerful virgin goddess Artemis was exceedingly popular during the early Empire. She and her cult are mentioned by numerous ancient writers, including the author of Luke-Acts (cf. Acts 20.28). As Jean-Pierre Vernant argues, Artemis's divinity is two-dimensional:

> Daughter of Zeus and Leto, sister of Apollo, holder like him of the bow and the lyre, Artemis has two sides. She is the Huntress, the one who runs in the woods, the Wild One, the Archer, who shoots wild animals with her weapons and whose arrows, when used among humans, sometimes strike women unexpectedly to bring them to sudden death. She is also the Maiden, the pure Parthenos, dedicated to eternal virginity, the one who leads, in joyous dance, music, and beautiful song, that gracious chorus of adolescent girls she makes her companions—the Nymphs and Graces.[155]

Most relevant to our study, Artemis is the protector and helper of *parthenoi*.[156] Helen King notes that Artemis is especially associated with the transitions that young *parthenoi* negotiate as they become *gynaikes*.[157] Each transition—menarche, marriage, and childbearing—involves the shedding of blood. The goddess whose own blood is never shed assists women whose social duty is to bleed, that is, to become fertile, to have sexual intercourse in marriage, and to bear children. By refusing participation in the spheres to which women's lives are assigned, Artemis empowers others to become fully incorporated themselves.

The permanent liminality of her sexual status is echoed in other dimensions of her divinity. As goddess of the hunt, Artemis oversees a liminal activity, one that signals the crucial boundary between the wild and the civilized. As Vernant argues, Artemis ensures that the realms remain permeable, yet distinct, "since the hunt allows passage from one state to the other."[158] As the patron of childbirth, the "Mistress of the Margins" navigates another process steeped in liminality. Marking the maturation of a woman and the beginning of new life, childbearing reflects the culmination of a social contract (marriage) and the perpetuation of human culture.[159] The anomalous sexuality of both Athena and Artemis enables each to perform a role that sustains, rather than defies, patriarchal cultural norms. Artemis ushers women, as they navigate the transition from *parthenos* to *gyne,* into the roles that Hellenistic culture assigns them. Athena presides over the generation and sustenance of culture.

Not deities themselves, but those who served a goddess, the Vestals were sacred women. Although they retained the option of marrying after completing their priestly terms (thirty years), their extended virginity was nonetheless extraordinary. As virginal priestesses, the Vestals exercised privilege and power regularly denied other Roman women—they were free from guardianship and exercised the right to make a will while their fathers were yet living.[160] Suetonius notes that, as an incentive for parents to offer their daughters for priestly service, Augustus expanded the privileges of the Vestals.

The powerful presence of the priestesses was of such magnitude that contact with them could be a matter of life and death. As Plutarch remarks,

> When they go out they are preceded by lictors with the fasces, and if they accidentally happen to meet a criminal being led to execution, his life is spared. The Virgin must swear that the meeting was involuntary and accidental and not planned. Anyone who goes underneath a Vestal's litter when she is carried is put to death.[161]

Finally, the power of the Vestal Virgins was exhibited in their priestly ministrations. Although little of their sacred task in known in detail, it was only these virgins who were able to "carry out sacred rites which it is the law for a Vestal priestess to perform on behalf of the Roman people, on the same terms as her who was a Vestal on the best terms."[162]

Lest we mistake the power of the Vestals and the virgin goddesses as absolute as their virginity, Mary Lefkowitz reminds us that "[a]lthough the virgin goddesses were worshipped for their power over so many aspects of human life, they act only within limits defined by Zeus and with his approval, or with the co-operation of another god."[163] So, too, the Vestal Virgins remained under the discipline of the Pontifex Maximus.[164] It was he who retained the power of life and death over the priestesses. Whereas virginity was associated with the extraordinary power of Athena, Artemis, and the Vestals, the exercise of such power was constrained by, and served, patriarchal norms. Thus even in myth, females who defied male authority and were characterized by self-definition and self-determination were portrayed as dangerous:

> A confirmed mortal virgin who resisted the advances of a god might get away simply with metamorphosis into a tree or flower, but women who consciously denied their femininity, like the Amazons, or who killed their husbands and fathers, like the women of Lemnos, were regarded as enemies and monsters. (Aeschylus, *Libation Bearers* 632–38)[165]

Virginity as Purity

The notion of purity remains difficult to define. As Robert Parker's influential study of pollution and purification in early Greek religion reveals, "the language of 'purity'" is used in various contexts to "indicate resistance to several distinct forms of contamination," whether physical, moral, or sexual.[166] Even in the context of discourse concerning sexuality, the relationship between purity and sexual status remains ambiguous. Greek religious sensibilities rarely associated illicit sex, in particular, with cultic impurity. In cases where Athenian adulteresses were denied access to the temple, it was dishonor, rather than impurity, that caused their exclusion.[167] Nevertheless, Greco-Roman notions of purity were sometimes linked to abstinence and sexual status. As Parker and others reason, sexuality can function as a measurable means of distinguishing between the sacred and profane spheres of human activity—"the closer a mortal comes to sacred objects, the more acute becomes his need for sexual purity."[168] Thus abstinence and sacred encounter are associated in certain Jewish traditions, as well. Philo, an admirer of the Therapeutae, contends that Moses entered into a period of celibacy prior to an encounter with God.[169]

Only occasionally required of laity, limited periods of abstinence were more often associated with priests, who needed to prepare themselves for their sacred duties. Requisite extended virginity, as in the case of certain priestesses, was the exception rather than the rule: "It is because they are not the rule that we hear specifically from Pausanias of 'virgin priestesses' and the like."[170] Whereas the virginity that led to marriage could signify the more general purity of youth (including sexual inexperience), extended virginity could indicate the discrete purity possessed by the female subject. As was the case with the Vestal Virgins, whose purity was said to have reflected that of the sacred fire and the objects handled in the course of their ministrations, such virginity was particular and distinct.

In contrast to pagan religious discourse, Satlow finds that the Jewish Scriptures regularly present illicit sex as defiling. Yet the cultic significance of such encounters remains ambiguous:

> In the Hebrew Bible, certain non-marital sexual liaisons were considered "impure" or defiling. . . . An adulteress is termed "defiled," as is a woman who is divorced from her first husband, remarries, and then divorces her second husband and returns to her first husband. The biblical use of this term is not entirely clear. It might, on the one hand, designate a ritual status, "defiled" as opposed to "pure." Alternatively, it might simply be another way of saying that she sinned.[171]

Here again the rhetoric of purity is imprecise. Such lack of precision, however, only heightens the impact of the condemnation it conveys. For what clearly matters most is not the nature of the impurity itself, but the fact that such sexual activity results in dramatically negative consequences. It sets the subject apart, either imposing or reflecting a change in her status. Indeed, illicit sex committed by a female (premarital as well as extramarital) is often compared with harlotry (*z'nut*). Such stern rhetoric not only confirms the notion that illicit encounters defile a woman, it redefines her (cf. Lev 21.7; Deut 22.21).

Unlike the rape victim, a virgin who has engaged in illicit sex is defiled by an act of her own agency. As the defilement of her body reflects her intention, both are implicated. The false virgin, guilty "because she committed an outrage in Israel by playing the harlot in her father's house" (Deut 22.21), can be condemned to death. So too can the virgin who consents to intercourse with someone other than her betrothed (Deut 22.23–24).

Whether the language of impurity and defilement relates to a specifically cultic context or implies sin in a general sense, it clearly identifies illicit sex as a serious transgression that reflects poorly on the subject. Citing M. Sot. 1.5, 3.3, and M. Ned. 11.12, Satlow observes that "(i)n each of these examples, as with many of the uses of the term 'defilement' in this context, the words are direct quotations attributed to women: 'I am defiled,' she says, meaning that she has committed adultery."[172] What is most compelling about the declaration is that it not only identifies the woman's act, it identifies the woman herself.

Virginity as Salvation

Purity implies the absence of corruption. In some instances, it signifies salvation itself. In contrast to both the temporary purity that commonly precedes religious ritual and the extended purity of the Vestals, "purity in life" distinguished such archaic Greek cults as Pythagoreanism and Orphism. As Parker notes, at the very least, moderation and self-control were hallmarks of the sexuality practiced in these circles. Reaching beyond a concern for "singleness of heart" or the attainment of virtue, their ascetical practices reflected a desire to transcend the fleshly corruption of human existence. It is this concept, the notion that the flesh is something to be transcended, that represents the antithesis of what Boyarin identifies as ancient rabbinic understanding of the body. According to such pagan thinking, "[e]ncasement in flesh was in itself a punishment, but during this imprisonment further purifications were necessary in order to escape from the 'dire cycle of deep grief' (incarnation)."[173]

The identification of sexuality with corruption permeated some early Christian discourse. As Peter Brown argues, the implications that Christians drew from this formulation were quite diverse. For example, in *On the Veiling of Virgins,* Tertullian

> made plain profound divergences in Christian attitudes to sexuality and to the possible meanings that might cluster around the act of sexual renunciation. . . . The uncanny, non-normal state of dedicated virgin girls, raised above shame and splendidly unveiled, stood for a fleck of divine glory in a dark world.[174]

Yet the implication that "to have renounced sexual activity meant something more than to have brought sexual urges under control by rigorous self-discipline" and that "[r]enunciation and baptism into the Church declared the power of sex null and void" was foreign to Tertullian.[175] For him, the believer was still squarely located in the present age, that is, in the territory of sexual desire and fleshly corruption. To deny such a reality was dangerously misguided, for Christians were not yet free from the pull of sexual desire.

Thus Tertullian advises his hearers to aspire toward the control, rather than the denial, of sexual desire. Accompanying such exhortation was the popular belief that sexual desire waned with age. Whereas marriage occurred in youth or young adulthood, continence could be practiced in, and after, one's marriage. Continence, Tertullian exhorts, is "superior to virginity. . . . For constancy of virginity is maintained by grace; of continence, by virtue."[176] It is blessed to never have known sexual pleasure in the first place, but it is virtuous to resist pleasure one has already discovered.

Because procreation only perpetuated "the cycle of grief" in which humanity found itself, in some Encratite circles, sexuality came to symbolize nothing less than bondage to death itself. Having been taught by the serpent to engage in sexual intercourse, and thus having become like irrational animals, Adam and Eve had plunged humanity into an animal-like existence that led only to death.[177] Hence sexual renunciation symbolized both a return to original humanity and the human "ability to undo the power of death."[178] Some second-century Christians became proponents of a realized eschatology that was linked to sexual abstinence. For them, continence following baptism embodied one's participation in the new age and served as evidence of salvation itself.

The relative popularity of such belief emerges in Clement of Alexandria's *Miscellanies:*

> To those, on the one hand, who under a pious cloak blaspheme by their continence both the creation and the holy Creator, the almighty, only God, and teach that one must reject marriage and begetting of children, and should not bring others in their place to live in this wretched world, nor give any sustenance to death,

our reply is as follows. . . . When Salome asked the Lord: "How long shall death hold sway?" he answered: "As long as you women bear children." Her words do not imply that this life is evil and the creation bad, and his reply only teaches the ordinary course of nature. For birth is invariably followed by death.[179]

Some circles of faith argued for a union of soul and Spirit so complete and so powerful that it would render sexual union for Christians obsolete. For Tatian and other like-minded Encratites, marital sex signified nothing less than *phthora* (corruption) and *porneia*.[180] Tatian reasoned that once Adam separated from union with God and the Spirit, he became subject to corruption and death. Sexual union with Eve, therefore, was a necessary consequence of sin. As Peter Brown shows, it was precisely this union that Christians were required to abandon.[181]

Clement opposed Encratite belief by supporting marriage and procreation as part of God's providence. On the one hand, he vigorously argued against the presence of sexual desire in marriage. On the other, he allowed for conjugal sexuality. Severing sexual intercourse from desire, Clement did not idealize virginity.[182] Virginity as a means and sign of salvation acquired greater significance and precision in later writings, such as those of Origen and Gregory of Nyssa. As Peter Brown details, developments in Christian understandings of the body saw the emergence of "a fully fledged notion of virginity" during the mid-third to the mid-fourth century.[183] Earlier Christian discourse, with its concern for the relationship between sexuality and salvation, only set the stage for more rigorous formulation.

The virgin in antiquity is not a single cultural symbol, nor does she bear a single valence. Rather, she is multidimensional, connoting a spectrum of images and meanings. A brief survey of Greco-Roman, Jewish, and Christian discourse of the first two centuries of the Christian era reveals that the *parthenos* functions as a topic of interest and concern across a wide range of contexts. Whether viewed primarily as a body or as an acting subject, the virgin signals the negotiation of a highly charged transition toward physical and moral maturity. Her physical incompleteness is mirrored by a moral unprovenness. But ideally presumed physical integrity and sexual inexperience is matched by the presumption of ethical integrity and ignorance of the baser dimensions of life. She is at once vulnerable, powerful, chaste, and desirous. Because none of these images is exclusive, to speak of the *parthenos* is to refer to a constellation of connotations.

Constraining the Virgin

The *Parthenos* in Ancient Narrative

Three

In this chapter we consider several ancient narratives that feature virgin protagonists: the Greco-Roman novels *Daphnis and Chloe* and *Leucippe and Clitophon;* the Jewish novel *Joseph and Asenath;* and the Christian Apocryphal Acts *The Acts of Paul and Thecla* and *The Acts of Peter.* Just as the literature surveyed in the previous chapter reveals the multiplicity of images and connotations associated with *parthenos* and *parthenia,* ancient narrative also afforded the *parthenos* significant complexity. The narratives portray the virgin as both erotic and chaste, wild and socialized. She bears the potential for each characterization, and the tension that results from such possibility figures prominently in fictional representation of the virgin. In portraying the *parthenos* in terms of both the female body and female subjectivity, ancient narratives expose not only the multivalence attributed to, but also the ambivalence evoked by, female sexual status.

The Ancient Novels

Although the narratives with which we are concerned are identified as ancient fiction, the definition and nature of the genre remain ill-defined. As Tomas Hägg and Bryan P. Reardon have noted, "Antiquity never created a special term for its 'novels,'" but in the last centuries before the common era, a "new type of prose literature" emerged in the eastern Mediterranean world.[1] In contrast to such well-established genres as tragedy and historiography, this new literature neither generated nor inspired a poetics of fiction. Rather, the novel "was not born in any context of theory or critical interest, but in spite of theory critics' interests."[2]

Despite its theoretical invisibility, the number of extant papyri attests to the popularity of ancient fiction. Although the majority of texts exist in only fragmentary form, five complete novels have survived. Three of these, including *Daphnis and Chloe* and *Leucippe and Clitophon*, were composed during the Roman revival of Greek culture and composition known as the Second Sophistic (50–250 c.e.).[3] Though in the midst of a cultural movement that was both conscious and intentional, "not even then did the genre acquire a new name; when works of this kind are sometimes alluded to, either very general terms are used, such as 'fictitious' or 'dramatic' tales (*plasmatika, dramatika*), or they are characterized in more detail for a particular purpose."[4]

Modern critics have tried to compensate for the oversight of their ancient predecessors by offering their own theories to explain the genealogy of the ancient novel. Drawing upon genres that are well-established in ancient literary discourse, including historiography, erotic poetry, and travel narratives, interpreters have argued for various origins of the novel.[5] As one interpreter declares, "The novel has always been the most polyphonic, heteroglossic of genres. . . . The Greek novels exploit the broadest spectrum of intertexts."[6] Despite, or perhaps in light of, a proliferation of exclusive theories concerning the novel's origins, none is fully persuasive. A now more commonly held view concludes that the novel is "too complex a phenomenon to be reduced to a single impetus."[7]

Unlike the sources considered in the previous chapter, the novels were popular reading. Even in a culture where literacy was reserved for the educated, it is likely that a greater number of persons would have read or heard the novels than would have read either the medical writings of Soranus or the disputations of the elder Seneca.[8] Indeed, the very accessibility that figured in the novels' popular appeal may also have contributed to their rather diminished literary status. J. R. Morgan observes that although "people of some sophistication bought and enjoyed novels, they seem to have read them within a frame of cultural values which somehow consigned the pleasures of novel-reading to the categories of the insignificant or in some way ambivalent."[9] Both he and Hägg cite Julian's recommendation that while history is useful and beneficial reading,

> we must reject all the fictions (*plasmata*) composed by writers of the past in the form of history (*en historias eidei*), narratives of love (*erotikai hypotheseis*) and all that sort of stuff. (*Ep.* 89.301b)[10]

Although the novels may not have served as the stuff of "serious" reading, they were indeed *read*. And, in light of their rather broad reach, these literary equivalents of our modern day "B" films remain integral to any consideration of popular notions of virginity. Why were the novels popular? Citing their high entertainment value, interpreters note that novels are rife with "contingent detail whose effect is to render the action concrete and specific."[11] For the single, defining action of tragedy they substitute complex plots of fast-paced actions and stunning turns of events. The novel conveys a sense of immediacy that enhances its ability to entertain and delight the reader.

Perhaps as appealing is the novel's cultural immediacy. Therefore interpreters have also considered the cultural impetus behind the novels' composition.[12] As Reardon argues, the novels mirror the age in which they were produced. They reflect a host of physical conditions and cultural preoccupations such as "the archaizing trend, the dominance of rhetoric, and the impulse towards religion, or religiosity."[13] Richard I. Pervo notes how the novels "were *koine* both culturally and linguistically. Just as that Greek dialect blended various elements, so novels reflected the various and sometimes contradictory features of cosmopolitanism."[14] The cultural forces and issues engendered by an increasingly pluralistic empire yielded an eclectic literary pattern. Merging a new genre with traditional motifs,

> [t]he newness of novelistic worlds could be illusory in several senses. In response to upwardly mobile audiences endued with all the old-fashioned virtues, novelists tended to reinforce existing values. Characters, even regal or historic persons, were repainted to reflect the values of novel readers, and life was repainted to reflect their wishes.[15]

Through the medium of fiction, the ideal could become real.[16] Against tremendous odds, the novel's male and female characters triumph in the face of life's many twists and turns.[17] Laden with images that border on the incredible, the novels negotiate the ideal. As Brigitte Egger, Judith Perkins, and Cooper have shown, the novels serve to reinforce social conventions and norms concerning marriage, family, and the social good.[18] The value and connotations of female sexual status are illustrated in stories of fictive characters struggling with *eros* but in ways that ultimately serve the larger society.

ANCIENT NARRATIVE AS A FOCUS OF INVESTIGATION

In his discussion of Greco-Roman culture as a "culture of the self," Foucault bypasses a thorough review of the novels. Consideration of "the strategic place of erotic narrative in the discourse of desire" is left to Simon Goldhill, who faults Foucault for treating the novels "as merely a repository of 'some of the themes that will subsequently characterize erotics' (as if the novel were just a stage on the journey from Plato to Jerome)" and for failing to appreciate "the complex and sophisticated ways in which these fictions engage with the real."[19] For Goldhill, "the novel's bricolage is itself a particular construction of the arts of living and the care of the self."[20] Novels demonstrate a distinctive repertoire of ways in which the self can be represented as an ethical subject. Because they can afford to "ironize and eroticize as well as represent and explore the relations between philosophy, sexuality, and nature," the ethics of the novels are sometimes subtle, even convoluted.[21] Whereas Foucault maintains the image of an ancient sexuality devoid of playfulness, Goldhill finds in the novels evidence of moral austerity as well as its counterpoint. The novels convey a sometimes amusing manipulation of the philosophical that is not only self-conscious but self-serving.

Thus Goldhill infuses Foucault's reading with necessary nuance. Even as he criticizes Foucault for positing an overly rigid trajectory of the development of sexual ethics in late antiquity, Goldhill implicitly confirms much of what his predecessor asserts. The ethical flexibility that Goldhill finds exhibited in the novels represents not moral anarchy, but variations on a theme. A concern for sexual ethics permeates novels that lend the "culture of the self" greater subtlety, tension, and humor.

Numerous interpreters have observed that the novels generally identified as romances follow a particular sequence of events. As Reardon notes,

> [A] handsome youth and a beautiful girl meet by chance and fall in love, but unexpected obstacles obstruct their union; they are separated, and each is launched on a series of journeys and dangerous adventures; through all their tribulations, however, they remain faithful to each other and to the benevolent deities who at critical junctures guide their steps; and eventually they are reunited and live happily ever after.[22]

The theme of these stories is the love relationship that must endure a series of threats to its integrity. When the stories are taken together, the heroine tends to be characterized in the following manner: she is introduced at the beginning of the story; she is described as being very beautiful; she is Greek and white; she is a woman of social standing; she is guarded in a domestic environment; she is chaste.[23] While variations occur across the different novels, two features are constant: the heroine's beauty and chastity.

Egger observes that whereas the Greek novel assigns to male characters a range of narrative functions, female characters are limited to only four roles. Like their male counterparts, they respond to "the workings of *tyche* and subordinate themselves under her power," but they do so in a much more constrained way.[24] Female characters appear in the role of the female protagonist; her anti-type, the female antagonist; her friend or confidante; or her mother.[25] Furthermore, in the world of ancient fiction, women are portrayed within a world of men and most often in relation to male characters. Their primary orientation is toward their male, not their female, counterparts.

In the novels, the heroine's beauty is of a supernatural order. Indeed, such protagonists

> depend entirely on this erotic omnipotence for social and physical survival. After all, it is the only real asset they possess. This attractiveness is of course double-edged: while it gets them into enormous difficulties in the first place, they can also use it (unconsciously, as is stressed) in order to gain control over the men who hold the real authority, and thus apparently invert the true conditions of power.[26]

Since *eros* cannot be fully controlled by the human subject, this display of eroticism renders the heroine both vulnerable and powerful. For *eros* itself is represented as a driving force, one that compels both men and women to act and that brings the need for *sophrosyne* into focus. Thus chastity functions as the "main generic characteristic of the female protagonist."[27]

Most relevant for this study is the observation that in the novels in which the heroine is wed early in the story and then separated from her husband, her eroticism remains implicit (i.e., it is indicated by the ways in which other characters behave toward her). However, in Achilles Tatius and Longus, where the heroine is a *parthenos* and marries only in the latter part of the story, "the two authors allow the heroine some erotic experience."[28] As a *parthenos*, the central female character is charged with a more explicit eroticism, a factor that figures in the images of virginity that permeate these stories.

Like the novels under consideration here, the contemporaneous narratives *Joseph and Asenath* (JosAs) and the Christian *Acts of Paul and Thecla* and *Acts of Peter* also portray *parthenoi*. Indeed, it was the text's references to *parthenos* that first caused New Testament interpreters to take notice of JosAs.[29] Although numerous interpreters have observed the formal and thematic affinities that JosAs and the Acts share with the Greco-Roman novels, examination of JosAs and the Apocryphal Acts does not depend on the precise determination of their genre.[30] It is sufficient to consider them the literary kin of the novels.

The Acts have long been read in the context of the novels.[31] Having cited the travel motifs, erotic themes, and other features that the Acts share with the Greco-Roman narratives, Ernst von Dobschütz left a lasting impression on the interpretation of the Acts. Indeed, echoes of his early assertions concerning the reciprocity of Christian sensibilities and the romance[32] can be heard in Reardon's recent discussion of the interplay between genre and religious culture:

> romance authors and other writers alike are often imbued with religious sentiment, in different ways. . . . That is not a one-way street. Romance absorbs such influences, but romance itself spreads outward and invades the field of religious belief. Just as rhetorical prose affects Christian apologetic in the second century . . . , so we find in the period an increasing number of Christian and para-Christian narratives of adventure . . . they are what Christian ideology could make of the romance form.[33]

It is precisely this phenomenon of shared cultural motifs, images, and interests that bears relevance for the present investigation. What Pervo conveys about the novels is true of all the literature we have placed in view:

> Writers for popular markets give people what they like and plenty of it. Where nondevotees see wearying repetition, admirers detect subtle differences or the joy of repeated pleasures. . . . The recurrence of plots, motifs, and incidents is an indication of their appeal and thus helps establish what was popular.[34]

Recurring images are popular images. In exploring the images of virginity that appear in the Acts, we may assume that we are encountering ancient popular perspectives on female sexual status.

Parthenoi and *Parthenia* in Ancient Narratives

Following a brief synopsis of each narrative in view, we turn now to a consideration of ancient fictive portrayals of virginity and virgin heroines. While each text exploits different aspects of virginity in order to achieve its narrative goal, all of the narratives give particular attention to the body of the virgin protagonist.

LEUCIPPE AND CLITOPHON

Synopsis

Of the two pagan novels with which this study is concerned, Achilles Tatius's *Leucippe and Clitophon* bears the closest resemblance to other romances.[35] Except for the later Heliodorus, it is the novel that demonstrates the greatest interest in *parthenia*. The story unfolds as follows: Handsome Clitophon encounters beautiful Leucippe and immediately falls in love with her. Through a series of encounters that he carefully manipulates, Clitophon wins Leucippe's love. Following a rendezvous in Leucippe's bedroom that is abruptly interrupted by the virgin's mother, the lovers flee, only to be caught up in a series of adventures that leads to their separation. Although her life and her virginity are repeatedly threatened by a string of male antagonists, Leucippe manages to preserve both until she and Clitophon are finally reunited.

Representing the Virgin Body

Throughout *Leucippe and Clitophon*, virginity is represented as a singularly female phenomenon. Although Leucippe's virginity is questioned several times, even to the point of public testing, Clitophon's virginity never becomes a point of public controversy. Rather, Clitophon himself raises the question of whether virginity bears any relevance for male sexuality. Writing a letter to Leucippe after a long period of separation from her, Clitophon defends himself against the presumption that he has been unfaithful: "You will learn that I have imitated your *parthenia*, if that word has any meaning for men as it does for women" (5.20). For Clitophon, *parthenia* clearly refers to female sexuality.

The significance of virginity and of the virgin body, in particular, reveals itself at the very opening of Achilles Tatius's narrative. Before introducing the reader to either Clitophon or Leucippe, the narrator directs the reader's attention to a painting. As interpreters have observed, the narrator's *ekphrasis* (description/interpretation) of the painting foreshadows the sea travels upon which Leucippe and Clitophon, compelled by Eros, will later embark: "the picture was of Europa; the sea was Phoenicia's; the land was Sidon. On the land were represented a meadow and a chorus of *parthenoi*, on the sea swam a bull, and on his back was seated a beautiful (*kale*) *parthenos*, sailing on the bull towards Crete" (1.1).[36] The chorus of virgins exude both joy and fear as Zeus, transformed into a bull in order to abduct Europa, and the *parthenos* are led away by the child-god, Eros. The narrator's detailed and erotically charged description of the virgin's body serves as one of the most striking aspects of this *ekphrasis*.

Following the opening, Clitophon takes over the story's narration. Thus it is his voice and his gaze that introduce Leucippe into the narrative. Recalling how Leucippe and her mother had been sent by Leucippe's father to take refuge at the home of his brother (Clitophon's father) during a time of war, Clitophon details his first encounter with Leucippe. Recounting how he had been struck by the virgin's beauty from the very first, Clitophon remembers that he had only once before beheld such beauty and tells of a painting he once saw of Selene riding a bull. The identification of Leucippe with the opening *ekphrasis* of Europa cannot be missed (some manuscripts even read "Europa" instead of "Selene" for the painting that Clitophon recalls).[37] The association of Europa/Selene/Leucippe enables the reader to envision Leucippe. As the narrative focuses on both the heroine's sexual status and her physical appearance, it indirectly but effectively "hints at details of Leucippe's body, a feature otherwise not delineated in the GN [Greek novels]." Egger continues,

> Europa is wearing clinging, revealing clothes, and if I read the
> rhetorically convoluted illustration of her figure correctly, she
> (and that is, also Leucippe) has a deep-seated navel (?), a narrow
> waist, curvaceous hips and a small bust. This is the only (and
> indirect) account of a heroine's (as well as antagonist's) physical
> build, which has, just as the analogy of Europa herself, strong
> erotic implications: all the other authors confine themselves to
> her face, hair, and mention of her tallness.[38]

Thus the opening *ekphrasis* and Clitophon's description of Leucippe combine to reveal a pronounced narrative interest in the
virgin body. Leucippe's erotic beauty is underscored from the
very moment that she is introduced into the story.

The virgin's beauty wields its power over the men with
whom she comes into contact. Beginning with Clitophon, a series of male characters seek to secure Leucippe's beauty for themselves, often going to extreme measures in order to do so. Upon
seeing Leucippe, Clitophon is immediately rendered love-sick
by his desire for the *parthenos* (1.9). Gazing upon her while an
after-dinner entertainer sings the song of Apollo and Daphne,
Clitophon murmurs to himself, "Look here, Apollo himself
loves a *parthenos;* unashamed of his love, he pursues the virgin—
while you hesitate and blush: untimely self-control (*akairos soph-
roneis*)! Are you better than a god?" (1.5). As Goldhill demonstrates, the episode is doubly programmatic. On one hand, it
illustrates the power of erotic speech (*erotikoi logoi*), for Clitophon's passion is stirred by the song's lyrics. On the other, it
"stages the 'cultivation of the self,' that central process in Foucault's construction of ancient sexuality, but stages it as a cultivated irony about self-representation."[39] Such irony is most
pronounced in the narrator's declaration, "In spite of all our admonitions to moderation (*eis sophrosynen*), models excite us to
imitation, particularly a pattern set by our betters" (1.5). Actions,
not admonitions, inspire imitation.

Thus Leucippe's compelling eroticism becomes cause for
Clitophon's clever triumph over *sophrosyne*. She evidences the
kind of beauty that every *parthenos* desires. As Kleinas reminds
Clitophon, "every parthenos wants to be beautiful (*kale*)" (1.9).

Yet Leucippe exercises no more control of her erotic power over others than do the men who encounter her. The source of such power is her body, not her agency. Rendering her both powerful and vulnerable, this unregulated eroticism is permeated with ambivalence. As in the painting of Europa/Selene/Leucippe that opens the novel, the compellingly beautiful virgin captures the viewer's gaze. But neither the virgin nor the bull controls the scene that the painting depicts. It is Eros alone who determines their fate.

The narrative exploits the novelistic convention of the well-guarded *parthenos* who remains indoors. Sure enough, Leucippe's movements are limited to the interior of her uncle's home, but Clitophon lives in the house as well. Even as he is kept at a distance by the watchful eye of Leucippe's chambermaid, Clitophon has at least visual access to the virgin. When this proves frustrating for him, he is reminded by a friend of his unusual good fortune, "Other lovers must be content with occasional glimpses of some well-guarded (*teroumenes*) *parthenos*" (1.9).[40] Finally, after scheming with two household slaves, themselves lovers, Clitophon obtains a private audience with Leucippe—in her bedchamber.

Here again the narrative focuses explicitly on Leucippe's body. Just as Clitophon reaches the virgin's bedroom, Leucippe's mother, Pantheia, dreams of her daughter's destruction:

> She was being disturbed by a dream, in which she saw a bandit with a naked sword seize her daughter, drag her away, throw her down on her back, and slice her in two all the way up from her stomach, making his first insertion at her modest spot (*apo tes aidous*). Pantheia was so distressed and frightened that she leaped up just as she was and ran the few steps to her daughter's bedroom, just as I was lying down. (2.23)

The image of genital (*ta aidoia*) mutilation graphically illustrates the notion that virginity can be stolen and virgins destroyed. The violation of virginity signals the dissolution of the virgin.

That fornication dismembers a virgin's honor is evidenced by Pantheia's fury at her daughter. Raging that it would have been better had Leucippe been raped than for her to have freely surrendered her virginity, Pantheia concludes, "My dream misled me; the truth was worse than I saw. . . . [H]e pricked you deeper than a sword could have" (2.24). She is most concerned about the mutilation of Leucippe's honor.

Even as the violence of these images suggests that virginity remains subject to violation, the narrative demonstrates that representation of male power over the virgin body is not always sexual. The heroines of the Greek novels do not willingly travel by themselves; rather they are taken and possessed by men. Leucippe is repeatedly escorted, abducted, and held against her will. Twice she is almost murdered by pirates at sea—the first time by disembowelment and the second time by decapitation (3.18; 5.7). The narrative's gratuitous violence underscores the vulnerability of the virgin body to male brutality.

Following the second attempt on Leucippe's life, Clitophon discovers what he mistakenly believes to be Leucippe's decapitated body. His lament sheds light on a theme that resonates throughout the narrative: the male desire to possess the *parthenos*. [41] Taking the remains of the virgin body into his arms, he declares that he has utterly lost (*apollymi*) her. With Leucippe's head seemingly lost at sea, Clitophon laments, "I have been left the smaller part of you in the guise of the greater, whereas the sea, in a small part of you, possesses (*kratei*) all of you" (5.7). In retaining Leucippe's head, it is the sea that has laid claim to Leucippe.

Indeed, part of the allure of any *parthenos* is that she has not yet been *had*. How is it then, that Leucippe "belongs" to Clitophon? Here Clitophon mourns that he can no longer kiss Leucippe's lips. Indeed, having remained a *parthenos*, Leucippe had become his *gyne* in kisses only. In this way, she had permitted Clitophon alone partial access to her: "[t]hough only the lips come into contact, a geyser of pleasures spouts up from the very soul" (4.8). The erotic power of Leucippe's kiss had been like that ascribed to the virgin in general, for as Clitophon observes, a kiss is pleasurable precisely because it is insatiate (*akoretos*, 4.8). The pleasure Leucippe's kiss had bestowed intensified with the increased want it engendered. Therefore Clitophon's desire to possess Leucippe had only increased with the partial access he had acquired. Having refused to allow any other man to kiss her, upon her supposed death, Clitophon grieves the sea's possession of his virgin.

An earlier attempt on Leucippe's life likewise underscores the significance of her sexual status. Having been identified as a *parthenos,* Leucippe is about to be offered as a purification sacrifice by the pirates who have abducted her (3.12). Unbeknownst to both her captors and Clitophon (and the readers!), Leucippe and her companion, Menelaos, trick the pirates into thinking that they have indeed killed her. After believing that they have plunged a sword into the virgin's heart and cut open her body, the pirates proceed to consume what they mistake for Leucippe's entrails. Horrified at the men dividing among themselves the secrets (*ta mysteria*) of Leucippe's body, Clitophon cries out, "oh strange communion service!" (3.16). The trope neatly exposes his sense of loss. Not having experienced all *ta mysteria* of Leucippe's love himself (1.9, 18; 2.19), Clitophon is rendered a voyeur who must watch other men enjoying *ta mysteria* of his virgin. He bewails his inability to collect all the component parts of her body and despairs that her "insides are inside the outlaws" (3.16). It is no wonder that when he later finds Leucippe alive, he happily exclaims that she is *holokleros* (3.18). John J. Winkler's translation catches the innuendo—Clitophon declares the virgin "intact and sound." Her mysteries yet await Clitophon's discovery.

Leucippe's virgin body is also susceptible to internal physical sufferings. After having survived two attempts on her life, the heroine is tricked into drinking an aphrodisiac and falls into a seizure and a state of dementia (4.9–10, 15–17). Before the horrid deed is revealed, the unwitting Menelaos tries to reassure Clitophon that Leucippe's symptoms are natural: "young blood seething in its own strength may boil over the veins (*to gar haima pante neazon kai hypo polles akmes anazeon hyperblyzei pollakis tas phlebas*) and rise inside the head, where by flooding it impedes the circuits of rational thought" (4.10). Although Leucippe's virginity is not explicitly cited as the cause of her condition, Menelaos associates the ailment with her youth. His explanation resonates with ancient medical discussion of virginity and the dangers of "hot" desire.[42]

Finally, cultic associations with virginity also permeate the narrative. Mortals and divinities alike strive after the virgin's body. The pirates' attempt to sacrifice Leucippe is prompted by cultic requirements: only the body of a *parthenos* will suffice as a purification sacrifice (3.12). Just as deities may demand the sacrifice of the virgin, so may goddesses offer to protect her. Thus Leucippe receives the repeated assistance of the virgin Artemis. It is Artemis who leads Leucippe's father, Sostratos, to his lost daughter, and promises Leucippe, "Do not be sad, you shall not die, for I will stand by you and help you. You will remain a virgin until I myself give you away as a bride" (4.1).[43] Later, Leucippe takes refuge in Artemis's temple, a sanctuary open only to men and to virgins, under penalty of death (8.13).

Virginity and the Ambivalence of Desire

Although the narrative repeatedly underscores the erotic power of Leucippe's beauty, its portrayal of the virgin's own erotic self-awareness is fraught with ambivalence. At times, arousal of Leucippe's desire depends upon Clitophon's savvy manipulation. At other times, the virgin acts directly on her desire for Clitophon. In still other instances, she exhibits a sexual modesty that contradicts the openly erotic behavior she has previously displayed. The narrative portrays a virgin whose erotic expression is sometimes overt, but more often covert. Moreover, it suggests that the cultivation of female eroticism is itself cause for ambivalence. When the erotic power of a woman is judged to be *too* cultivated, it is viewed negatively by her male counterparts.

Like every young man, Clitophon is self-taught (*autodidaktos*) in the ways of *eros* (1.10). Like every young virgin, Leucippe needs first to believe that she is loved before she will imitate a suitor's love by expressing her own (cf. 1.9, *erasthai pisteusato kai tacheos se mimesetai*). Furthermore, virgin modesty (*aidos*) dictates that erotic discourse must be indirect. Following advice that he should "never mention anything Aphrodisiac" directly to a *parthenos*, because virgins, unlike (experienced) women (*gy-*

naikes), are embarrassed by such speech (1.10), Clitophon must find a way to seduce Leucippe through indirect *erotikoi logoi*. Upon meeting Leucippe in the formal garden of his family's home, Clitophon provides her with an erotic lesson (*erotikos*, cf. 1.19) on nature. By describing in detail the evidence of Eros's power in nature, Clitophon cultivates the seed of erotic desire that is natural to the virgin (1.16f).

According to Shadi Bartsch, the naturalness of Leucippe's eroticism mirrors the heightened sensuality of the garden where Clitophon finds her. Recalling A. R. Littlewood's observation that the gardens in the novel correspond to the personalities of particular characters, Bartsch adds:

> Leucippe's ambivalent safekeeping of her virginity may be said to be indicated beforehand by the eroticism of the garden that symbolizes it. What Littlewood has failed to mention, however, is that Europa's garden is described in equally erotic terms; and this in turn draws our attention to a new correspondence between her and Leucippe, and a new foreshadowing of the latter by the former. Europa is represented as strangely calm; although her handmaidens are distraught and evince a mixture of joy and fear, Europa—who as it is mounts the bull of her own will in the myth—is seated calmly on the back of the swimming bull.[44]

The garden, natural and yet requiring cultivation, reflects the virgin sexuality that Clitophon aims to harvest for himself.

The balance between the contributions of nature and culture to the development of female eroticism is a precarious one. Although Leucippe's sexuality needs to be nurtured, if it were to become too cultivated, it would be judged false. In a single but significant scene, Clitophon and two male friends debate the relative benefits of homoerotic and heteroerotic love. For Clitophon, woman's eroticism is rooted in nature (*physis*). But, as Goldhill notes, his companions quickly turn Clitophon's arguments from nature on their head. Instead they praise the love and kisses of boys:

> precisely because they have no female *sophia*, no *techne*, "no devastating spell of lips' deceit"; rather, they are kisses of nature, *tes physeos ta philemata*. The appeal to nature which for Cleitophon had meant the natural physical response of the

female—a response framed by those kisses of animal's mouths and the physiology of snogging—here becomes reconstituted as the "naturalness" of boys as opposed to the cultured deceptiveness of women.[45]

In contrast to the modesty, or shame (*aidos*), of boys and *parthenoi* (cf. 1.10), women (*gynaikes*) exude experience and deceit. Thus Leucippe, the *parthenos,* is portrayed as sexually aware but not sexually knowing. She remains a virgin, one whose erotic power renders her far more threatened than threatening.

Achilles Tatius affords Leucippe a fair degree of erotic expression and self-awareness. She is, after all, a willing participant in a late-night rendezvous with Clitophon. So, too, does she ask Clitophon to take her away with him. Ultimately, though, Leucippe's self-awareness is placed in the service of her virginity's preservation, not its relinquishment. It is because she is aware of her erotic appeal and desire that she can boast of the virginity she retains. When, in a scene reminiscent of the Elder Seneca (*Controv.* 1.2), Leucippe's *parthenia* comes under question because of the extensive amount of time she has spent in the company of pirates, the heroine presents a bold defense of the virginity she managed to protect against all odds (6.21). She declares that her single weapon against violation is the freedom (*eleutheria*) she wields. The irony is clear—the very eroticism that deems her virginity worthy of praise is also that which compels others to pursue her at all costs. As in the painting of Europa, the virgin who exudes erotic power is led not only by her own volition, but by the forceful whims of Eros. Yet in the midst of external, even violent, pressure, Leucippe exercises her power to resist. Such is the nature of the virgin's freedom.

Therefore the exercise of Leucippe's freedom is juxtaposed with the practice of virtue. Leucippe's virginity is evidence of both. When Pantheia (correctly) accuses Leucippe of having plotted a rendezvous with a male lover, the ensuing tension between mother and daughter revolves around issues of honor and shame. The *parthenos,* having fallen victim to neither force nor seduction, protests that her mother should not find fault with her *parthenia:* "Of one thing I am sure: no one has disgraced my virginity" (2.25). Virginity preserved connotes honor retained.

When Pantheia challenges her daughter's version of the event that has transpired, Leucippe offers to take a virginity test (*dokimasia parthenias*). Pantheia, citing the familial disgrace brought on by such a public event, refuses the virgin's counter challenge. The narrator then provides a lengthy description of Leucippe's state of mind. The scene rings with the dissonance created by Leucippe's behavior and her moral indignation:

> Leukippe was caught in emotional chaos. She was vexed, ashamed, angered: vexed at being caught, ashamed at being criticized, angered at not being believed. Shame, grief, and anger are three waves rising in the soul. . . . Under the stress of so many afflictions, Leukippe did not put up with her mother's attack. (2.29)

As Goldhill notes, there is "something of a tension between (Leucippe's) passionate defence of her virginity to her mother and her willingness to indulge her passion for Cleitophon."[46] Though she exhibits no remorse for having plotted a forbidden rendezvous with Clitophon, Leucippe is overcome with shame and anger at her mother's accusations. In short, her erotic activity becomes a source of shame only when it is suspected by others. As the narrator (Clitophon) explains that Leucippe leaves to escape the sting of Pantheia's accusations, he colludes with her by failing to acknowledge her fraudulence. Thus the scene displays the same kind of moral equivocation and ironic self-representation that initially surfaced in Clitophon's first monologue.

As the story continues, the preservation of her honor dominates Leucippe's actions. She flees from her mother's insults and defends herself against increasingly violent attempts on her virginity. Leucippe's honor is finally secured when she proves her virginity in a public test. After following Leucippe through her many adventures, only careful readers will recall that it was the protagonist's own willingness to participate in a clandestine affair that signaled the first threat to her virginity.

Throughout the narrative, then, Leucippe's virginity remains of central interest. Guided by Clitophon's narration, the reader's focus rests upon Leucippe's virgin body from the moment she is introduced. Beautiful and compellingly erotic, it is an object of pursuit and often violent intention. Leucippe's body —powerfully beautiful, vulnerable, and unknown—belongs to the realm of mysteries. It is up to Leucippe, with some divine assistance, to guard and protect the mysteries of her virgin body. Therefore she is portrayed as a moral agent, a virgin who must maintain her honor. The cultivation of her sexual desire is accompanied by a sense of shame. As Leucippe's erotic awareness is fraught with ambivalence, the narrative succeeds in both exploiting the virgin's eroticism *and* promoting her exercise of *sophrosyne.*

DAPHNIS AND CHLOE

Synopsis

Whereas *Leucippe and Clitophon* opens with the narrator's description of a painting, the story of *Daphnis and Chloe* is itself an *ekphrasis* of a painting that the narrator purports to have seen while hunting in Lesbos.[47] Since the painting tells a "story of love," the narrator packages the tale as an offering to Eros, the Nymphs, and Pan. He writes for the sake of his reader's pleasure (*terpnos*), promising that his story will

> cure the sick, comfort the distressed, stir the memory of those who have loved and educate those who haven't. For certainly no one has ever avoided Love, and no one will, as long as beauty exists, and eye can see. As for me—may the god (*Eros*) let me write about others' passions but keep my own self-control (*sophrosyne*). (Prologue)

From the very beginning of the novel, then, the narrator betrays his awareness of both the pleasures and the "potential dangers of erotic fiction" (*panta erotika*).[48] The ambivalence of *eros* is obvious—pleasure is possible, but *sophrosyne* is needful.

The story follows Daphnis's and Chloe's development from infancy: after each child is orphaned, they are raised by the couples who discover them. Daphnis is raised by the goatherd Lamon and his wife, Myrtale. Chloe is raised by the shepherd Dryas and his wife, Nape. The children grow up together, sharing their play as well as their rural chores. As they mature, each becomes "more beautiful than country children usually are"

(1.8). The story details the love that develops between them. Although natural, their erotically charged relationship remains stunted until they are finally educated in the ways of love.

Paideia *and Virginity*

The story of *Daphnis and Chloe* contrasts the naturalness of *eros* emerging in a bucolic setting with the socialization and cultivation of *eros* that can occur only through instruction (*paideia*). As Froma I. Zeitlin argues, Longus's "major innovation in plot is to center a romance on the extreme youth and naïveté of his lovers and to link up the 'natural' forces of *eros* to processes of education, both innate (*physis*) and acquired by skill (*techne*), as well as the teaching (*paideia*) of others."[49] The coupling of nature and *paideia*, rather than their polarization (as was evidenced to some degree in Achilles Tatius), allows Longus to underscore the significance of *mimesis*. As Zeitlin recognizes, *mimesis* can refer to the imitation of nature or art, or both. Such was the hallmark of the Second Sophistic. Both kinds of imitation combine in the erotic education of Daphnis and Chloe. The maturation of their sexuality is nurtured by both nature (*physis*) and social convention:

> the boldness of Longus' experiment suggests that at a certain level of analysis, love and letters are inseparable, that one's only means for apprehending any experience of *eros* is already entirely shaped and determined by the cultural system of representations, including and especially stories about love.[50]

Likewise, Winkler observes that the narrative "is not about the natural growth of erotic instinct but about the inadequacy of instinct to realize itself."[51] Longus situates the virginal figure of Chloe in this complex mix of nature and culture. It is she, especially, who evidences the negotiation of these forces. To an extent that exceeds even that of Achilles Tatius, Longus allows Chloe a significant degree of erotic self-awareness. It is she, not Daphnis, who first senses the erotic beauty of the other and the desire which it engenders. Yet, it is also Chloe upon whom the greatest sexual constraint is imposed. The very *paideia* that lends Chloe a more informed eroticism also delimits the social boundaries within which her natural sexuality may be expressed.

This *parthenos* exudes an eroticism whose expression depends upon a process of acculturation that, in the end, imposes severe restrictions upon her. Thus the portrayal of Chloe's sexuality is also permeated with ambivalence.

In the bucolic setting of the narrative's first book, the presence of nature and the absence of social convention combine to afford Daphnis and Chloe much freedom of movement. Often alone in the outdoors, the protagonists grow up side by side, schooled only by their surroundings. Nature is their teacher: "Everything was possessed by the beauty of spring; and Daphnis and Chloe, impressionable young creatures that they were, imitated (*mimeomai*) what they heard and saw" (1.9). For Egger, the centrality of the natural realm and the marginal significance of larger social realities is reflected in Longus's portrayal of Chloe:

> That this protagonist is actually a slave is stated in so many words only very late in to the narrative. The first mention of the existence of a master who can determine his servants' fate (their marriage, station, even death) is made at the end of Book 3; characteristically, it functions as a major obstacle to the love relationship. Before that, there is no intrusion of the urban lords into the pastoral world: it seems autonomous, undisturbed by outside masters. . . . This semblance of freedom is part of the unique appeal of the story.[52]

In the same manner, Daphnis and Chloe "live in a special realm, free of parental as well as social control. . . . The narrative is focused on an absence of restrictions."[53] Chloe, in particular, exercises a range of activities. She does everything with Daphnis. They work and play together, sharing in all things with one another.

Longus immediately follows this description of their activity with the notice that "[w]hile they were playing these games, *Eros* contrived to make things serious" (1.11). Following his heroic rescue of a goat, Daphnis goes with Chloe to the shrine of the Nymphs and proceeds to bathe himself. Watching Daphnis closely, Chloe begins to see him differently:

> His hair was dark and thick, and his body was tanned by the sun; you could have imagined that his body was taking its color from the shadow of his hair. It seemed to Chloe, as she gazed at him,

that Daphnis was beautiful (*kalos*); and she thought that since he hadn't seemed beautiful to her before, the bathing must be the cause of his beauty. (1.13)

Afterward, Chloe feels nothing but the desire to see Daphnis bathing again. Here Daphnis's body and beauty function as the compelling objects of Chloe's desire. After persuading Daphnis to take another bath, Chloe again experiences an unidentifiable longing. The narrator explains that her thoughts are the beginning of *eros,* but she remains in ignorance: "She didn't know what was happening to her; she was a young girl brought up in the country and hadn't heard anyone speak of love" (*kai oude allou legontos akousasa to erotos onoma,* 1.13; cf. 1.15). She feels ill and blames her condition on the stream in which Daphnis took his bath. She complains to the Nymphs because they do nothing to save her, a *parthenos.* From the moment that Chloe is identified as a *parthenos,* she is portrayed as a female bound by *eros.*

No sooner has Chloe been called a *parthenos* than the question of her marriage is introduced into the narrative. For the first time in the story, concern for social convention intrudes upon the seemingly autonomous world of the protagonists. Just as the narrator repeats that Chloe is ignorant of the name *eros,* he introduces Dorcon, a youth who knows not only *eros* but also its works (*erga,* 1.15). He immediately sets out to marry Chloe, and in the context of a beauty contest between him and Daphnis, each man addresses Chloe directly: *parthene* (1.16). It is for the *eros* of a *parthenos* that the two youths compete. In the midst of the contest, Chloe spontaneously kisses Daphnis. In contrast to the virgin, Daphnis's first sexual response is generated by events inspired by both nature *and* culture.

The socialization of Chloe's sexuality takes several forms. Just as the possibility of marriage is introduced with the recognition of Chloe as a *parthenos,* so is the possibility of rape. Twice the narrative refers to violence as a means by which Dorcon can obtain Chloe (1.15, 1.20). In the following chapter, Daphnis's father, Lamon, recounts the story of how Pan tried to rape the beautiful virgin (*parthenos kale*) Syrinx (2.35). In Longus's narrative world, sexual norms and conventions signal danger for the *parthenos*.

As in other literary contexts, here *parthenia* is of monetary value. Chloe's mother, Nape, fearing that her daughter will lose her *parthenia* to a shepherd in exchange for mere apples or roses, debates with Chloe's father the ways in which they can best use their daughter's virginity for monetary gain (3.25). As a virgin, Chloe is a valuable commodity.

In addition to representing the social valuation of *parthenia*, Longus's tale emphasizes the necessity of socializing the virgin through *paideia*. In a series of comic scenes, the protagonists attempt to satisfy their sexual desire for one another, only to demonstrate repeatedly their ignorance of how to do so. When they try to imitate the mating behavior of the goats, rams, and ewes, Daphnis and Chloe discover the inadequacy of nature's schooling (3.14). Nature instills desire, but only culture provides the means for its fulfillment. *Eros* requires the *mimesis* of human culture.

Eventually, Daphnis and Chloe receive instruction in the erotic arts. After the elder Philetas tells them about *eros,* they are better equipped to recognize the ache they feel when they are apart from one another: "Lovers feel pain—and so do we. . . . Surely this is 'love'" (2.8). Having learned from Philetas that "[t]here is no medicine for Love, no potion, no drug, no spell to mutter, except a kiss and an embrace and lying down together with naked bodies" (2.7), Daphnis and Chloe delay trying the "third remedy" out of natural modesty. When by accident they fall into a horizontal embrace, they still don't know how to consummate their mutual desire. Their frustration is comical: "They did not know what to do next and thought that this was the limit of love's satisfaction. So they spent most of the day in this futile way" (2.11).

The completion of Daphnis's education is left to Lycaenion, a *gyne* from town (*ex asteos,* 3.15). In sharp contrast to Daphnis and the virgin Chloe, Lycaenion is a sophisticated townswoman. Recognizing Daphnis's love for Chloe, even while desiring him for herself, Lycaenion seduces Daphnis by offering to teach him *ta erotos erga:* "If you want to get rid of your troubles and try out the pleasures you are searching for, come and give yourself to me as a pupil (*mathetes*)" (3.17). Daphnis quickly accedes and the narrator recounts the lesson that Lycaenion teaches him (*paideuein*, 3.18).

Lycaenion's lesson does not conclude until she offers Daphnis a final and critical word:

> You've still got this to learn, Daphnis. Because I happen to be an experienced *gyne,* I didn't suffer any harm just now (long ago another man gave me this lesson and took my virginity as his reward). But if Chloe has this sort of wrestling match with you, she will cry out and weep and lie there, bleeding heavily. But don't be afraid of the blood; when you talk her into giving herself to you, lead her to this spot so that if she cries out, no one can hear her, and if she weeps, no one can see her, and if she bleeds, she can wash in the spring. And remember—I made you a man before Chloe did. (3.19)

The irony implicit in Lycaenion's "lesson" does little to soften her message.[54] Sexual intercourse will injure Chloe. Goldhill, in particular, notes how Lycaenion's language resonates with ancient portrayals of first intercourse. Her lesson is characteristic of the "pervasive imagery linking violence and penetration *throughout* Greek culture, and the pervasive imagery associating ᵗhe wedding-night with violent seizure and even death."[55] As has been noted, this is not the first time that Longus links violence with sexuality.

Thus Lycaenion introduces two essential elements of Daphnis's education. The first is the violence associated with sexual intercourse. The second is the passive sexual role assigned to Chloe. In no previous episode has the reader been led to imagine that Chloe would need to be "talked into" engaging in sexual intercourse. As she has been the first of the two protagonists to exhibit any erotic inclination, Chloe's passion for Daphnis has been overt. Now Lycaenion implies that for the *parthenos* who would become a *gyne,* an informed sexuality is a passive and painful one. When Daphnis returns to Chloe, his ardor is somewhat dampened by the memory of Lycaenion's word about "the blood" (*to haima*). Fearing that one day he will no longer be able to exercise *sophrosyne*, he limits how often Chloe can undress. Puzzled by Daphnis's stilted passion and disadvantaged by her ignorance of what transpired between him and Lycaenion, Chloe is indeed rendered increasingly passive.

Following events that lead to the disclosure of their true (and socially distinguished) identities, Daphnis and Chloe are brought together in marriage. The story concludes as the protagonists finally consummate their passion for one another. But just as the narrative draws to a close, there occurs a curious shift in tone:

> At that time, when night came, everyone conducted them into the bed-chamber, some playing pipes, some playing the flute, others holding up great torches. And when they were near the door, they sang with harsh, rough voices, as though they were breaking up the earth with forks, not singing a wedding hymn. . . . Daphnis did some of the things Lycaenion taught him; and then, for the first time, Chloe found out that what they had done in the woods had been nothing but shepherds' games. (4.40)

Noting the suddenly harsh description of the wedding guests' singing and the reappearance of Lycaenion's name in this closing scene, Winkler remarks that the episode is "ominous." He wonders whether we may "presume that Daphnis and the reader have not forgotten . . . her careful description of defloration as trauma—the screams, the tears, the pool of blood?"[56] Given the violent imagery that echoes throughout this final scene, how is the reader to understand Chloe's experience of becoming a *gyne*?

As Goldhill shows, the narrative directly links Lycaenion and Chloe:

> For Lycaenion's "instruction"—*epaideuse*—leads to Chloe "learning"—*emathe*—about "children's play"—*paidion paignia*. . . . The etymological connection between *paideusis* and *paides* and *paignia*—"education", "children", "play"—is stressed in these pointed repetitions: as play is to seriousness, so childhood is to adulthood, and education is the transition.[57]

The ending of the novel signals the completion of Chloe's education. The *parthenos*, with her instinctive eroticism, has become a *gyne*—a passive and wounded partner for Daphnis. The seriousness of the transition is underscored by its implied violence. The novel's ending reveals precisely why virginity is portrayed with ambivalence. On the one hand, the eroticism of the virgin is natural and playful. On the other, it requires the assistance of *paideia*, wherein *mimesis* is critical for a mature and socialized sexuality. The virgin must finally submit to culture, adopt the passive role of a *gyne*, and learn the injury of first intercourse. To learn (*mathein*) the *erotos erga* is to suffer (*pathein*). It is the sustenance of culture and society, not erotic love, that the novel most promotes. Thus Cooper is surely right in seeing the novel as a means of "harnessing desire . . . to a moral: at the tale's end, the marriage feast must be celebrated, and the work of maintaining and renewing the city must begin."[58]

Longus's narrative invites the reader to focus on both the body and the subjectivity of the virgin. The narrative casts the growing desire within Chloe's body as a phenomenon of *physis*. It also underscores the subjectivity of the virgin and the importance of her learning her proper sexual (read: social) role. By itself, the body cannot attain the *telos* of its desire. Rather, the virgin must learn to imitate that which is found in human culture. It is *her* body that is injured in first intercourse and it is the *parthenos*, last of all, who must learn that adult sexuality is a civic duty and not a child's game.

JOSEPH AND ASENATH

Synopsis

The text of JosAs can easily be divided into two parts: the story of Joseph and Asenath's meeting and marriage (1–21); and the story of Pharaoh's son's attempt to engage Joseph's brothers in a plot to kill Joseph and claim Asenath for himself (22–29).[59] The plot of chapters 1–21 develops details found in Genesis 41.46, 50–52; chapters 22–29 represent the rather extensive embellishment of material found in Genesis 41.53ff, 45.26–46.7, and 47.27.[60] It is the first part of JosAs (1–21) that is most relevant for this study, for it is here that Asenath is portrayed as a *parthenos* of Egypt.

The story of JosAs 1–21 unfolds as follows: Asenath, the daughter of Pentephres, priest of Heliopolis and the satrap of Pharaoh, is a beautiful *parthenos* who refuses to be seen by any man. Likewise, she refuses to greet Joseph, the "Powerful One of God" whom Pharaoh appointed "king of the whole land." However, upon seeing Joseph from her chamber window, Asenath immediately falls in love with him. Now it is Joseph who refuses Asenath and refrains from kissing the "strange woman." Distressed by Joseph's rejection, Asenath repents of her idolatry and experiences a religious conversion. Finally a heavenly man appears to Asenath to confirm her acceptance by the Lord God and to announce her impending marriage to Joseph. When Joseph and Asenath meet again, Asenath recounts all that has happened and Joseph returns her love with his own. The two marry, and the narrator closes the section by announcing the births of Manasseh and Ephraim.

Conversion and the Re-Contextualization of Asenath's Virginity

Virginity is an important dimension of Asenath's portrayal. In this text, as in other literature, *parthenia* connotes images of the virgin as both a body and a subject. Here, however, Asenath's sexual status connotes different images at different points in the story. In some cases, *parthenia* is evaluated positively. At other points in the story, it is cause for despair. Therefore this narrative, too, maintains a fairly ambivalent attitude toward virginity.

The protagonist's sexual status is mentioned when she is first introduced into the narrative. By immediately coupling virginity and beauty, the text focuses the reader's attention on Asenath's body. She is "a *parthenos* of eighteen years, very tall and handsome and beautiful (*kale*) to look at beyond all the *parthenoi* on the earth" (1.4). Already eighteen years of age, Asenath has retained her virginal status for several years. Moreover, she is nothing like the daughters of the Egyptians, resembling instead the daughters of the Hebrews, "as tall as Sarah and handsome as Rebecca and beautiful as Rachel. And the name of that *parthenos* was Asenath" (1.5). The link between beauty and virginity is confirmed when the text, in a singular instance, refers to Joseph, too, as a *parthenos* (4.7).[61] The virgin's beauty is the cause of her fame (1.6).

For all its significance, Asenath's beauty remains hidden. Unseen by any man, the virgin daughter of Pentephres resides in a tower adjoining her father's house. There she is waited upon by seven virgins who were born on the very same night as was she. They, too, are beautiful, and they converse with neither a man (*aner*) nor any male child (*paidion arren*, 2.6). Furthermore, no one sleeps in Asenath's bed but she: "And in this bed Asenath slept, alone; and a man or another woman never sat on it, only Asenath alone" (2.9). It is in this tower that Asenath's virginity is fostered (*he parthenia autes etrepheto*, 2.7) and all the ornaments of her virginity (*pas ho kosmos tes parthenias autes*, 2.4) stored.

Coupled with attention to Asenath's body is the narrative's portrayal of the virgin's pride and arrogance. Emphasis on her arrogance is the first indication that Asenath's virginity, in and of itself, is insufficient to render her an ideal heroine. Soon after introducing her, the narrator adds, "And Asenath was despising and scorning every man (*aner*), and she was boastful and arrogant with everyone" (2.1). If this is not enough to cast doubt on Asenath's character, the next reference to her boastfulness certainly is. When Asenath refuses her father's request that she meet Joseph, the narrator remarks, "Pentephres was ashamed to speak further to his daughter Asenath about Joseph, because she had answered him daringly and with boastfulness and anger" (4.12). Asenath, the proud *parthenos*, is cause for her father's shame. The early chapters of the narrative associate Asenath's virginity with her beauty, sexual independence, and arrogance.

While Asenath's boastfulness remains an important motif throughout the narrative (cf. 6.2–8; 7.7ff; 11.6; 12.5; 13.13; 21.12, 16–21), perhaps more important is the rhetorical constellation of virginity, arrogance, and religious conversion.[62] For once Asenath has repented of her arrogance, virginity stops being a sign of independence and pride and becomes rather a sign of humility and submission to the God of Israel.

Asenath first becomes aware of her arrogance when she spots Joseph from her tower window. Compelled by his beauty, she finds that Joseph evokes the same response that Asenath elicits from other men ("for who among men in earth will generate such beauty [*kallos*]?" 6.4, 7.2–3; cf. the description of Asenath in 1.4–6). She grieves how she has spoken to her father: "What shall I now do, wretched (that I am)? . . . What a wretched and foolish (girl) I (am), because I have spoken wicked words about him to my father" (6.4). Her desire to remain hidden from view is motivated now by shame rather than pride: "And now, where shall I go and hide from his face/in order that Joseph the son of God does not see me because I have spoken wicked (things) about him?" (6.5) The man of whom she once said, "Why does my lord and my father speak words such as these, to hand me over, like a captive to a man (who is) an alien, and a fugitive, and (was) sold (as a slave)?" (4.9) is now the one whom she desires to serve: "And now, let my father give me to Joseph for a maid-servant and slave, and I will serve him for ever (and) ever" (6.8).

That Asenath's virginity alone gives her little reason to boast is indicated by Joseph's refusal to greet her with a kiss. Although Joseph agrees to meet Asenath after Pentephres assures him that his daughter is a *parthenos* "hating every man, and there is not any man who has even seen her, except you today" (7.7), he inevitably pushes Asenath away, for "it is not fitting for a man who worships God to kiss a strange woman" (8.5). He will love her as a sister (7.8), but he will only kiss "the sister (who is born) of his mother and the sister (who is born) of his clan and family and the wife who shares his bed, (all of) who(m) bless with their mouths the living God" (8.6). As Burchard observes, "virginity paves the way toward acceptance by God, but it does not by itself warrant it."[63] Joseph recognizes Asenath's virginity, but more is required of the virgin who would be his *gyne*. Joseph prays for Asenath and asks the Lord to "bless this *parthenos* and renew her by your spirit" (8.9).

After she departs from Joseph, Asenath repents of having worshipped idols. Thus begins Asenath's conversion from the foreign/strange woman to the pious and wise woman of the Hebrews.[64] For seven days she fasts, weeps, dresses in mourning clothes, and remains in silence and isolation in her tower (10.2–17, 11.2). She even refuses the company of her seven virgin attendants. On the eighth day, she at last speaks to herself and reveals that her virginity has become cause for *lament:* "What shall I do, miserable (*tapeine*) (that I am)/ or where shall I go;/ with whom shall I take refuge,/ or of what shall I speak,/ I the *parthenos* and an orphan and desolate and abandoned and hated?" (11.3). On the one hand, she grieves that her family rejected her when she turned away from their gods. On the other, she mourns that "all people hate me,/ because I, too, have (come to) hate every man, and all who asked for my hand in marriage" (11.6). An orphaned and isolated *parthenos,* Asenath now places her hope in the compassion and mercy of the God of the Hebrews (11.10–14).

She prays to the Lord God, confessing in the midst of her prayer: "And I, Asenath, daughter of Pentephres the priest,/ the *parthenos* and queen,/ who (was) once proud and arrogant . . . am now an orphan, and desolate, and abandoned by all people" (12.5). The virgin implores the Lord God to rescue her in the same way that a father would save his child (12.7–8, 13). As a *parthenos* who has lost the guardianship of her father, she asks, "Have mercy upon me, Lord,/ and guard me, a *parthenos* (who is) abandoned and an orphan,/ because you, Lord, are a sweet and good and gentle father" (12.14). She prays for pardon, "because I sinned against you in ignorance (*en agnoia*)/ being a virgin (*parthenos*)" (13.13). Asenath repeatedly identifies herself as a *parthenos,* a self-designation that connotes not boastfulness and arrogance, but humility, vulnerability, and ignorance. The *parthenos* of former privilege has been transformed into a *parthenos* of *tapeinosis* (cf.13.1, 21.21).

Asenath receives a visit from a heavenly man who not only confirms God's acceptance of her but also announces her impending marriage to Joseph. The man instructs Asenath to take off her mourning clothes and put on her "new linen robe" and the "twin girdle of (her) virginity" (14.12). He then tells her to remove her veil and repeatedly addresses her as "chaste virgin" (*ei parthenos hagne semeron,* 15.2; cf. 15.4, 6, 10, and 19.9), a title by which she has not previously been addressed. Since she has repented and has been assured of God's acceptance, Asenath's virginity has come to signal not only physical integrity but religious and moral purity. Thus the man announces good news to the chaste virgin: her name is now "written in the book of the living in heaven" (15.4), she will marry Joseph (15.6), and her name will be "City of Refuge" (15.7). Moreover, when he declares that Repentance herself is the "guardian of all virgins" (15.7), his description of her resembles the transformed Asenath. Repentance is "exceedingly beautiful, a virgin pure and laughing always, and she is gentle and meek" (15.8). Thus Asenath's virginity, "consonant with the requirement of the adjuration of angels," serves as the embodiment of her repentance and conversion.[65] She is now not only a virgin, she is a pure virgin, the one who calls herself "the humble" (18.7).

When Joseph meets Asenath again, he fails to recognize her, for now she possesses "a heavenly beauty" (20.6).[66] Realizing that she is Asenath, the converted virgin, he calls to her, "And now, come to me chaste virgin (*he parthenos hagne*), and why do you stand far away from me?" (19.9). Following their marriage and the birth of their sons, Asenath sings a psalm that reflects the narrative's evolving construction of virginity:

> I have sinned, Lord, I have sinned; before you I have sinned much./ I was prospering in my father's house,/ and I was a boastful and arrogant *parthenos*/ . . . I have sinned, Lord, I have sinned; before you I have sinned much. And I spoke bold (words) in vanity and said, "There is no prince on earth who may loose the girdle of my virginity."/ . . . I have sinned, Lord, I have sinned;/ before you I have sinned much,/ until Joseph the Powerful One of God came. / He pulled me down from my dominating position/ and made me humble after my arrogance, and by his beauty he caught me. (21.12, 19, 21)

Asenath's relationship to Joseph reflects her standing before the Lord God. Having repented of her idolatry and arrogance, she became worthy of Joseph and favored by God. Thus her *parthenia* took on greater meaning and value only after her conversion. Alone it had been of little advantage.

Like the pagan novels, JosAs portrays the *parthenos* in terms of both her body and her subjectivity. At the beginning of the narrative, Asenath is identified as a beautiful virgin whose body remains hidden from men. As the story unfolds, her moral and spiritual disposition takes center stage, so that Asenath's eventual repentance and conversion lend greater value to her virginity. When she is a worshipper of idols, her sexual status connotes arrogance. When she is penitent, it signals dependence and ignorance. Upon her conversion, it evidences holiness and acceptance by the Lord God and Joseph. The significance of this virgin's sexual status clearly rests with her status in the cult.

ACTS OF PAUL AND THECLA

Synopsis

The first part of the *Acts of Paul,* the *Acts of Paul and Thecla,* narrates the events of Paul's ministry in Iconium.[67] There he meets Thecla, a *parthenos* who becomes an adherent of his gospel. When her mother (Theoclia) and fiancé (Thamyris) become alarmed by Thecla's attachment to Paul and rejection of marriage, they bring Paul before the governor, charging that he "makes virgins averse to marriage" (16). After the governor summons Thecla, she is condemned by her mother and sentenced to be burned. By divine miracle, Thecla escapes death and travels to Antioch with Paul, who fears that temptation may yet overcome the virgin. After refusing another male suitor in Antioch, Thecla is again brought before the governor and condemned. As she enters the arena where she is to be devoured by wild beasts, Thecla prays and throws herself into a pit of water in order to be baptized. Instead of being killed by either the seals in the pit or the beasts in the arena, Thecla is miraculously saved again. Following her release, she returns to Paul. After she announces that she is going to Iconium to teach, Paul tells her, "Go, and teach the word of God" (41).

Virginity as Chastity: Subversion of the Social Order and Sublimation of the Erotic

Whereas the phrase *parthenos hagne* occurs only in the latter half of the first part of JosAs, chastity and virginity are juxtaposed from the very beginning of the *Acts of Paul and Thecla.* As virginity connotes chastity, and vice versa, it is not surprising that the narrative displays significant interest in Thecla's body and ambivalence toward its erotic potential. The eroticism that so permeates the ancient novels finds expression here in terms of religious devotion.

In the Acts, the body is the site of purity/chastity (*hag-notes*). The narrative opens with Paul teaching the "word of God about abstinence (*enkrateia*) and the resurrection" (5). Among other pronouncements, Paul declares:

> blessed are those who have kept the flesh (*sarx*) chaste (*hagne*) for they shall become a temple of God . . . blessed are those who have wives as not having them, for they shall experience God . . . blessed are the bodies of the virgins (*makaria ta somata ton parthenon*) for they shall be well pleasing to God and should not lose the reward of their chastity (*tes hagneias auton*). (5–6)

Immediately following Paul's blessing of the *parthenos,* the narrator introduces Thecla, a certain *parthenos* who watches from her window the women and virgins making their way to Paul. The implication is clear. Thecla has an opportunity to receive the blessing awarded only to *parthenoi.* Having been persuaded to remain *hagne* (cf. 27, 31), she commits herself to the preservation of her *parthenia.* Unlike Asenath, Thecla will never yield her virginity to marriage.

As an adherent of Paul's teaching, Thecla is twice brought before the governor, twice condemned to death, and twice saved by divine intervention. In the first instance, the virgin is brought naked into the arena to be burned. Upon seeing Thecla, the governor weeps with admiration at the power (*dynamis*) within her (22). Later, when she, again stripped of her clothes, confronts the beasts in the arena, the governor weeps that the creatures "were to devour such beauty *(kallos)*" (34). When Thecla emerges unharmed in the arena, the governor summons her and demands that she be clothed. Thecla responds, "He who clothed me when I was naked among the beasts will in the day of judgement clothe me with his salvation" (38). As has been noted, "Thecla reinterprets her nakedness away from its traditional significance, removing it from the governor's power and aligning it with her strength as a confessor of Christ."[68] At once the governor decrees the release of "the pious Thecla, the servant of God"

(38). In the context of impending martyrdom, the beauty of Thecla's virgin body connotes *dynamis* owing less to the *eros* she evokes and more to the chastity, piety, and resistance she promotes.[69]

That Thecla is also an object of erotic desire, however, is evidenced in men's reactions to her. Like the virgin protagonists of the novels, she encounters the requisite suitors and sexual predators. In contrast to the novels, the narrative focuses primarily on the social response that Thecla's celibacy provokes. As Thamyris weeps "for the loss of a wife" (10), his jealousy, loss, and anger (15) express the intense distress caused by Thecla's refusal to marry. Just as he mourns the loss of a *gyne,* Theoclia grieves the loss of a child (*teknon*), and the maidservants weep over the loss of a mistress (*kyria,* 10). The entire household (*oikos*) is affected by Thecla's refusal to marry. All of society retains a vested interest in its *parthenoi.* Thus Paul, whose teachings threaten the very social order and fabric of Iconium, is brought before the governor (9, 15, 20).

As Cooper and others have shown, the Apocryphal Acts parody the ancient social norms and attitudes that the novels serve to reinforce. The heroines of the Acts play strategic roles in essentially male contests for power and honor, so that Thecla's continence signifies Paul's victory over the social norms represented by Thamyris and the governor.[70] Virginity, and all that it connotes, is the means by which the narrative represents Christian subversion of Greco-Roman socio-cultural norms.

Yet in contesting values of the dominant culture, the narrative exploits conventional images of the virgin. The presumption of Thecla's virginal eroticism and sexual vulnerability is sublimated but not challenged by the narrative. For not only do Thamyris, Alexander, and the governor repeatedly notice Thecla's beauty, but Paul, too, remains mindful of Thecla's erotic potential. When Thecla wants to accompany Paul in his work, he warns her about the possibility of another trial (*peirasmos*) of her chastity: "Times are evil and you are beautiful" (25). Because she is not yet baptized, Thecla is presumed sexually vulnerable. Thus when Paul sees Thecla traveling in mixed company, he immediately assumes that a new *peirasmos* has come upon her (40).

Even as it signifies purity and blessedness, *parthenia* connotes a dangerous sexuality. It is only after learning that she has been *sealed* (cf. 25) by baptism that Paul commissions the virgin protagonist: "Go, and teach the word of God" (41).

Melissa Aubin traces the masculinization of Thecla that leads the protagonist to gird herself and turn her woman's mantle "into a cloak after the fashion of men" (40). Aubin observes that Thecla "completely sheds her tokens of femininity," but most relevant to this study is the way in which such transformation functions to verify the tokens of Thecla's virginity. Given Paul's anxiety over the necessity of the virgin's baptismal sealing, the narrative reveals that the masculinization of Thecla falls just short of completion. An idealized female who subverts the dominant social ideology, but whose virginal erotic potential must yet be constrained by an external source, Thecla resembles, at most, a masculinized *parthenos* who never fully transcends her engendered identity.[71]

The narrative's ambivalence toward Thecla's eroticism is evidenced by the way in which it recontextualizes the very language and imagery of *eros*. As Rosa Söder and others observe, the relationship between the woman and the apostle in the Apocryphal Acts is often characterized by a number of features found in the romances.[72] Here these include repeated emphasis on the virgin's beauty, Thecla's nocturnal visit with Paul, her bribery of the prison guard, and Paul's awareness of how other men respond to her. The narrative infuses their relationship with a fair degree of erotic tension and reads much like a romance. Nevertheless, it also mitigates such tension by carefully circumscribing the context of their relationship—Paul and Thecla are united by the Word that Paul preaches.

By identifying Thecla's desire for Paul as hunger for his teaching, the Acts sublimates the eroticism of the *parthenos* and recasts it as religious devotion. When Thecla first hears Paul (the text emphasizes that she hasn't yet seen him), she responds as if she were love-struck—with *epithymia, pathos,* and *ekplexis* (9–10). Just as Tatius's Pantheia shames Leucippe, Thecla's mother pleads with her daughter to return to her betrothed "and be ashamed" (10). And because the virgin "so loves the stranger," her betrothed becomes enraged. Like the female protagonists of the novels, Thecla praises the deity when she is reunited with the male object of her desire (24).

The narrative strains to qualify its erotic overtones. Thecla is not Paul's lover; rather she is likened to a lamb in search of its shepherd (21). When she visits Paul in prison (at night no less), she kisses only his "bonds," being "bound" to him not by *eros* but by affection (19). By implying that it is Paul's teaching that inspires the virgin's devotion, the text manages to contain the sexual undercurrents it so teasingly exposes by sublimating the novelistic motif of *erotikoi logoi* (cf. Tatius, Longus). It is precisely because Paul's *logos* serves something other than *eros* that it can both seduce and save this *parthenos*. Thecla's body recalls the beauty and power of her novelistic counterparts, but as a subject, she is denied the explicitly sexual *eros* that they enjoy.

From the beginning of the Acts, chastity is associated with the retention of *parthenia*. Despite the narrative's sublimation of the erotic, Thecla's body, the locus of purity and the spark that sets off social conflict, remains of great interest. When she imposes distance between herself and social convention (e.g., marrying and sustaining the household), members of her household and civic community act to regain control of her. Thus the narrative also emphasizes her willingness to risk dishonor for her fidelity to Paul. As an acting subject, this apocryphal protagonist is no passive *parthenos*.[73]

ACTS OF PETER

Synopsis

Two brief scenes at the opening of the *Acts of Peter,* the stories of Peter's Daughter and the Gardener's Daughter, are relevant to our study.[74] Each recounts events concerning an unnamed virgin. The first story shows that it is better for Peter's daughter, a beautiful virgin, to remain paralyzed on one side than to be physically restored to her original condition. In order to demonstrate that his daughter's paralysis is preferable, Peter heals his daughter and then returns her to her paralyzed state. The second story recounts how it would have been better for a gardener's

virgin daughter to have remained dead than to have been re-
vived. For after she was raised from the dead, she was seduced by
a strange man and never seen again.

The Virgin as a Body

In each of these brief episodes, virginity is of absolute value.
Indeed, virginity so embodies purity that its loss signals nothing
less than radical defilement. The virgin is portrayed primarily
in terms of her body, and the preservation of her sexual status is
of utmost importance. The virgin body is valued insofar as it
is pure.

In the first story, Peter recounts how he received a vision on
the day that his daughter was born: "'Peter, this day has been
born for you a great affliction, for this daughter will harm many
souls, if her body remains well!'" He then relates how when
his daughter became ten years of age, she "became a stumbling
block to many." The narrative implies that even at the age of ten,
a female child possesses a dangerous eroticism. Indeed, it is after
seeing the girl bathing with her mother that a man by the name
of Ptolemy seeks to make her his wife. Here certain details of
the story are lost because the text is corrupt, but eventually Peter
and his wife discover the girl paralyzed, and they rejoice. The
narrative so associates the loss of *parthenia* with defilement that
bodily injury is received with gladness: "We carried her away,
praising the Lord that he had kept his servant from defilement
and violation and . . . " Although the episode with Ptolemy leads
to the girl's paralysis, she is spared defilement, that is, the violation of her virginity. The virgin bears no name, demonstrates no
action, and utters no speech. She is a body, an object of concern
and an object upon whom both mortals and the deity stake a
claim. Later in the story, a heavenly voice refers to the girl as "my
virgin." The girl's sexual status serves as the summation of her
identity. It is the Lord to whom she belongs.

Likewise, the second story tells of how a peasant man asked
Peter to pray for his only daughter, a virgin. After the apostle
prayed "that the Lord would bestow upon her what was expedi-
ent for her soul," the virgin fell dead. The man, "failing to recognize the worth of the heavenly grace," implored Peter to re-

vive his daughter. Peter fulfilled the man's request, only for the virgin to be seduced soon thereafter. The narrative clearly implies that in a world so threatening to a virgin's chastity, early death is a blessing. Here again, the virgin bears no name and exercises no agency. She is portrayed as an object of seduction and destruction rather than a moral agent.

Like the Greek novels, these brief scenes assume both the sexual vulnerability and the erotic power of the virgin. The virgin, even at the age of ten, is desired by men. She exudes a sensuality that is dangerous to both herself and others, for "God has not given the vessels for corruption and shame." By wedding the divine intention of creation with the retention of chastity, virginity connotes not only chastity but also incorruption. Even as these brief accounts elevate the importance of virginity above that of the body, it is the body of the *parthenos* that remains their singular focus. The bodies of these virgin daughters are so powerfully erotic, and the exercise of agency so conspicuously absent, that death and physical impairment, not moral choosing, are the only ways to avoid corruption. Less tolerant of the tension that results from imagining a *parthenos* who can desire and be desired and still choose to act rightly, these early Christian texts preserve the virgin body and sacrifice the virgin as moral agent.

Like other literary evidence from the early Roman Empire, ancient novels focus on both the body and the agency of the *parthenos*. They demonstrate not only the complexity and range of images by which the *parthenos* is presented but also the varying permutations that such portrayals involve. While figures such as Chloe and Leucippe are allowed a certain degree of erotic agency, the narratives nevertheless seek to contain and delimit such eroticism. In so doing, they variously emphasize the significance of both the virgin body and her subjectivity. The value of Asenath's *parthenia* is also portrayed in terms of her body and her agency, but the significance of her sexual status remains subject to qualification. Finally, the *parthenoi* of the Apocryphal Acts exude the same physical attributes as do virgins in the other narratives, but the significance of their *parthenia* differs. For Thecla and the unnamed virgins in the *Acts of Peter*, *parthenia* is both an expression of chastity and a denial of *eros*. Yet whereas Thecla exercises direct agency, the virgins in the *Acts of Peter* demonstrate none, so that their sexual status serves as the very sum of their identity.

Each of the narratives surveyed here underscores the erotic potential of the virgin body. Whether the virgin's eroticism is evaluated positively or negatively, whether it is highlighted or sublimated by the narrative, and whether or not the virgin's body remains of primary interest, such concern permeates the novels and Acts. The images of the *parthenos* that appear here resonate with those that occur in the medical and philosophical literature surveyed in chapter 2. The virgin body is the locus of beauty, *eros*, and desire. As the narratives place these meanings in service to larger themes and rhetorical aims, they emphasize to varying degrees the virgin subject.

Despite such range, some of the images that are prominent in the discourse surveyed in the previous chapter rarely occur in the narratives. Association of the *parthenos* with priesthood and prophecy is conspicuously absent. She is not an active conduit of the divine. Only the barest traces of this image appear in the novels and Acts. While Leucippe is aided by Artemis, prepared as a purification sacrifice, and permitted entrance into a sanctuary open only to virgins and men, she functions as neither the site nor the minister of divine encounter. Chloe, like Daphnis, is affected favorably by the intervention of a deity, but she is afforded no cultic significance. Asenath is redeemed as a chaste virgin, and although her chastity renders her acceptable before the Lord and Joseph, she functions as neither a priest nor prophet. Thecla is the character ascribed the most sacred role. Having procured the sealing of her *parthenia* in baptism, she becomes a teacher of the Word, but no prophetic or priestly function is assigned to her. Her body is more a living testimony to Paul's teaching on virginity than it is the locus of sacred encounter. Rather than promoting the sacred function of the body, the *parthenoi* of the Acts illustrate the significance of preventing bodily defilement. In none of the narratives considered here does the *parthenos* function as the instrument of either priesthood or prophecy.

Ancient narratives demonstrate the complexity and multiplicity of images of virginity in the early Empire. Whether portrayed in terms of body, agency, or both, the virgin is a figure charged with meaning. Each of the narratives we have discussed exploits different connotations associated with virginity. We turn now to a consideration of how *parthenia* figures in the portrayals of Mary in Luke-Acts and the Protevangelium of James.

The Virgin Speaks

Four

Having reviewed ancient literary images of virginity, we may now address the ways in which extratextual images of virginity inform the construction of the *parthenos* Mary in Luke-Acts. Presuming the significance of cultural notions of female sexual status, this examination engages Robbins's notion of intertexture:

> Intertexture is a text's representation of, reference to, and use of phenomena in the "world" outside the text being interpreted. In other words, the intertexture of a text is the interaction of the language in the text with "outside" material and physical "objects," historical events, texts, customs, values, roles, institutions, and systems.[1]

The interplay between ancient images of virginity "outside" Luke-Acts and the construction of the virgin "inside" the text constitutes, in part, the intertexture of Mary's characterization. Therefore my analysis takes into account textual clues that Luke-Acts provides about Mary, the ancient contexts with which they resonate, and the valences with which they can be infused.

Beginning with the scene that introduces Mary, readers may examine Luke's portrayal of Mary in terms of both the information that readers retrieve from the text and extratextual data that readers can assimilate and negotiate in the act of reading. Here my concern is less with authorial intention, that is, with what Luke may have intended to convey, and more with what readers familiar with ancient images of virginity can make of the Marian character indicators that the narrator supplies. I consider the scenes in which Mary figures in two stages: first, I provide a general overview of Mary's portrayal, including the impressions, questions, and expectations that the text generates for readers familiar with the images of virginity I reviewed in chapters 2 and 3; then I explore how the progression of textual cues that the narrative provides not only underscores the polyvalence of *parthenia* but reinforces some nuances and suppresses others in respect to Mary. The initial overview of each scene allows us to consider the range of impressions and possibilities that readers confront and negotiate in the act of reading. The discussions that follow show how particular valences associated with virginity especially advance and serve the construction of the Lucan Mary.

Virginity and the Lucan Portrayal of Mary

Several scenes in Luke 1–2 feature the character Mary: the annunciation to Mary (1.26–38); Mary's visit with her kinswoman Elizabeth (1.39–45); Mary's hymn of praise (1.46–56); the birth of Jesus (2.1–7); the shepherds' visit with Mary, Jesus, and Joseph (2.15–20); Mary and Joseph's presentation of Jesus in the temple (2.22–40); and Mary and Joseph's discovery of the boy Jesus in the temple (2.41–51). Mary reappears briefly as Jesus' mother in 8.19–21, and she is present at the opening of Acts (1.14).

The scenes that occur in Luke 1–2 have long been appreciated for the way in which they advance the so-called step parallelism of Luke's portrayal of John and Jesus. Therefore they are often read in terms of Luke's presentation of Jesus as the Gospel's central protagonist and John as the prophet subordinated to him. Yet it is Mary, not Jesus or John, who figures most prominently in Luke 1–2. Here she appears in all scenes but one that concern the identity, life, and destiny of Jesus (2.8–14). While she functions as a secondary figure in the Gospel as a whole, Mary so occupies the foreground of Luke's early chapters that a reader's impression of her lasts well beyond Luke 1–2. Indeed, with his direct and unelaborated reference to Mary in Acts 1.14, the narrator assumes that readers will be able to call this particular character immediately to mind.

Luke uses an array of direct and indirect textual cues to portray Mary. Character indicators, in general, fall into two main categories: direct indicators and indirect indicators. Direct character indicators are those that the implied narrator explicitly provides through description and evaluation, including references to gender, appearance, age, and affect. Indirect character indicators illustrate, rather than describe, who a character is and what he or she does. As Gowler observes, "indirect description does not overtly announce character traits, but displays or exemplifies those traits or qualities."[2] It is left to the reader to derive significance from such data. Indirect character indicators include the speech and actions of characters, the environment in which they appear, and their interaction or association with other characters.

At the forefront of Mary's characterization stands mention of her sexual status—she is introduced to the reader by the designation *parthenos* (Lk 1.27). Although this initial scene serves as the only instance in which Luke explicitly identifies Mary as *parthenos*, singularity need not render such description insignificant. Just as personal titles can conjure a whole complex of images, so can other character indicators do the same. As Hochman observes, literature "has the capacity to charge relatively limited quantities of information with a sense of significance and to consolidate them into patterns of meaning."[3] It is this very principle that undergirds any discussion of "the Virgin."

Thus a single phrase like "to be or not to be" can bring to mind the essence of an entire Shakespearean play, and a word like "rosebud" can recall a whole host of images and valences embedded in the classic film *Citizen Kane.* The phenomenon is not foreign to Luke. In Acts, the narrator uses the phrase "signs and wonders" (*terata kai semeia*) to signal the presence of prophetic activity.[4] Therefore, beginning with Luke 1.26–38, we can consider how Lucan references to *parthenos* and *parthenia* interact with other textual clues to lend shape to the characterization of Mary.

Luke 1.26–38

Overview

Luke introduces Mary as the recipient of divine visitation: "In the sixth month the angel Gabriel was sent from God to a *polis* of Galilee named Nazareth, to a virgin betrothed (*parthenon emnesteumenen*) to a man whose name was Joseph, of the house of David; and the virgin's name was Mary" (1.26–27). Gabriel, the angel of the Lord who announced Samson's birth (Judg 13.3) and visited Zechariah with the news of John's birth (Lk 1.11–20), is sent to Nazareth to visit Mary, a seemingly insignificant resident of an equally insignificant Galilean town. Whereas the older couple resides in Jerusalem, the socio-religious center of Israel, Mary lives in "Galilee of the Gentiles" (1 Macc 5.15).[5] In contrast to the priestly family of Zechariah and Elizabeth (1.5–6), Mary is strikingly ordinary. Yet she is visited by Gabriel, one of only two angels named in the Septuagint and the one who figures prominently in biblical tradition as the bearer of eschatological revelation (Dan 8.15–16, 9.2–27). Thus in the space of two verses, Mary is thrust onto center stage of Luke's narrative.

With two references to her as a *parthenos* (1.27), Mary's sexual status is quickly brought into the foreground. As Brown notes, Luke calls Mary neither *pais* (child/girl), *paidiske* (young girl), nor *korasion* (little girl), any of which would convey youth over sexual status. Therefore the double occurrence of *parthenos*, "the normal understanding of which is 'virgin,'" is significant.[6] Mary is also given a name. Called *Mariam*, rather than the alternative *Maria*, the virgin stands in the intertextual shadow of the first female prophet in the Jewish scriptures (Exod 15.20; Num 26.59). Since Luke introduces Mary as a virgin betrothed to a man (1.27), the representation of Mary as an object of social exchange may very well figure in this scene. With the high regard for marriage evidenced in such diverse ancient texts as the Mishnah and the *lex Julia*, Mary's sexual status strengthens her image as one whose requisite virginity is soon to find its *telos* in marriage. Just as Asenath's identity is shaped by her relationship to a man called Joseph, so is Mary portrayed in terms of her betrothal to one similarly named. But in contrast to the narrator of JosAs, Luke is conspicuously silent in regard to Mary's family of origin.

The dialogue that ensues between Mary and the angel Gabriel provides additional information that advances the characterization of Mary. When the angel meets Mary, he proclaims, "Greetings, O favored one! The Lord is with you" (*chaire kecharitomene, ho kyrios meta sou*, Lk 1.28). His speech, reminiscent of angelic greetings in the Septuagint (Judg 6.12), identifies Mary as one visited by the presence of the Lord. Mary is further distinguished by the elegance of Gabriel's greeting, as the title *kecharitomene* conveys a sense of divine benefaction toward one who, in this case, bears little or no social and cultic standing.[7] As a character indicator, Gabriel's language makes explicit what his appearance implies—the virgin of Nazareth is somehow a figure of significance.

Despite the marked absence of any physical description of Mary, erotic overtones associated with virginity might well be detected in this initial portrayal of a *parthenos* alone with a stranger in the *polis* (properly "city," but in this case, "town") of Nazareth (cf. Deut 22.23–24). Readers familiar with the literary motif of virgins remaining indoors and out of the (male) public eye (cf. 2 Macc 3.19; 3 Macc 1.18; *Leucippe and Clitophon; Joseph and Asenath; Acts of Peter*) might raise an eyebrow at the intimacy suggested by the encounter. Although she is engaged to Joseph, a descendent of David, it is Gabriel with whom Mary appears in Luke 1.26–38. When she is troubled by the angel and wonders what sort of greeting he brings, readers may at once recognize the tension that accompanies a scenario involving a *parthenos* and a male stranger. Given the sexual violation of virgins illustrated in ancient fiction and myth (*Daphnis and Chloe; Leucippe and Clitophon; Acts of Paul and Thecla; Acts of Peter;* cf. *Metamorphoses*) and assumed in ancient discourse (Seneca the Elder; Mishnah), Luke's portrayal of Mary easily calls to mind the juxtaposition of violence and virginity. The situation in which Luke presents Mary can conjure images of seduction, lust, and violence that both human and divine figures perpetrate against *parthenoi.*

The angel's proclamation, "Do not be afraid, Mary, for you have found favor (*charis*) with God" (1.30), expands upon his initial greeting and confirms Mary's special standing. The imperfect tense of the verb, *heurisko,* indicates that the assignment of divine favor precedes Gabriel's appearance. Like Noah, Abraham, and Moses, Mary has "found favor with God," but unlike her forebears, she has yet to demonstrate the obedient faith that earned them such attribution (Gen 6.8, 18.3; Exod 33.12–17; see also Tob. 1.13). In contrast to Elizabeth and Zechariah, neither has Mary been described as particularly righteous or blameless (see reference to the former as *dikaios* and *amemptos,* 1.6). Mary's favor is conferred by divine initiative.

After having explicitly informed Mary that she has "found favor with God" (1.30), the angel reveals what is to come: she is to become pregnant and give birth to a son whom she will name Jesus (*kai idou syllempse en gastri kai texe huion kai kaleseis to onoma autou Iesoun,* 1.31). The focus of the message remains on Mary; *she* will conceive, *she* will bear a son, and *she* will name him. As in the stories of Sarah (Gen 18.1–15), Hannah (1 Sam 1.3–18), Manoah's wife (Judg 13.2–14), and Elizabeth (Lk 1.8–17), Mary receives the promise of a son who will be great in Israel. Moreover, her son is described in Messianic terms and destined for unsurpassed greatness: "He will be great and will be called son of the Most High and the Lord God will give to him the throne of his father David/ and he will rule over the house of Jacob forever, and of his kingdom there will be no end" (*houtos estai megas kai huios hypsistou klethesetai kai dosei auto kyrios ho theos ton thronon Dauid tou patros autou/ kai basileusei epi ton oikon Iakob eis tous aionas kai tes basileias autou ouk estai telos*, Lk 1. 32–33). Mary will bear the inheritor of the Davidic throne who will establish the everlasting kingdom promised to David by Nathan (2 Sam 7.1–17). Yet in striking contrast to other female recipients of angelic birth announcements, Mary is neither married, aged, nor barren. She is a virgin, seemingly potent and fertile, having suffered neither the punishing disgrace nor the futility of a barren womb. Her status as a *parthenos* marks her as a most unusual candidate for such an announcement.

Mary is further distinguished from her literary foremothers by the power she is given to name this remarkable child: *kaleseis to onoma autou Iesoun* (1.31). Because naming was formerly reserved as a male prerogative (cf. Zechariah's role in 1.13, 62–63), Mary's naming of Jesus easily captures readers' attention. Clearly, the virgin is being singled out in a most unusual way.

As Luke describes the virgin's cognizance of the angel's greeting and narrates her consent to the divine word, "Behold the slave of the Lord (*doule kyriou*); let it be to me according to your word (*rhema*)" (1.38), Mary is portrayed as an acting subject. In ancient literature, virgins are required to navigate carefully their moral and ethical development. Virgins are figures whose honor and purity are tested (Seneca the Elder; Dionysius of Halicarnassus; Aulus Gellius; Tertullian) and proven by the choices and actions they welcome or resist (cf. Deut 22.23–24). What are readers to make of Mary's response to Gabriel?

Looking back over the entire scene, a reader sees that Mary is primarily associated with male figures. She is the recipient of Gabriel's visit, poised to marry into the house of David, and told that she will bear a son. Furthermore, it is a male character, Zechariah, whose encounter with Gabriel in Luke 1.11–20 prefigures and provides a contrast to her own interaction with the angel. Finally, the character with whom she is primarily associated is here a male-constructed deity. It is *ho theos* who sends Gabriel to Mary, and it is *ho kyrios* with whom she finds favor and to whom she functions as *doule* when she declares herself the Lord's slave (1.38). The only female figure with whom Mary is associated in this scene is her kinswoman Elizabeth.

Thus an interesting constellation of textual clues emerges in this introductory scene. The images of virginity evidenced in ancient texts make possible a range of meanings that readers must negotiate in constructing an image of Mary. Amidst the convergence of character indicators that occur in this scene, what does Mary's *parthenia* connote and how does it inform her portrayal?

THE VIRGIN MARY AS AN OBJECT OF DIVINE ACTIVITY AND AN EXEMPLAR OF FAITH

Mary's sexual and marital status are the first direct Marian character indicators that Luke provides for his reader (1.26–27). In contrast to Elizabeth's infertility, the virgin's betrothal signals not only her nubility but also her expected fecundity. Luke's reminder of Elizabeth's shame in the verse preceding our passage (1.25) only sharpens the difference between the women. Given the patriarchal social setting in which Elizabeth and Mary appear, Gabriel's announcement that Mary is favored (1.28) is quite apt.

Beyond his initial introduction of Mary, however, Luke ceases to emphasize the virgin's relationship to Joseph. Having established that Mary is both engaged and a *parthenos,* the narrative focuses instead on the relationship between Mary and the male-configured deity. It is with *ho theos* that the virgin maintains her primary relationship, and it is by divine, not human, initiative that she will bear a child who will be called "son of God," rather than son of Joseph (1.32, cf. 3.23). By the end of the scene, Mary explicitly identifies herself not as the slave of Joseph, her beloved, but as the *doule kyriou* (1.38).

Therefore the sequence that begins with the identification of Mary as Joseph's betrothed ends with Mary primarily configured as the Lord's slave. Unlike Asenath, who asks the Lord to commit her to Joseph as a *paidiske* and *doule* (JosAs 13.15), and the lover who makes himself a slave to the object of his erotic love (cf. *Leucippe and Clitophon* 8.17), Mary belongs solely to the Lord. By minimizing Mary's family of origin, the narrative highlights an unusual social exchange: rather than presenting the virgin as the object of exchange between a father and a husband, the story illustrates the subversion of a husband's authority by the deity. The Jewish notion that God controls the womb (cf. 1 Sam 2; Lk 1.25) is raised to a new level. God so governs Mary's reproductive role that the participation of a human male is completely omitted.[8] This is only intensified by Mary's task of naming the child that will be born to her. The deity neither receives Mary at the hands of her father nor does he, like Artemis or Fortuna Primegenia, merely guide the *parthenos* through her transition to *gyne* (wife) and *meter* (mother). This deity claims Mary for his own purposes, and the virgin consents. By circumventing the normative role of husband and father, Luke's narrative sows the seed for later apocryphal depictions of virgins who disavow marriage out of devotion to the Gospel. Mary exemplifies the virgin whose primary relationship with the deity eclipses social norms.

The precise nature of the relationship between Mary and the deity is ambiguous. Mary's question about how she is to conceive implies that her impending pregnancy is imminent (1.34). Yet in contrast to scenes recorded by the elder Seneca and depicted in the novels, Mary does not offer a defense of her virginity. Rather she simply declares, "I know no man" (*andra ou ginosko*, 1.34), pointing to her virginity as a seemingly obvious obstacle to any imminent fulfillment of the divine word.[9] As David Landry notes, it is the seeming physical impossibility (cf. 1.37, "for with God, nothing is impossible" [*hoti ouk adynatesei para tou theou pan rhema*]) of this unprecedented annunciation (contra the message to Zechariah in 1.13–17) that justifies Mary's initial and immediate response, "How can this be?" (*pos estai touto*, 1.34). Hence, unlike Zechariah (1.20), Mary is not punished for posing her question to the divine messenger.[10]

While the narrative stops short of implying that Mary must surrender her *parthenia* in order to conceive Jesus, Gabriel reveals that the virgin's body is to become a site of divine activity: "the Holy Spirit will come upon you/ and the power of the Most High will overshadow you/ therefore the child to be born will be called holy, the son of God" (*pneuma hagion epeleusetai epi se/ kai dynamis hypsistou episkiasei soi/ dio kai to gennomenon*

hagion klethesetai huios theou, 1.35).[11] Schaberg, like Seim, notes
the resonance between this verse and Acts 1.8, wherein the risen
Jesus tells his apostles that they will receive power (*dynamis*)
when the Holy Spirit comes upon (*eperchomai*) them. She errs,
though, in assuming that such language is merely figurative.[12] In
Acts 1.8, the sending of the prophetic Spirit is quite a physical
phenomenon. As Schaberg herself maintains, several texts in the
Septuagint show that "the verb carries the notion of onrushing,
overpowering vitality where it is used in a positive sense."[13] In
keeping with such imagery and in light of ancient views of the
virgin body as the site of sacred encounter, we may therefore
understand Gabriel's message quite literally. As her body has
been chosen to serve as the object of God's "overpowering vitality," Mary will be overcome by divine power. She will conceive at the initiative of the divine will and by the activity of
its Spirit. While the scene certainly pales in comparison to the
exaggerated sexual imagery in Lucan's account of prophecy at
Delphi, Luke deftly couples the prophetic Spirit's generative
agency with the notion of *dynamis* ("the *pneuma hagion* will
come upon you, and the *dynamis* of the Most High will overshadow you," 1.35).[14] Through the Holy Spirit and the *dynamis*
of the Most High, Mary's body will soon become a site of sacred, procreative activity.

    As numerous interpreters have observed, Gabriel's message
fails to narrate an explicitly carnal and erotic encounter between
Mary and the deity.[15] Nonetheless, Luke's account underscores
the overwhelmingly dominant role that the deity exercises in
Mary's pregnancy. As Bow observes, Luke merges Jewish and
Greco-Roman birth narrative traditions to narrate "an almost-
but-not-quite physical impregnation of Mary by the divinity."[16]
In keeping with birth stories of Greco-Roman heroes that credit
divine parentage for their protagonists' great accomplishments,
Jesus' identity as "son of the Most High" (1.32) is rooted in
Mary's supernatural pregnancy. Yet, like biblical and post-biblical
Jewish birth narratives that feature figures who "have a special
relationship with God because God chose them for a special
role," Luke focuses most on the deity's purpose in siring a son
with the virgin.[17]

As I noted above, Luke's ambiguous narration of the annunciation is accompanied by hints of the virgin's sexual vulnerability. The same factors that function to provide Mary with the little status she possesses (virginity and betrothal) mark her encounter with the stranger as especially threatening—biblical law rendered betrothed virgins in the *polis* culpable in cases of illicit sexual encounter. Whether or not Luke's narrative sustains a direct allusion to Deuteronomy 22.23–24, the scene resonates with the image of virginity that the Septuagintal text assumes.[18] Whereas Zechariah had clearly been frightened by the angel's appearance, he was immediately reassured by Gabriel's first spoken words that he should not be afraid (1.12–13).[19] In Luke 1.28, the messenger's unusual greeting only compounds Mary's concern. Whereas the frightened responses of Zechariah and Mary both follow the literary convention of the annunciation-type scene, the narrator takes time to describe directly only what Mary is thinking: "But she was greatly troubled at the saying, and considered in her mind what sort of greeting this might be" (1.29). Although the text attributes no ill intent to Gabriel, the virgin is nonetheless wary. Her response is illustrative of her character and infuses a distinct perspective into the narrative.[20] Overtones of the virgin's vulnerability function more as a Marian character indicator than as evidence of an untoward encounter. Mary's reaction underscores her self-awareness and advances her construction as a righteous and thoughtful *parthenos*.

Luke's attention to the virgin's subjectivity is heightened by an absence of interest in Mary's physical appearance. Despite its pronounced focus on the virgin body, the narrative resists the kind of erotic description often given to virgins in the novels and refrains from attributing any physical beauty or sensuality to the virgin protagonist. Indeed, no mention at all is made of Mary's appearance. Neither does the narrator ascribe to the virgin any erotic inclination or affect. In contrast to the novels that focus on the *dynamis* of a virgin's beauty and desire, the only *dynamis* identified in this scene is that of the Most High (1.34). The Gospel avoids the eroticized male gaze of the novels.

As the scene furthers the construction of Mary as an acting subject, the virgin accepts the angel's word by identifying herself as the Lord's slave: *idou he doule kyriou genoito moi kata to rhema sou* (1.38). Like other "servants of the Lord," Mary believes the word of God (1 Sam 3.9, 10; 18.30; 19.4; 2 Sam 3.18; Isa 49.3; Jer 2.14). The narration of her response, unparalleled in biblical birth narratives, serves to convey a sense of agency that counters the representation of Mary as vulnerable object.[21] Although no response is sought by the angel, Mary makes a choice in a situation where none is demanded. By offering her consent, the virgin asserts her own voice into the scene. Following Aristotle's discussion of character as that which reveals choice, it is here that Luke most develops Mary's *ethos*. The virgin defines who she is.

In contrast to the *parthenoi* of pagan myths who are tricked and impregnated by lustful deities, Mary consents to a pregnancy that is announced prior to its occurrence. By embracing God's surprising *rhema* (1.38), Mary risks dishonor to display the singleness of heart that was sometimes associated with virginity. Caring not for "the things of this world" but for "the things of the Lord, how to please the Lord" (1 Cor 7.32–34), the virgin accepts a pregnancy that is bound to be scandalous.[22] Thus as Mary accepts an exceedingly difficult call to motherhood and to faithfulness, Schaberg likens the scene to a commissioning.[23] Like the greatest of the prophets, Mary allows socially derived honor to be supplanted by divine vocation.

Luke 1.39–45

OVERVIEW

Following Gabriel's departure, Mary visits Elizabeth. Since Luke supplies no explicit reason for Mary's "haste," readers may wonder whether the virgin wants to confirm the angel's word about Elizabeth's unusual pregnancy (1.36; cf. 2.15–16, the shepherds go with haste to see the thing that the Lord has revealed), seek female counsel, or hide her own imminent pregnancy (cf. 1.24). Not only does the virgin go quickly, she travels alone: "In those days Mary arose and went with haste into the hill country" (1.39). In Greco-Roman myth, only virgin goddesses (e.g., Artemis, Athene) demonstrate such autonomy.

Among mortals, lone virgins are vulnerable. In the novels, virgins left on their own run the risk of being kidnapped or assaulted. In the Apocryphal Acts they are subject to temptation. Given the anxiety that ancient literature exhibits in regard to unescorted virgins, Mary's journey stands out as an anomaly.

As the narrative focuses on the exchange between the two women, Elizabeth's speech functions as an indirect Marian character indicator. In the narratives that we previously reviewed, older female characters offer an important and distinct perspective for assessing their younger virgin counterparts. As idealized representations of woman's experience, their voices carry a measure of authority that readers use to evaluate the female characters with whom they interact. Pantheia's dream and subsequent accusations bring her virgin daughter Leucippe's ambivalence and deceit to light. So too, the perspective of the older and more experienced Lycaenion provides the key for understanding the nature and significance of Chloe's erotic education. In Luke's narrative, Elizabeth is uniquely positioned to provide information that is pivotal for Mary's characterization. Just as Gabriel cited the example of Elizabeth's pregnancy to assure Mary of the credibility of his message (1.37), Elizabeth's reception will serve to either validate or invalidate for Mary the divine word that she has believed.

THE VIRGIN MARY AS THE OBJECT OF PRAISE

Luke supplies no clear reason for Mary's visit with Elizabeth. Whether the virgin is motivated by curiosity, fear, shame, or another factor altogether, is not to be easily gleaned from the text. Whatever the case, it is the encounter itself to which the narrator draws the reader's eye. The visit between the kinswomen provides a clear contrast to the previous scene: Gabriel's greeting (*aspasmos*) troubled Mary, but the greetings (*aspasmoi*) that the women exchange are cause for joy (1.40, 41, 44; cf. 1.46–47).

Repeated reference to the older woman's remarkable pregnancy and the baby growing in her womb (*to brephos en te koilia autes*, 1.41, 44) validates the angel's assurance to Mary that nothing is impossible with God (1.37). Elizabeth's body serves as evidence that in Mary, God will indeed achieve the seemingly impossible. Furthermore, she voices the insight that both Mary and her child are blessed (*eulogemene, eulogemenos,* 1.42). Being filled with the Holy Spirit (*kai eplesthe pneumatos hagiou he Elisabet,* 1.41), Elizabeth prophesies what could have only been divinely revealed to her, that the virgin's body is indeed a site of divine blessing: "Blessed are you among women and blessed is the fruit of your womb!" (1.42). Divine initiative lends Elizabeth this remarkable insight. In contrast to the human (*en anthropois,* 1.25) reproach that she herself experienced, Elizabeth proclaims Mary blessed among women (*en gynaixin*).

Thus in the midst of highly questionable circumstances, the older woman opts not to question the virgin. Instead, Elizabeth immediately recognizes Mary's impending maternity, and rather than putting the virgin to shame, she elevates her younger kins-woman above even herself. Elizabeth, the wife (*gyne*) of a priest and an expectant mother herself, asks why it is "that the mother (*meter*) of my Lord (*kyrios*) should come to *me*?" (1.43). The re-gard that she shows for Mary and her child is consistent with the status that Gabriel ascribed to them in Luke 1.31–33 and 35. Just as Elizabeth's pregnancy served to confirm the credibility of the angel's word (cf. 1.36), her greeting validates both his mes-sage and the virgin's honor. Clearly no defense is required of this *parthenos.*

Elizabeth honors Mary further when she declares that the virgin is blessed specifically because she believed that "there would be fulfillment (*teleiosis*) of what was spoken to her from the Lord" (1.45; cf. 1.38).[24] Elizabeth's speech repeatedly casts Mary as both an object of divine activity and a woman of faith. Virginity, maternity, faithfulness, and blessing converge in Luke's portrayal of Mary.[25] Elizabeth's greeting not only reconfigures what Robbins and Seim rightly identify as a biblical tradition of rivalry between kinswomen, it validates Mary in the midst of circumstances that would ordinarily bring shame and reproach upon her.[26] Remarkably, despite her pregnancy, the virgin's honor remains intact.

Luke 1.46–56

OVERVIEW

In response to Elizabeth's greeting, Mary pronounces the only extended speech that the narrator attributes to a female. Thus the scene renders Mary a singular female character in Luke-Acts. Because Luke is known to use speeches to advance the Gospel's plot and develop its characters, the importance of Mary's speech as character indicator cannot be overestimated.

Here readers encounter the familiar scene of a virgin appealing to the divine. We may recall how the elder Seneca (*Controv.* 1.3) and Dionysius of Halicarnassus (*Ant. Rom.* 2.67.1–5) portrayed virgins praying to their gods for vindication. Likewise, Achilles Tatius's Leucippe seeks guidance from Artemis (*Leucippe and Clitophon*) and the virgin Asenath repents before the Lord in prayer (JosAs 12–13). In yet another instance, Diodorus of Sicily recounts how virgins utter divine speech (*Library of History,* 16.26.2–6). In each of these cases, *parthenia* figures significantly in the supplicant or seer's relationship with the deity. Just as virginity plays an important role in these other contexts, so might it figure as well in the Magnificat, Mary's speech in Luke 1.46–56.

Of particular interest is the relationship between Mary's sexual status and the *tapeinosis* to which she alludes (1.48). In contrast to early and modern interpreters who cite this reference to *tapeinosis* as reason to attribute the hymn to the infertile Elizabeth, readers familiar with ancient notions of virginity will recognize that the coupling of *parthenos* and *tapeinosis* is not altogether unusual. Ancient discussions of virginity envision contexts in which *parthenoi*, in particular, are construed as figures of *tapeinosis*. In JosAs, Asenath experiences the *tapeinosis* of being a *parthenos* who has been orphaned by her family and abandoned by her people (JosAs 11.3–6; cf. 11.10, 17; 13.1). She turns to the God of the Hebrews in the hope that he may see her *tapeinosis* and have compassion upon her (11.12). With Schaberg, who observes the Septuagintal use of the verb *tapeinoo* to signal the sexual humiliation of women (Gen 34; Judg 19.26–38; 2 Sam 13.16–19; Lam 5.11), we may also wonder whether the *tapeinosis* to which Mary refers is Luke's way of alluding to an unwelcome encounter that renders the virgin pregnant.

MARY AS VIRGIN PROPHET

Having been received by Elizabeth with elation and not reproach, Mary is filled with joy ("my spirit rejoices [*kai egalliasen to pneuma mou*] in God my savior," 1.47). She offers praise, not entreaty, to the deity who has already "regarded the *tapeinosis* of his *doulē*" (1.48). Although Luke does not specify the nature of Mary's *tapeinosis*, a term that generally refers to persons of low stature (Pss 21.22, 27; 24.1; 30.6–8; 118.50; 132.23; Gen 31.42; 1 Sam 1.11), the narrative has provided ample cause for the virgin to fear public shame: she is a betrothed *parthenos* who has consented to a pregnancy amid circumstances that, no matter how extraordinary, render her pregnancy illicit. Here Luke implies what Matthew makes explicit: the virgin's pregnancy is scandalous (Mt 1.18–25).[27] Schaberg's suggestion that Mary's circumstance is the result of an unnarrated, perhaps violent, liaison is undermined by a lack of narrative and extratextual evidence.[28] Yet her emphasis on the sexual vulnerability of virgins and the shame of an extramarital pregnancy sheds light on Mary's predicament. Regardless of its origin, her pregnancy threatens to diminish what little social status Mary possesses.

Mary's speech is rendered most coherent when it is read in narrative sequence as a response to her kinswoman's greeting.[29] In contrast to the *aspasmos* of Gabriel, Elizabeth's greeting elicits the virgin's celebration, for the one whose own pregnancy signaled her redemption from reproach sees *beyond* the potential *tapeinosis* of the virgin's pregnancy. Therefore, it is in response to Elizabeth, specifically, that Mary acknowledges God as *soter* (1.47). Her kinswoman's greeting demonstrates for Mary that the divine word is truly trustworthy. Rather than abandoning the virgin in her unusual situation, through Elizabeth God has shown regard for Mary's *tapeinosis*. As if to confirm such blessing, Mary proclaims, "all generations will call me blessed" (*makariousin me pasai hai geneai*, 1.48).[30]

Echoing Elizabeth's assertion that she is blessed (1.45), Mary utters a long speech declaring the fulfillment of what God has promised (*kathos elalesen*, 1.55) to Israel. In so doing, the narrative aligns the virgin's experience with that of an entire people and brings into view representation of the virgin body as a symbol of the body politic.[31] Like the Vestal Virgins, who function as a sign (*semeion*) of Rome's standing before its gods (*Ant. Rom.* 2.67.5), the graciousness that Mary experiences signals the salvation of Israel. The same Lord who acts as a father to protect his virgin daughter and avenge her against her opponents (cf. Isa 37.22; 2 Kings 19.21) "has shown strength with his arm" (1.51) and "has helped his servant Israel in remembrance of his mercy" (1.54). Just as Mary claims that God has shown regard for her *tapeinosis*, so does she proclaim the deity's exaltation of the *tapeinoi* (1.52). The exalted and exulting Mary personifies God's justice and faithfulness to virgin Israel (1.50–55). The *doule kyriou* emerges as the embodiment of God's "servant Israel" (1.54).

The narrative's new focus on Israel exposes another nuance of *tapeinosis*. The *tapeinoi* who are exalted by God stand in direct contrast to the mighty (*dynastoi*) removed from their thrones (1.52). As a *parthenos* with little or no social standing and much at risk, Mary is a fitting representation of an oppressed Israel whose liberation is dawning. Thus readers need not choose between the sexual and socio-political implications of *tapeinosis*. Both meanings coalesce around the Lucan virgin. Mary is both a female risking the humiliation of an illicit pregnancy and the embodiment of the biblical *tapeinoi/anawim*, the oppressed people of God.[32] Here the juxtaposition of *tapeinosis* and virginity does not so much develop an erotic dimension to Mary's character as it fuses the social-sexual shame imposed on *parthenoi* with the socio-political oppression endured by the body politic. The coupling of degradation and exaltation that Mary's portrayal connotes is comprehensive.

As a *parthenos*, Mary's character is particularly able to sustain multiple valences that interpreters too often seek to reduce to a single meaning. On one narrative level, Mary is the virgin honored rather than condemned by her elder kinswoman. On another, she functions as the representative of her people. The Magnificat serves to advance both the story of Mary and the Lucan metanarrative of God's relationship with the people Israel. The hymn's manner of inverting positions of social and political status reinforces the expectation that God will both vindicate Mary and save Israel.[33] By so doing, it furthers Luke's presentation of the Gospel as the continuation of the biblical saga of God's activity among Israel. Not surprisingly, then, the language of the Magnificat reflects that of the Septuagint.[34] Mary's speech locates her among other women of Israel who offer thanksgiving on behalf of the vindicated people of God (Judg 13.18, 16.17; Exod 15.21). Interpreters have especially recognized the affinity between Mary's speech and the Song of Hannah (1 Sam 2.1–20). Both merge the thanksgiving of a "maidservant of the Lord" (1 Sam 1.1) with that of the larger community, and both speakers bear sons destined to become great prophets in Israel.

Numerous interpreters recognize the voice of a prophet in Mary's speech.[35] As Brown and others have noted, the string of aorist verbs that make up the Magnificat are best rendered as prophetic constructions.[36] The prophetic dimension of Mary's characterization is critical, for as Paul Schubert first demonstrated, prophecy and fulfillment are at the center of Luke's plot.[37] Prophetic speech is uttered "through the Spirit" (Acts 11.28) by characters who are "full of the Holy Spirit" (Acts 7.55, 13.9). According to Johnson, proof from prophecy is the single most important literary device that Luke uses to cast the story of God's activity in Jesus and the believing community as the continuation of biblical tradition.[38] Thus the attribution of prophetic speech to the *parthenos* whose namesake is Miriam, the female prophet who uttered the Song of the Sea when her people were delivered out of Egypt (Exod 15), is most apt.[39]

Although the narrative itself does not explicitly correlate virginity and prophetic speech, ancient literary sources demonstrate the degree to which prophecy was associated with virginity and physical penetration was analogous with sexual intercourse. Plutarch and Lucan both underscore the erotically charged and consuming dimension of prophetic phenomena. Given the proliferation of such imagery for prophecy, Luke's reference to the overshadowing *dynamis* by which Mary conceives, and the prophetic speech that Mary utters, virginity can be seen as a significant building block in the characterization of Mary as a prophet.[40] Gaventa suggests that with Gabriel's annunciation in Luke 1.35, the Spirit may be "responsible not only for Mary's pregnancy but also her speech."[41] That the virgin's lack of social standing fails to keep her from magnifying the Lord with her soul (*psyche*, 1.46) only increases her resemblance to Plutarch's ideal seer: lacking technical skill, faculty, and experience, Mary is very much like the "pure virgin *psyche*" that the moralist upholds as the best instrument of prophecy (*Oracles at Delphi* 405C, D, in *Mor.* 5). The one who finds herself overshadowed and overcome by the divine *dynamis* proclaims nothing less than the divine word. The generative power of God manifests itself in Mary's pregnancy and speech. With her proclamation that God "has put the mighty down from their thrones and exalted those of low degree" (1.52) and "filled the hungry with good things, and the rich he has sent away empty" (1.53), Mary provides us a glimpse of the Gospel that her son, Jesus, later announces: "Blessed are you poor, for yours is the kingdom of God. . . . Blessed are you that hunger now, for you shall be satisfied" (6.20, 24). Reflecting the social reversal that Mary declares, the Lucan Jesus adds warning that is absent from Matthew's parallel account: "But woe to you who are rich, for you have received your consolation. Woe to you who are full now, for you shall hunger" (6.24–25).

The setting of Mary's proclamation, the house (*oikos*) of Zechariah, is important for two reasons. On one hand, it provides a domestic setting for the encounter that occurs between the older woman and the virgin. On the other, it introduces a motif that will be developed throughout Luke-Acts, namely, the proclamation of God's word in the *oikos*. As John H. Elliott observes, temple scenes frame the third Gospel (Lk 1.5–23, 24.50–53). But Acts, the narrative where "literally, the church spreads 'from house to house,'" begins and ends with household scenes (1.12–14, 28.30–31).[42] As the two-volume narrative unfolds, it becomes clear that "the Christian *oikos* is rather a decisive alternative to the temple."[43] When Mary utters the prophetic word in the *oikos* of Zechariah, she signals the beginning of the household's significance as the setting of proclamation, prayer, and gathering.

The scene closes with Mary leaving the house of Zechariah after only three months' time (1.56). She presents a striking contrast to Elizabeth, who remains hidden throughout the pregnancy that signals the end of her humiliating infertility (1.24–25). The virgin whose own pregnancy is illicit and dishonorable ventures forth into the public arena, assured of the blessing that is to come.

Luke 2.1–7, 15–20, 22–40, 41–51; Luke 8.19–21

OVERVIEW

Mary appears in five more scenes in Luke's Gospel. Four of the scenes occur in the second chapter: the birth of Jesus (2.1–7), the visitation of the shepherds (2.15–20), the presentation in the temple (2.22–40), and the boy Jesus in the temple (2.41–51). In each of these scenes, Mary is identified primarily in terms of her relationship to Joseph and Jesus. She repeatedly appears in the company of one or both. At no time does she speak or act independently. While Luke never refers to Mary as a wife (*gyne*), the narrative does specify that she is pregnant (*egkuos*, 2.5).[44] After she gives birth to her son, Mary undergoes the post-partum purification rites prescribed in the law of Moses (2.22). In the final Gospel scene in which she appears (8.19–21), Mary and Jesus' brothers try to approach Jesus through the crowd whom he is teaching. No longer called by name, Mary is identified only as Jesus' mother (*meter*). The one who served as an exemplar of faith in Luke 1 is aligned here not with Jesus' disciples, but with his brothers. As Gaventa observes, the family of Jesus stands at the boundary between the insiders (Jesus' disciples) and the outsiders (the crowd). When Jesus, having learned that his family is looking for him, declares, "My mother and my brothers—these are the ones who hear the word of God and do it," the family's relationship to Jesus remains couched in ambiguity.[45] This bears significance for the characterization of Mary.

Readers familiar with ancient narratives that feature *parthenoi* who eventually marry can assess the development of Mary's characterization in light of other virgin protagonists. The hero and heroine of *Leucippe and Clitophon* are cosmopolitan figures. Both born to families of means, they are raised in the cities of Tyre and Byzantium. Although Achilles Tatius devotes little time to the couple's married life, the narrator does indicate that they divide their time between their respective home cities. Longus's protagonists live and work in a pastoral setting throughout the greater part of his narrative. The discovery of the couple's true identities allows Daphnis and Chloe to finally wed. Daphnis, the son of the wealthy and virtuous Dionysophanes, marries Chloe, the daughter of the affluent Megacles. They worship the gods Nymph, Pan, and Love, and they raise two children, a son and a daughter. Finally, after Asenath, the virgin daughter of Pentephres, marries Joseph, she gives birth to two sons. The story maintains its focus on Asenath, whose beauty inspires Pharaoh's firstborn son to plot her kidnapping. When the four brothers of Joseph who join in on the plan are found out, it is Asenath who argues for their pardon and prevents the other brothers from avenging their evil. She serves as the exemplar of beauty and mercy born of piety.

With these images in mind, we can reconsider the characterization of Mary in Luke 2 and 8. As she fulfills the maternal role to which she consents, how closely does Mary resemble the virgin of Luke 1 and how does she compare with the protagonists of the novels? How does the transition from *parthenos* to *meter* inform the construction of Mary?

FROM VIRGIN TO MOTHER

At the start of Luke's Gospel, Joseph's procreative role is supplanted by the angel's announcement that Mary will conceive of the Holy Spirit. As the story continues, the relationship between Mary and Joseph remains largely undeveloped. They function together as the parents of Jesus, but not as a husband (*aner*) and wife (*gyne*) to one another. Luke makes no mention of their love or desire for one another and recounts no dialogue shared between them. The narrator refers to Mary and Joseph as the parents of Jesus soon after the child is born (2.27), but leaves the couple's marriage ceremony completely unnarrated. Indeed, as Joseph travels to Bethlehem not with his wife, but with "Mary, his bethrothed" (*Mariam te emnesteumene auto*, 2.5), the narratives implies what Matthew makes explicit—that the couple has not yet wed and that Mary is still a *parthenos* (cf. 1. 27; Mt 1. 24–25). By noting that she is pregnant (*egkuos*, 2.5), the narrative reconfirms Mary's extraordinary pregnancy and emphasizes her new familial role. For the rest of the Gospel, she is identified as *meter*. Like the prophetess Anna who lived with her husband "seven years from her virginity" (*apo tes parthenias autes*, 2.36), Mary is never identified as *gyne*. It is the unexpected transition from *parthenos* to *meter* rather than the usual progression from *parthenos* to *gyne* that dominates Luke's portrayal of Mary.

Unlike the ancient novelists, Luke makes no mention of any significant change in Mary's socio-economic status as she navigates the transition from *parthenos* to *meter*. Rather, Mary gives birth in a manger "because there was no place for them in the inn" (2.7). The contrast between this virgin and the protagonists Leucippe, Chloe, and Asenath, all of whom enter into comfortable if not opulent circumstances, could not be sharper. Whereas Leucippe and Clitophon divide their time between two cities, and Chloe and Daphnis own many flocks in the land where they reside, Mary has no fixed location or *topos*. Although she and Joseph travel to Bethlehem, the *polis* of David from whence Joseph's family hails, they are welcomed there by no one. The first characters to visit Mary, Joseph, and the baby are mere shepherds (2.15–16). Whereas Longus's protagonists ultimately transcend their status as shepherds, Mary's affiliation with persons of "low degree" remains unaltered.

In her religious piety, however, Mary does resemble the protagonists of the novels and Acts. Not only does she observe the Mosaic law (2.22–23), she also raises her son according to the law and customs of Moses (2.22, 27, 39–40, 41–42). By carrying out the religious responsibilities of a *meter*, Mary fulfills the duties expected of a mature female.

Mary's cognizance is repeatedly underscored by the narrator: "But Mary kept all these things, pondering them in her heart" (*he de Mariam panta syneterei ta rhemata tauta symballousa en te kardia autes*, 2.19). When Mary witnesses the shepherds recounting their angelic vision (2.17–19), Simeon blessing the baby Jesus (2.28–33), and the boy Jesus speaking of his father's house (2.49–51), she is amazed at what she hears (2.18, 33) and keeps *panta ta rhemata en te kardia autes* (2.51). Whereas the *parthenos* Mary believed the *rhema* of the angel and trusted in its fulfillment (1.38, 45), the mother is left only to ponder the things that continue to unfold in her midst, especially those matters that she does not understand ("and they did not understand the saying that he spoke to them" [*kai autoi ou synekan to rhema ho elalesen autois*, 2.50]). Thus in Luke 2, Mary's characterization takes a turn that culminates in Luke 8.19–21. By calling Mary's comprehension into question and then distancing Jesus' mother from her son's ministry (Lk 8.19–21), the narrator casts increasing doubt on Mary's place in God's ongoing plan. While Mary fulfills her duties as *meter*, she no longer demonstrates the insight of a prophetic *parthenos*. Readers will have to wait to see if Mary has a place in her son's ministry.

Finally, Mary's role as the mother of Jesus comes with a cost. In a narrative that underscores the suffering that precedes the exaltation of God's people, Mary is portrayed as one who will also suffer. Just as her son is set "for the fall and rising of many in Israel" (2.34), Mary learns from the prophet Simeon that her own *psyche* will be pierced by a sword so "that thoughts out of many hearts will be revealed" (2.35). The virgin *psyche* that praised the deity in Luke 1.46–55 is now the suffering *psyche* of a *meter*.

Although Luke neither depicts Mary's reaction to Jesus' death nor places her at the foot of the cross, Simeon's oracle may be understood in light of the anguish that Mary is bound to experience upon her son's death. Noting how "Greco-Roman letters of consolation often employ the imagery of a sword in discussion of the grief of mothers upon the loss of a child,"

Gaventa underscores the narrative implications of Simeon's prophecy (2.34–35).[46] Mary is destined to suffer the wound that Seneca describes for a grieving mother as "most serious; it has not merely torn the outer skin, but pierced your very breast and vitals" (*Helv.* 3.1).

Simeon's reference to a *psyche*-piercing sword also calls to mind the biblical image of the *romphaia* of judgment that passes through the land (Ezek 14.17; cf. *Sibylline Oracles,* 3.314–18; 3.672–73). The implicit re-identification of Mary and Israel (cf. 1.46–55) is noteworthy. Just as Mary's recognition of God as *soter* signaled the advent of Israel's consolation (*paraklesis*) and sparked the virgin's joy (1.46–55, 2.25), so does Simeon's recognition of Jesus as the salvation (*soteria*) of God (2.30) portend division among Israel and incur the mother's wounding.[47] Here as in Luke 1.46–55, Mary functions as a character in two simultaneous narratives, the story of God's activity in Jesus and the story of God's plan for Israel.

In the book of Judges, maternal imagery expresses the prophetic vocation of the heroine, Deborah, who "arose as a *meter en to Israel*" (Judg 5.7). Mary's prophetic role, however, yields to her maternal identity. In contrast to Luke 1.54–55, Mary voices no particular insight in these later scenes. As *meter,* she is only the recipient of Simeon's oracle (2.34–35). But whether she is identified primarily as a prophesying virgin or a mother who marvels at what she hears (2.33), Mary's identification with Israel lends coherence to her characterization. The *parthenos* who spoke prophetically of the fulfillment of God's promises to Israel (1.46–55) and the *meter* who suffers with Israel (2.35) are integral components of a single character.

Acts 1.14

Mary as Witness

Mary is present in the opening chapter of Luke's second volume. She is the only figure who appears at the beginning of both Luke and Acts and witnesses the entire span of Jesus' life and ministry. In Acts 1.14, Mary is counted among those who await the sending of the Holy Spirit. She has persevered in faith since before Jesus' birth and even after his death. In the short space of one verse, Luke answers the question implicitly posed by Mary's lack of understanding in Luke 2.18–19, 33, 49–51, and Jesus' ambiguous pronouncement in Luke 8.19–21: will Jesus' mother remain a person of faith? Appearing now in Acts 1.14, Mary embodies those who "having heard the word (*logos*), hold it fast in a noble and good heart and bear fruit with patience" (Lk 8.15). Through her steadfastness and presence among the gathered community, she fulfills Jesus' own definition of *meter* ("My mother and my brothers are those who hear the word [*logos*] of God and do it," Lk 8.21).

Appearing among the company of others "constantly devoting themselves to prayer," Mary is reminiscent of Anna, the female counterpart to the prophet Simeon (Lk 2.36–38). Like the widow prophetess who prayed and fasted night and day in the temple, Mary prays continually in the *oikos* where the community of faith has gathered. Like Anna, she appears apart from her husband. If we understand Mary to be included among all those (cf. *pantes*, Acts 1.14, 2.1) upon whom the Spirit of prophecy is poured in Acts 2.1–4 (cf. 2.17–18), then she, like Anna, is associated with prophecy in her later years.[48] At Pentecost, the believing community is collectively assigned the prophetic role that the virgin Mary evidenced, for a brief moment, in Luke 1.46–55. With this vision of God's people in place, Mary's characterization comes full circle to reach its completion. The one who prophesied the eschatological activity of the Lord on behalf of her people now witnesses the outpouring of the Spirit upon the whole community.

The portrayal of Mary in Luke-Acts is that of a multi-faceted character. As interpreters have long noted, she is virgin, mother, prophet, and disciple. Consideration of Luke's identification of Mary as a *parthenos* in light of ancient notions of virginity demonstrates the way in which Mary's sexual status advances her overall characterization. Multiple connotations of virginity coalesce in the Lucan portrayal of Mary. In the first place, Mary appears as a betrothed virgin who is about to enter into marriage, the social *telos* of the *parthenos*. Secondly, Mary's portrayal hints at the sexual vulnerability generally attributed to virgins. Then, as the object of divine initiative, the virgin is chosen to give birth to the *huios theou* (1.35). Together these connotations yield another, that is, the taboo against illicit pregnancy. The prohibition of illicit sexuality and the pregnancy to which the virgin Mary consents combine to explain the *tapeinosis* to which she alludes. Furthermore, the familiar metaphor of the body politic as a *parthenos* in need of divine guardianship emerges in Mary's personification of Israel.

The association of virginity and prophecy advances the image of Mary as a prophetic figure. Although the prophetic Spirit is said to be poured "upon all flesh" (*epi pasan sarka*, 2.17–21)— daughters (*thygateres*) as well as sons, and female as well as male slaves (*doulai*)—Luke limits his portrayal of women's prophetic activity to only seven characters in his two-volume saga. Interestingly, each of the seven women is either a virgin, a widow (Lk 2.36–38), or a woman well advanced in age (1.18). Despite the programmatic function of Acts 2.17, only Anna and Philip's four virgin daughters (*thygateres tessares parthenoi*) are identified explicitly as female prophets (*propheteuousai*, Acts 21.9). Thus Luke's narrative suggests not only that the Spirit's interaction with women is limited but that it is predicated upon the absence of female erotic activity. As Seim notes, "In Luke-Acts chastity is never explicitly stated as a prerequisite for revelations by the Spirit or the gift of prophecy. . . . It is, however, remarkable that out of the seven concrete cases of prophesying women who are mentioned in Luke-Acts . . . six are said to be chaste."[49] At no time does the writer identify the sexual or marital status of the numerous male characters who demonstrate prophetic ability in Luke and Acts. Luke's apparent identification of sexual abstinence with female prophetic activity helps to explain the silence of female slaves and the stigmatization of their speech that F. Scott Spencer observes in Luke and Acts.[50] Like other literature that we reviewed in chapter 2, despite the prominence of Acts 2.17–21, Luke-Acts may quite simply assume the sexual activity of female slaves. Given this pattern in the narrative, it is not surprising to find that Mary speaks prophetically only when her identity is primarily that of *parthenos*. When narrative interest shifts to focus instead on her maternity, Mary suddenly demonstrates a notable lack of insight. The Spirit visits her again only after she, like Anna (2.36–38), appears without a husband (Acts 1.14). Mary the virgin prophesies. Mary the young married mother of Jesus does not. Therefore we should not only understand Mary's virginity in light of her prophetic activity, we should comprehend Mary's prophetic capacity as being largely dependent on her sexual status.

Even as the Lucan narrative exploits images of virginity evidenced in ancient literature and discourse, the portrayal of Mary differs from that of other *parthenoi*. Although the virgin Mary is betrothed to a man, she is aligned more closely with the deity than with her betrothed. It is God who causes Mary to conceive and it is the deity, not her husband, to whom she pledges herself as a *doule*. The object of this virgin's devotion is a deity, not a man. And in contrast to Greco-Roman accounts of deities who sire the children of *parthenoi,* the God who shows unsolicited favor toward Mary also shows regard for her *tapeinosis.* She is neither abandoned, nor eroticized, nor exploited as an object of lust.

The portrayal of Mary as a *parthenos* is complex. As her sexual status figures significantly in her characterization as betrothed virgin, mother, prophet, and faithful disciple, readers need not choose between Marian constructions. When Mary's body is singled out for the fulfillment of God's plan, she exemplifies the virgin body as the site of divine activity. She models the agency that virgins can exercise when she infuses the scene of divine encounter with unsolicited consent and when she is later praised for her belief in the divine word. Hence Mary is both an object of divine initiative and an exemplar to be honored and praised. While she is no less an object of use and exchange than the *parthenoi* of other narratives, she is praised not for an erotic power over which she has no control, but for her active response to the deity and the events that unfold around her.

In comparison to the virgin protagonists of the narratives reviewed in chapter 3, Mary's characterization is especially multivalent. This may be due, in part, to the nature of the Gospel genre. While Luke-Acts functions and can be read as a unity,

Luke's story, by the narrator's own admission (Lk 1.1–4) draws on multiple traditions and sources. Thus Luke's identification of Mary as a virgin, almost certainly a pre-Lucan tradition, serves both the continuation of an earlier Christian tradition and the specific aims and innovations of a new Gospel story. Because the multivalence of *parthenia* allows Luke's *parthenos* to function as both a singular character and a symbol of Israel, Mary's portrayal serves not only Luke's story of Jesus but also his larger metanarrative of God's relationship with Israel. That Mary can function in both capacities as *parthenos* only heightens the opportunity to exploit virginity's multivalence and the virgin's role in the narrative. Appearing at the openings of both Luke and Acts, Mary bridges the two volumes, and as a symbol of Israel, she helps connect the entire narrative to previous biblical tradition. While she is a minor character in the overall saga of Luke-Acts, Mary's role as *parthenos* is nonetheless an essential one.

Defying Nature

Five

Whereas Luke's emphasis on Mary's virginity is exclusive to the opening chapter of his Gospel, the Protevangelium of James demonstrates a sustained interest in Mary's sexual status. Mary is the apocryphal text's central protagonist as it chronicles the annunciation of her birth, her infancy and early childhood, her maturation and marriage to the widower Joseph, and the birth of her son, Jesus. As Bow observes, PJ is the only narrative in earliest Christian tradition that recounts the birth of a female protagonist.[1]

By providing us with this expanded story of Mary, PJ implies the insufficiency of the Lucan account. In much the same way that the synoptic gospels put common source material to different use, PJ borrows, rearranges, and expands upon tradition evidenced in the Lucan and Matthean infancy narratives. This recontextualization of canonical tradition testifies to the intentionality of PJ's composition.

The language of the text, like that of Luke, is often cast in Septuagintal hues. Not surprisingly, there is also a good deal of linguistic affinity between PJ and the literature of the New Testament, particularly the Matthean and Lucan birth narratives. Therefore characters and images in PJ often resonate with those in the Septuagint and the New Testament.

Mary's characterization is clearly one of PJ's primary concerns. As a character indicator, *parthenia* is one among many textual cues that serve a reader's construction of Mary. The narrator of the Protevangelium identifies Mary as a *parthenos* fairly early in the narrative and sustains her characterization as such throughout. In order to examine the implications of Mary's sexual status for her overall characterization, I give consideration to a majority of the narrative, section by section. As in the previous chapter, overviews of each section highlight the impressions and possibilities that readers familiar with the multivalence of virginity in antiquity can negotiate. The discussion that follows each overview focuses on the developing construction of Mary's character, particularly her representation as a *parthenos*. Although the greater part of this chapter focuses on the portrayal of Mary once she has been identified as a *parthenos*, I begin with a discussion of the beginning of Mary's story.

PJ 1.1–6.14

OVERVIEW

The opening chapters of PJ detail precisely what Luke omits from his story—information concerning Mary's social background and family history, including the names and identity of her parents, their occupation and circumstances, and the story of Mary's own birth. From the start, this Mary stands in stark contrast to the lowly virgin of Lucan tradition. Mary's father, Joachim, a figure significant enough to be included "in the records of the twelve tribes of Israel" (*en tais historias ton dodeka phylon Israel*) is introduced as "a very rich man" (1.1–2; cf. Sus 4). Indeed, so great is his wealth that he doubles his gifts to the

Lord, offering one portion on behalf of all the people, and the other as a sin-offering for himself (1.2–3). Nevertheless, despite their piety and wealth, Joachim and his wife, Anna, suffer from the stigma of infertility, knowing that "all the righteous ones of Israel" bear children (1.7). After both Anna and Joachim receive an angelic message that Anna is to give birth (4.1, 4), Joachim witnesses a sign that his sins have been forgiven (5.1–3). Thus the divine promise of Mary's birth signifies the parents' righteousness. Prosperous and firmly embedded in the traditions of Israel, Anna and Joachim are reminiscent of the biblical Sarah and Abraham (cf. PJ 1.18, 2.9) and the Lucan Zechariah and Elizabeth.

Like her literary foremothers, Anna suffers the *tapeinosis* of a barren womb (2.1, 5; 5.8; 6.11–13) prior to conceiving Mary. Just as Hagar ridiculed Sarah, so does the servant Juthine berate the yet infertile Anna (2.6). Anna's humiliation ends when, in a brief annunciation scene, an angel of the Lord appears to her and says, "Anna, Anna, the Lord God has heard your prayer. You will conceive and give birth, and your child will be spoken of in all the world" (*lalethesetai to sperma sou en hole te oikoumene*, 4.1; cf. Lk 1.31). The announcement indicates that Mary will be a special child, indeed. Anna immediately embraces the news and, like Hannah (1 Sam 1.11, 28), she vows to bring (*prosago*) the child, be it a boy or girl, as a "gift to the Lord my God, and it will serve him its whole life" (4.2). Soon she learns that Joachim, too, has received an angelic message, "Look, your wife Anna is pregnant" (*en gastri eilephen*, 4.4). When he returns home, Anna rejoices, "Now I know that the Lord God has blessed me greatly. Behold, the widow is no longer a widow, the barren one, behold, is pregnant!" (4.9).[2] Having been miraculously conceived, Mary is destined for a special purpose in Israel. But unlike other biblical figures whose births were announced by divine messengers, Mary is female.

The birth of Mary is a significant interest of the text, as is indicated by its variant Greek titles, *Genesis Marias, Apokalypsis Jacob* (cf. de Strycker), and *Genesis Marias tes hagias theotokou kai hyperendoxou metros Iesou Christou* (cf. Tischendorf). The scene that recounts Mary's birth includes exclusively female characters. After Anna gives birth, she asks the midwife, "What have I delivered?" (5.6). When she hears the response, "a female" (*theleian*), Anna exclaims, "My soul (*psyche*) has been magnified this day." In an obvious adaptation of Luke 1.46, Anna states that she herself is honored by the birth of this female child. Finally, she names the baby *Maria*. In contrast to the Lucan *Mariam*, Anna's child does not bear the name of the Hebrew prophetess.

Almost immediately after she is born, the child (*he pais*, 6.1, 7, 9, 10; 7.1 [twice]) demonstrates exceptional physical growth and agility. Mary's parents raise her at home before bringing her to live in the temple of the Lord (*en to nao kyriou*, 6.3). They care for Mary without ever referring to her as their daughter (*thygater*), and they ensure the child's purity by confining her to a bedchamber-turned-sanctuary (*hagiasma*), insulated from anything profane (*koinos*) or unclean (*akathartos*). Thus it is only after completing the customary rites of post-partum purification that Anna offers her breast to the infant. In the bedchamber where her feet are kept from touching the ground, Mary enjoys the company of no one except "the undefiled daughters of the Hebrews" (6.5).

An enormous banquet in honor of her first birthday serves as the single occasion in which Mary is permitted to interact with others (6.6). She is blessed by the priests, who pray that Mary will be granted the "ultimate (*eschatos*) blessing that has no successor" (6.9). Female characters celebrate the blessing Mary brings; male characters confer blessing upon her.

In contrast to Luke-Acts, PJ does not attempt to supplant the temple with the *oikos*. Instead the *oikos* becomes an extension of the temple so that Mary's home environment functions as nothing less than a sanctuary. Therefore when Mary is later welcomed to the temple by the *oikos Israel* (cf. PJ 7.9), the narrative implies continuity in Mary's care and environment. Upon arriving at the temple, Mary has simply moved from one sacred space to another.

Looking back over the first six chapters of the narrative, we can see that PJ's readers encounter a rapid succession of direct and indirect Marian character indicators, including the miraculous nature of Mary's birth, her physical growth, purity, lineage, and family wealth. Although she is not yet identified as a *parthenos,* the wealth and prestige of her family resembles that of virgins like Asenath, Chloe (at least as revealed late in Longus's tale), and Leucippe. The narrator of PJ clearly devotes a great deal of attention to Mary's origins. The presumed apologetic function of the text notwithstanding, readers are left to absorb the rhetorical impact of an almost dizzying compilation of positive character indicators. To what effect might the text be positioning the reader's construction of Mary?

In Praise of Mary

In chapter 1, I commented on the correspondence between character indicators and various *topoi* used in ancient epideictic rhetoric. In a similar vein, Hock notes significant correspondence between the *topoi* that occur in the early chapters of PJ and the rhetorical conventions of the *egkomion*. Citing Lucian's criticisms in *How to Write History* as evidence that by the second century, "*historia* was becoming *egkomion*," Hock shows how PJ uses the form of *historia* (cf. 1.1) to serve encomiastic purposes.[3]

By speaking of Mary's lineage in terms of race (*genos*), providing details about her parents (*pateres*) and ancestry (*progonoi*), and including illustrations of her upbringing (*anatrophe*), the narrative highlights those aspects of Mary's character that the ancients considered most worthy of commendation. As Hock observes, Mary's *anatrophe* is especially detailed, receiving "special emphasis because it becomes thematic."[4] The description of the child's origins and upbringing in PJ 1–6 establishes the basis for seeing Mary as one who is praiseworthy.

In contrast to Luke-Acts, where Mary is at best a secondary character, PJ's extraordinary protagonist is the narrative's raison d'etre. Like the heroines of the novels, she is a figure of socioeconomic, familial, and cultic status that not only is rendered in direct and indirect detail, but explicitly recognized by all the characters with whom she interacts. From the very opening of the narrative, the reader is prepared to construct a Mary who will stand in sharp relief against the unknown virgin of Luke's account.

PJ 7.1–9.11

The narrative continues to chronicle Mary's *anatrophe* with a development that reveals ignorance of Jewish cultic traditions: Joachim and Anna bring the three-year-old Mary to actually live "in the temple of the Lord" (*en nao kyriou*, 8.2). On the way there, the child is accompanied and guarded by the "undefiled daughters of the Hebrews" (7.4). Each carries a lit torch to prevent Mary from glimpsing her surroundings, lest she should "turn back and have her heart captivated by things outside the temple of the Lord" (7.5). Mary clearly continues to live and move within carefully circumscribed boundaries.

Upon her arrival at the temple, the priest blesses Mary, saying, "The Lord God has exalted your name among all generations (*emegalynen kyrios ho theos to onoma sou en pasais tais geneais*). In you the Lord will disclose his redemption to the people of Israel during the last days" (7.7–8). Rendered in the aorist, his blessing either identifies Mary as one whose name has already been magnified or functions prophetically to foreshadow Mary's future exaltation. Just as Luke's Simeon proclaimed the dawning of God's salvation when he beheld Jesus in the temple (Lk 2.30), so does PJ's priest immediately recognize that in Mary the deity will reveal redemption to Israel. The child who was promised to God is now received in the manner of a pure and unblemished temple offering (cf. Lev. 4). Thus Mary embodies Joachim's "double-offering" (1.3). With her miraculous conception having already signaled the forgiveness of her father's sins, she is destined to participate now in the redemption of her people.

To the delight of the *oikos Israel*, Mary dances on the steps of the very temple altar. Like Jesus in the *Acts of John* (95–96), she dances before the people gathered around her and delights all those in her presence. In contrast to her former home environment, she moves about freely in the temple. Her behavior indicates that she is quite at home in this most sacred space, where nothing profane or unclean touches her and where she is "fed like a dove, receiving her food from the hand of an angel" (8.2). In the temple, Mary communes with the divine.

All goes seemingly well for Mary until she reaches the age of twelve. Without preparing the reader to anticipate a problem, the narrator writes, "And when she turned twelve, there was a meeting of the priests" (8.3). The priests force Mary to leave the temple "lest she pollute the sanctuary of the Lord our God" (*mepos miane to hagiasma kyriou tou theou hemon,* 8.3–4). Their sudden concern for the purity of the temple suggests the imminent onset of the young girl's menarche, a phenomenon that would render both her and the temple unclean (Lev 15.19–33). Thus the narrative demonstrates a decidedly new concern by underscoring Mary's potential as both an object *and* subject of defilement. The text's recourse to Jewish custom, following its inarguably unorthodox yet unproblematized premise of Mary's residing in the temple, only underscores the degree to which sexuality, and not religious observance, figures as the primary cause of crisis. The problem is not the temple. Surprisingly, the problem is Mary.

After the high priest Zechariah prays for divine guidance, Mary, the "virgin of the Lord" (*parthenos kyriou,* 9.7), is entrusted to the care of the aged widower Joseph, who takes (*paralambano*) Mary into his keeping (*teresis,* 9.7–11). Thus the text first identifies Mary as a *parthenos* when she is cast out of the temple and placed under the charge of a male overseer.

Looking back over PJ 7.1–9.11, we can see that the unusual circumstances in which Mary is raised are rather striking— what kind of girl lives in the temple? And under what conditions should she be cast out of the temple? Readers may wonder whether and to what degree Mary's portrayal resembles the Vestal priestesses who entered the temple between the ages of six and ten, or the haughty solitude of the virgin Asenath. We may also ask how the character indicators of environment and age figure in Mary's characterization. Readers familiar with ancient discussions of *parthenia* know the frequency with which female sexual maturation was construed as problematic. Medical writers, philosophers, and religious writers alike posited female puberty as a life stage rife with physical, moral, and spiritual danger. Given such concerns, we can examine whether and how particular cultural understandings of virginity interact with the Marian character indicators provided by the narrative.

MARY AS THE PURE VIRGIN OF THE LORD

Much in this narrative sequence resonates with the dedication of young girls to the Vestal priesthood. Like the temple fire whose purity the Vestals reflect, Mary is pure (*amiantos*, 10.4; cf. Gell. *NA* 1.12). She exudes the purity and chastity of Dionysius's Aemilia (*Ant. Rom.* 2.67.1–5), and she is of both honorable lineage and sound physical condition (cf. *NA* 1.12). Furthermore, like the Vestals, Mary belongs not only to the deity, but to the people. After Joachim and Anna dedicate Mary to the temple, they vanish from the narrative, leaving the child's care in the hands of the *oikos Israel.* In many ways, Mary's portrayal befits that of a young priestess.

In the company of the temple priests, however, Mary performs no priestly duties. The narrative clearly establishes Mary as the embodiment of purity, but refrains from ascribing to her the privileges and obligations of the priesthood. Perhaps the greatest obstacle to envisioning Mary as a priestess is that far from functioning as a requisite of her temple residency, Mary's virginal status precedes and even necessitates her departure from the sanctuary. Whereas the *parthenoi* dedicated to Vesta remained at the temple as long as they retained their *parthenia,* Mary is cast out of the temple just as she comes to be identified as the "virgin of the Lord."

The narrative's concern for what Gaventa calls Mary's sacred purity, then, is not aimed at characterizing Mary as a priestly virgin. Rather, it is a means of locating Mary in the context of holiness. Moving from the shelter of a bedchamber-sanctuary to the very temple of the Lord, separated from anything common or unclean, eating a heavenly diet, and interacting only with the religious elite, Mary emerges as a holy child. As Saul Olyan remarks, "the notion of uncleanness has no meaning apart from the notion of holiness; pollution is only a consideration vis-à-vis the holy."[5] In the portrayal of Mary, purity signals nothing less than holiness.

Therefore the sudden representation of Mary as potentially polluting (and its dependence on Mary's gender) is immediately striking. Having previously narrated the very celebration of Mary's female identity by Anna and the women who witnessed Mary's birth (5.6), the text initially presented gender as a significant and positive Marian character indicator. Here, however, it is precisely Mary's identity as a female that prevents the narrative from asserting without equivocation the protagonist's purity. In this scene, sexual status and gender suddenly converge as cause for grave concern.

Observing how biblical rhetoric concerning purity and impurity marginalizes women in the text, Olyan has noted that "the pollution of menstruation and parturition is restricted to women of childbearing age. In the world of the text, preadolescent and post-menopausal women would not be directly affected by these gendered impurities."[6] By implicitly identifying Mary's approaching menarche as a problem, PJ follows the rhetoric of biblical precedent. Even as one who formerly embodied exceptional holiness, Mary's identity as a pubescent *parthenos* renders her nonetheless as threatened and threatening as any other female. Thus the very narrative that praises Mary perpetuates an androcentric assessment of its heroine.

Repeated references to Mary's age, another direct character indicator, illumine the concern for life stage that Olyan identifies as relevant for the conceptualization of purity. Mary is brought to the temple at age three and removed from it at age twelve. Interestingly, both ages, three and twelve, can be connected to particular notions of female sexuality. As the Mishnah seems to suggest that only a hymen ruptured before a girl reaches the age of three can regenerate and that females are legally recognized as sexual beings at the same age, we may detect in the narrative's reference to Mary's age an implicit guarantee of the child's sexual purity and anatomical integrity. And whereas the threat of defilement that the nearly twelve-year-old Mary posed for the *hagiasma* (8.4) can be explained by her approaching menarche, a more generalized anxiety over female sexual maturity also figures in this scene. For the impending crisis that Mary's body imposes is not fully resolved by the virgin's removal from the sanctuary; she requires the additional safeguard of an aged widower's protection. Recalling how virginity in antiquity was considered most pertinent when it was threatened, we can see why Mary is not identified as a *parthenos* until she is about to leave the temple. As the sexually maturing young woman goes out into the world, she approaches concurrent sexual danger.[7]

In literature that construes the *parthenos* as both sexually potent and vulnerable, marriage is often the means by which she is simultaneously protected and sexually contained. Both the Mishnah and Soranus attest to a girl's thirteenth year as the age of marriageability, with the former recounting how a twelve-and-a-half-year-old daughter leaves the jurisdiction of her father to become legally attached to her betrothed or spouse (M. Nid. 5.7). It is at this very juncture in her young life that Mary leaves the temple to begin life with the aged (and sexually unthreatening) Joseph. Having become literally and figuratively "out of place" in the temple, the virgin becomes the object of yet another social transaction that resembles the transition from *tutela impuberis* to *tutela mulieris* and signals the end of Mary's childhood.[8]

The identification of Mary as *parthenos* enables the narrative to resume its focus on *her* purity, rather than that of the temple. Here, as in Luke's narrative, Mary's primary relationship is with the deity. At a marriageable age, she becomes Joseph's ward, rather than his wife. Beginning a new life under Joseph's care, Mary is called the virgin of the Lord (*parthenos tou kyriou*). It is this designation, rather than any sacred environment, that now sets her apart, signals her difference, and testifies to her holiness. No mention is made of her physical beauty or her sexual desirability. She remains the chaste virgin *tou kyriou* whose sustained sexual status signals her unique holiness.

PJ 10.1–12.9

OVERVIEW

In Joseph's absence, Mary performs the domestic chores of spinning and retrieving water from a well (11.1). She is summoned along with other "true virgins from the tribe of David" to complete the task of spinning the thread for the temple veil (10.2). These indirect character indicators serve as the narrative's only illustration of the protagonist at work. Not all the ancient narratives we reviewed portray the *parthenos* at work. While Chloe works alongside Daphne, neither Asenath nor Leucippe is associated with any kind of labor. What is the significance of Mary's work?

It is in the midst of drawing water outside that Mary is greeted by an unidentified voice saying, "Greetings, favored one! The Lord is with you. Blessed are you among women" (*chaire kecharitomene, ho kyrios meta sou, eulogemene sy en gynaixin*, 11.2). The message echoes both Gabriel's greeting in Luke 1.28 and the priestly blessings uttered on Mary's first birthday (PJ 6.7, 9). In contrast to Luke's account, the virgin is greatly disturbed because she cannot tell whence the voice is coming. Retreating indoors, Mary is encountered by an unnamed angel (contra Luke's Gabriel), who tells her not to be afraid because she has found favor in the sight of the Lord of all (*heures gar charin enopion tou panton despotou*, 11.5). Confirming the narrator's description of Mary in PJ 7.9, the angel echoes Luke 1.29 and adds, "You will conceive by (the Lord's) word" (*syllepsei ek logou autou*, 11.5). Mary responds not in fear, but in doubt, wondering whether she will actually give birth in the manner of all (read: all other) women (*kai genneso hos pasa gyne genna?* 11.6).

After Mary consents to the divine word in language that recalls her Lucan counterpart, *idou he doule katenopion autou, genoito moi kata to rhema sou* (11.9), she presents her finished spinning to the high priest and leaves to visit Elizabeth. The high priest praises Mary with words that invoke a recurring theme, "Mary, the Lord God has exalted your name and you will be blessed by all the generations of the earth" (12.3).

Elizabeth, too, greets Mary with joy. But in contrast to Luke's account, she refrains from praising the virgin for having believed the divine word, and Mary utters no joyous response to her kinswoman. Instead the narrator comments that Mary has forgotten the very mysteries (*epelatheto ton mysterion*) that the angel revealed to her (12.6). After three months with Elizabeth, Mary's womb begins to swell. Both visibly pregnant and frightened, the now sixteen-year-old Mary returns home to hide her pregnancy from the "sons of Israel" (12.8). In sharp contrast to Luke 1.46–56, the scene closes in tension rather than triumph.

THE VIRGIN AS THE SITE OF DIVINE ACTIVITY

As Hock observes, it is in these scenes that PJ "takes up the next encomiastic topic: Mary's adult pursuits, skills, and habits."[9] Whereas Mary's spinning illustrates that she has undertaken the task expected of a proper young woman, her specific role of spinning the thread for the temple veil conveys the elevated cultic status that she continues to enjoy. Just as Chloe's work exemplified her socio-economic status, Mary's labor underscores the special cultic status afforded her.

As with Chloe, the context of Mary's domestic labor renders her particularly vulnerable. Readers will recall that Chloe was nearly sexually assaulted when she labored outdoors and that Clitophon initiated his seduction of Leucippe in the household garden. In keeping with the ancient view that *parthenoi* are safest when kept indoors, it is not only the unidentified voice, but also the outside environment that provokes Mary's anxiety. Thus she retreats inside. Citing the example of Susanna 15–27, Hock notes that when Mary takes refuge inside she "is behaving properly. Going outside puts a girl in danger, even if the well is regarded not as a public well but as one in her garden."[10] Mary responds in an honorable way to the potential threat she perceives.

Although the image of the *parthenos* as a potential object of rape or seduction figures in this scene, the effect of the angel's appearance is less startling than it is in Luke's narrative. For having been "fed by the hand of an angel" (8.2), this virgin is accustomed to encountering the divine. As the sexual tension of the scene is eased, rather than heightened, by the angel's appearance, Mary ceases to be afraid. Neither is she compelled to either mention her virginity or act in its defense. Indeed, rather than doubting the possibility of a virginal conception, she expresses concern about how she is to give birth—will she deliver in the same manner as other (ordinary) women (11.6)? Her question reveals anxiety about her bodily, not moral, integrity. The angel's reply, though reminiscent of Lk 1.35, answers quite a different set of concerns than its canonical parallel. Here the divine messenger tells Mary how she will give birth to Jesus: "the power of God will overshadow you (*dynamis gar theou episkiasei soi*). Therefore the child to be born will be called holy, son of the Most High" (11.7–8). Having already announced that the virgin will conceive by means of the divine *logos* (11.5), the angel informs Mary that the *dynamis* of God will overshadow her to facilitate the delivery, not the conception, of her child (11.7).[11]

Thus the generative role of the Holy Spirit, so prominent in Luke, is absent from this account. Although Mary's body will serve as the locus of divine activity, PJ minimizes any potential sexual overtones in the relationship between the virgin and the deity. Mary's purity, primarily a phenomenon of her body, is as carefully guarded in and by the narrative as ever.

Finally, Mary's ignorance of the mysteries revealed to her and Elizabeth's failure to praise the virgin for her belief both underscore the text's focus on the *logos* by which Mary *conceives*. In contrast to Luke, no emphasis is placed on the *logos/rhema* that the virgin either utters or trusts. Unlike the Lucan virgin, the apocryphal Mary demonstrates no prophetic capacity.

PJ 13.1–16.8

OVERVIEW

When Joseph returns home to find Mary in her sixth month of pregnancy and unable to explain its origin (13.10), he is anguished and frightened. That PJ is borrowing here from Matthew is undeniable. In an innovative stroke not owing to canonical tradition, PJ's Joseph goes on to lament both Mary's pregnancy and his own failure in protecting the virgin "from the temple of the Lord" (*ek naou kyriou tou theou*). Likening their situation to that of Adam and Eve, he asks, "Who has enticed the *parthenos* away from me and defiled her? Has the story of Adam been repeated in me?" (13.4). Soon Joseph turns on Mary: "How could you have done this (*ti touto epoiesas*)? . . . Why have you brought shame upon yourself (*ti etapeinosas ten psychen sou*), you who were raised in the Holy of Holies (*he anatrapheisa eis ta hagia ton hagion*) and fed by a heavenly messenger?" (13.6–7). His question not only makes Mary culpable, it recalls the marks of holiness that distinguish her from other women. The one who was raised in the Holy of Holies and fed by the hand of an angel would only have degraded (*tapeino*) herself had she had sexual intercourse with a man.

After weeping bitterly, Mary at last speaks and asserts her innocence (*kathara eimi ego*, 13.8). Like her canonical counterpart, she implies that she is yet a virgin (*kai andra ou ginosko*, 13.8; cf. Lk 1.34) and confirms the intrinsic relationship between her *parthenia* and her purity. But when Joseph asks whence her pregnancy comes, Mary, having forgotten what had been revealed to her, can only declare her ignorance.[12]

In response, Joseph becomes frightened. Not wishing to oppose the "law of the Lord" by hiding Mary's sin, neither does he want to hand "innocent blood over to a death sentence" (cf. Deut 27.25, 21.22) should the pregnancy indeed be of a heavenly origin (*aggelikos*, 14.3). Joseph's reflections confirm that the pregnant virgin's fear has been justified. He knows that the "sons of Israel" (cf. Deut 22.23–27) could judge her worthy of death. Thus the narrative frames potential threat to Mary's purity in terms of an even greater danger. The virgin's purity is worth her very life.

That night an angel speaks to Joseph in a dream and reassures him that Mary's pregnancy is "of the Holy Spirit" (cf. Mt 1.19–25). In so doing, the angel repeatedly refers to Mary as a child (*pais*) as if to convey a sense of innocence that *parthenos* does not.

Throughout PJ 13–16 Mary and Joseph defend their sexual purity. Having told Joseph, *kathara eimi ego kai andra ou ginosko* (13.8), Mary repeats the same claim to the high priest (15.13). Joseph, too, tells the high priest, "As the Lord lives, I am innocent where she is concerned" (*ze kyrios kathoti katharos eimi ego ex autes*, 15.15). Having learned that the virgin is pregnant, the high priest demands that both Joseph and Mary submit to a public test of their purity. Thus the very people (*pas ho laos*, 16.6) who celebrated Mary's first birthday (6.6) anticipate the virgin's disgrace. Despite the strict boundaries within which she has lived, Mary remains a wholly public figure. Finally, both Joseph and Mary are vindicated by an obscure drink test (Num 5.11–32; 17.1–11; Sotah 5.1) that confirms that they are indeed morally sound, and in Mary's case, "intact" (*holokleros*, 16.5).

The scene of a virgin's testing is surely a familiar one in ancient literature. Like the Vestals and priestesses whose chastity is questioned, Mary and Joseph appeal to God for their vindication. What is most unusual, however, is the testing of both Joseph and Mary. While Achilles Tatius's Clitophon attempted, with some irony, to claim *parthenia* for himself, and Asenath's Joseph was called a *parthenos,* neither character was expected to prove his sexual purity. Readers familiar with ancient narrative may rightly puzzle over the significance of Joseph's testing.

THE VIRGIN AS MORAL SUBJECT

Given ancient connotations associated with virginity and the sequence of events that confirm Mary's virginity, the juxtaposition of Mary and Eve in PJ 13 advances the portrayal of Mary as a moral subject by subjecting even her to the suspicions and concerns that surround *parthenoi.* As a story that works to satisfy both encomiastic and apologetic aims, the pairing of Mary and Eve serves as a subtle means of framing the protagonist as one who could fall victim to defilement and dishonor, but does not. Joseph's lament functions to expose the assumed weakness of all virgins without injuring the reputation of the one it seeks to uphold. By using Eve as a potential mirror image of Mary, the narrative deftly underscores Mary's difference while avoiding the kind of titillating detail the novels employ to depict virtuous heroines fending off seducers and sexual assailants. More than the text needs Mary to redeem Eve, it needs Eve to reveal Mary as the *parthenos tou kyriou.*

Sure enough, although she is pregnant, the virgin resolves to defend herself. In the face of mounting pressure from both Joseph and the high priest, Mary models the virtue expected of a true *parthenos.* When she is finally vindicated, both her bodily purity and *sophrosyne* are proven. Thus it is at this point in the narrative that Mary's *parthenia* functions as evidence not only of bodily purity or ascribed honor but of publicly demonstrated moral virtue. At last Mary comes into view as one whose actions befit her extraordinary upbringing. She emerges here as an exemplar of virtuous self-control.[13]

Given the significance of Mary's defense of her virginity, the importance of Joseph's claim of sexual innocence becomes clear (15.15). In contrast to both Asenath's husband (also named Joseph) and Clitophon, Joseph is a widower who demonstrates no erotic interest in any female, let alone his ward. Joseph never suggests that he is a *parthenos;* rather he asserts that he is innocent (*katharos*) . . . *ex autes,* that is, in respect to Mary. Joseph is put to the test in order to prove that he has not "violated the virgin he received from the temple of the Lord" (15.6). His innocence is sought less for its own sake and more as confirmation of Mary's virtue. Therefore even as Joseph is put to the test, it is with Mary's purity that the narrative is most concerned. When she is vindicated at last, Mary's moral purity is firmly established. As an adult, Mary has successfully guarded the status ascribed to her since her infancy. She is truly the Lord's virgin.

PJ 17.1–20.12

OVERVIEW

As in Luke's Gospel, Mary travels with Joseph to Bethlehem in order to be enrolled in the emperor's census. Here, though, Joseph expresses particular concern about how to enroll Mary—what should he call the virgin? His puzzlement underscores the degree to which familial role and sexual status are ordinarily intertwined. Joseph is too ashamed to enroll Mary as his wife (*gyne*) but he is also unable to claim her as his daughter (*thygater,* 17.4). Here we may consider the implications of Joseph's dilemma for the characterization of Mary. What bearing might Mary's sexual status have on her familial identity?

When it is time for Mary to give birth, Joseph goes in search of a Hebrew midwife, leaving Mary alone in a cave outside of Bethlehem. He and the midwife return just in time to witness the phenomena that accompany Jesus' birth. Seeing the cloud that overshadows the cave, the midwife announces that "salvation has come to Israel" (19.14; cf. Lk 2.29–32). As the light recedes to reveal a newborn baby, she proclaims a second miracle: a *parthenos* has given birth, something that her *physis* certainly does not permit (19.18). In the narrative's most remarkable turn, Mary remains a virgin—even after having delivered a baby.

Mary receives the ultimate confirmation of her sexual status when she passes a post-partum virginity test. Refusing to believe the midwife's claim that a virgin has given birth, another woman at the scene, Salome, inserts her finger into Mary (*eis ten physin autes*) to test her virginity (20.2; cf. 19.19). As the scene recalls Thomas's testing of Jesus in John 20.25, Salome's hand bursts into (clearly punitive) flames. She cries out, "I'll be damned because of my transgression and my disbelief; I have put the living God on trial!" (20.3). After she is healed by picking up Mary's newborn son, Salome rejoices that the child has been born to be king of Israel (20.10). Although the scene ends in language that praises the child, the weight of the scene clearly rests on this final and extraordinary confirmation of Mary's virginity. As the story reaches its climax, readers may well ask what this most unusual demonstration of Mary's sexual status adds to her characterization.

Virginity as Holiness

As Joseph searches for an appropriate way to identify Mary, the narrative underscores how sexual status and familial role can be mutually evocative. While a man's wife (*gyne*) is his sexual partner, his *parthenos* is usually his daughter (*thygater*). A *parthenos* who is not his daughter and a partner who is not his *gyne* fall outside of standard familial roles. In PJ, Mary never crosses the threshold from *parthenos* to *gyne*. Instead she occupies it indefinitely. Just as Mary was never a *thygater* to Anna and Joachim, she is never a *gyne* to Joseph. The Lord's virgin retains a familial status determined only by the deity (cf. 17.4; 19.8–9).

Readers familiar with ancient images of *parthenoi* will recognize in Mary connotations of virginity associated with cultic figures like the Vestals. Like the Roman priestesses, Mary's sexual status sets her outside the bounds of normal familial roles. Her special relationship with the deity (as the *parthenos kyriou*) disrupts the formation and maintenance of familial ties. Yet unlike the Vestals and virgin deities like Artemis and Athene, Mary exercises neither the privileges of the priesthood nor the powerful independence of a goddess. It is her sexual status, more than her cultic service, that sets Mary apart from other women.

Unlike Luke's Gospel, which underscores the goodwill exchanged between Mary and Elizabeth, PJ does feature agonistic relationships among its female characters. From the early example of Anna and Juthine (2.2–6) to Salome's testing of Mary, women in PJ contend with one another. These female characters are keenly aware of each other's status in the cult. Whereas Anna's slave, Juthine, ridicules Anna and asserts that it is the Lord God himself who has closed the infertile woman's womb, Salome doubts Mary's sexual status and imposes a serious test (*agon*) on the virgin of the Lord. Equally telling is the way in which the author reconfigures speech that was attributed to Elizabeth in the Lucan infancy narrative. In PJ as in Luke, Elizabeth refers to Mary as the "mother of my Lord" (*he meter tou kyriou mou*, 12.5), but here in the later text she fails to add, "blessed are you among women" (*eulogemene sy en gynaixin*, Lk 1.42). Instead, such praise is attributed to the male priests who pray that Mary will be given a blessing that cannot be surpassed (6.9). Here it is male-inscribed speech, not the admiration of other women, that elevates Mary.

As we have seen, the cultic status that Mary enjoys is established from the beginning of the narrative. Two elements in the account of Jesus' birth, the characters with whom Mary interacts and the virgin's bodily condition, advance this dimension of Mary's characterization. Just as the infant Mary keeps only the company of the undefiled daughters of the Hebrews, it is a Hebrew midwife whom Joseph brings to witness the birth of Jesus. Throughout her life Mary interacts only with the people of Israel. Even the doubting Salome is a descendant of Abraham. All of Mary's relationships are determined by the twin character markers of *genos* (race) and cultic status.

Above all, it is the condition of Mary's *physis* that confirms both her extraordinary virginity and her status as the *parthenos kyriou*. Although translators most often nuance the meaning of *physis* as "nature" or fail to translate the word at all, at least one interpreter has demonstrated that *physis* can refer specifically to genitalia.[14] It is this meaning that illumines the test that Salome imposes upon Mary. As Salome places her finger *eis ten physin autes* (20.2; cf. 19.19), the narrative reveals an anatomical definition of *parthenia* that corresponds to what one finds in Soranus. It is not only her sexual continence but Mary's bodily condition that allows her to retain the status of *parthenos*. Just as Mary's ante-partum *parthenia* is evidence of her moral virtue, her post-partum *parthenia* serves as an expression of a bodily integrity and physical purity that does indeed defy nature. In this sense, PJ presents a truly supranatural virgin birth. As in the case of the Vestals, virginity, chastity, and purity coalesce in Mary's portrayal so that she requires no post-partum ritual of purification. In contrast to Anna, who had to delay giving her breast to her infant daughter, the virgin suckles the baby Jesus as soon as he is born (19.16).

Finally, the scene signifies the fulfillment of the angel's promise to Mary. For when the virgin asked whether she would give birth in the manner of all other women (11.6), the angel assured her that she would not. Rather, he explained, the "power of God will overshadow (*episkiasei*) you" (11.7). Upon their return to the cave where Mary is giving birth to Jesus, Joseph and the midwife witness the power of God being present to Mary—they see a cloud overshadowing (*episkiazousa*) the cave just before the baby appears. The account confirms that the virgin surely did not give birth in the manner of other women. Having received the assistance of the divine *dynamis*, Mary retained her virginity. The miracle of the account is not simply God's presence with Mary, nor is it the birth of an extraordinary child. Above all else, it is the preservation of God's holy virgin.[15]

PJ 21.1–22.9

COMMENDABLE MATERNITY

When astrologers (*magoi*) visit Mary and the baby, the virgin is called *meter* for the first and only time in PJ (21.11). The *magoi*'s visit constitutes the single instance in PJ in which Mary interacts with anyone outside of Israel. These characters, in contrast to the Lucan shepherds, whom PJ omits, are figures of wealth and prestige. Just as the child Mary received the homage of the religious elite and enjoyed the bounty of her wealthy parents, so are she and her son the recipients of fine gifts and much honor. The narrative demonstrates that as *meter* and *parthenos*, Mary retains the honor ascribed to her since infancy. The apocryphal virgin bears no *tapeinosis*.

In the final scene in which she appears, Mary acts to protect her son from Herod's rage by wrapping him in strips of cloth and hiding him in a manger. As Hock observes, Mary's action illustrates courage not unlike that demonstrated by Zechariah (23.1–8, 23.9–24.11). Unlike the Lucan narrative, Zechariah's portrayal underscores Mary's virtue not by contrast, but by confirmation.[16] As a *meter*, Mary is no less virtuous than before. With this final illustration, the narrative concludes its praise of Mary.

In comparison to the Lucan Mary, the virgin of the Protevangelium is presented in a rather austere light. From beginning to end, she is the holy one of God destined to give birth to a son who, in turn, will be called holy. Miraculously given to Joachim and Anna, she is preserved for the Lord. From the day that she is born, Mary functions less as an active subject and more as an object of exchange and offering. Her birth is guaranteed in angelic announcements (4.1, 4); she is vowed to the Lord by her parents (4.2, 7); protected by them in their home (6.3, 7.4–5); placed under the guardianship of the temple priests (7.7–8.2); removed from the temple and placed under the guardianship of Joseph (8.3–12); and subjected to a series of accusations and tests (13.6–7, 15.10, 16.5, 20.1–2). She is often cherished by those who bear responsibility for her, yet she also poses a burden. Finally, she is a passive character whose bodily integrity is of paramount concern. The graphic depiction of Salome's exam underscores an interest in Mary's body that permeates the narrative from start to finish.

The focus on Mary as a holy figure renders her character

rather one-dimensional. Although she is destined to participate in the redemption of her people (7.8), she expresses no particular concern for Israel, offers no direct praise to God, and demonstrates little insight. Although Mary is aware of her distinct status among women (11.6), she is nonetheless ignorant of the significance of her pregnancy (12.6). The paradoxical juxtaposition of character indicators that present Mary as both exceptional and ignorant finds expression in the narrative's reappropriation of speech attributed to the Lucan Mary: the praise and vindication that the Magnificat expresses is assigned here to Anna (6.11), and the canonical virgin's declaration of blessedness is spoken here by the priest and the high priest (7.7, 12.2). Moreover, when Mary visits Elizabeth, she not only fails to utter prophetic speech, she wonders aloud, "Who am I, Lord, that every generation on earth will bless me?" (12.6). Over the course of the entire apocryphal narrative, Mary speaks infrequently and in only very brief phrases (11.6, 9; 12.6; 13.8, 10; 15.13; 17.9, 10). Far from possessing a prophetic voice, this Mary hardly speaks at all.

Nevertheless, the *parthenos* of PJ is ascribed greater cultic status than her Lucan counterpart. Rather than exploiting the prophetic connotations of virginity and continence, PJ draws heavily on the priestly image of the *parthenos* to advance Mary's construction not as priestess, per se, but as the locus of holiness itself. Just as the purity of the Vestals and the sacred fire were to reflect one another, Mary as subject and the virgin as object form reflecting images. However, as the narrative progresses, it becomes clear that Mary's purity is more often ascribed to her than achieved by her. Thus she is rendered more like the sacred things entrusted into the Vestals' care than the priestesses themselves. Mary's characterization as a *parthenos* rests on the conflation of two narrative concerns: (1) the guardianship of virgins and the requisite maintenance of sexual boundaries; and (2) the careful distinction of the holy and the common. Just as virgins require protection from sexual violation, so do sacred objects and spaces need to be guarded from pollution. As the *parthenos tou kyriou*, Mary represents both concerns. The retention of her virginity signals the holiness that distinguishes, elevates, and isolates her: "In a sanctuary sphere of varying degrees of holiness, the greater an area's or an object's sanctity, the more highly guarded it is and fewer are the persons who may approach it legitimately."[17] Therefore, she is not like Thecla, whose pure virginity, though austere, is replicable by other women. Mary is not a model for others to follow. The carefully circumscribed environment, movement, and condition of the virgin serve as a most effective means of illustrating the boundaries of holiness that only she can cross.

As PJ's encomiastic portrayal of Mary exploits particular images of virginity, it strengthens the connection between virginity and purity that came to figure significantly in later Christianity and Mariology. Just as Beard recalls how religious discourse reflects and depends upon cultural notions of gender, she also notes how "religion itself plays a minor part in actively constructing, defining, and negotiating those categories."[18] Moreover, she argues that "religion regularly acts as a privileged space, a key place within any particular culture for the definition of gender roles, for debate on gender norms and transgressions."[19]

In PJ, the portrayal of Mary not only depends on cultural notions of what constitutes virginity and what virginity connotes, it elevates a particular constellation of associations and images. That it takes a series of virginity tests to vindicate Mary only underscores the degree to which her sexual status serves as the necessary evidence of the holiness that the entire narrative seeks to affirm. As the story centers the reader's attention on a sequential pattern of accusations, defenses, and tests, the danger posed by failure to pass a virginity test becomes clear. Anything less than a sure demonstration of Mary's virginity threatens to annul former attestations to her purity. Thus in Mary's story, virginity becomes the expression of purity and holiness *par excellence*. As a result, sexual status eventually emerges as the defining aspect of the character. In effect, PJ not only portrays Mary as a sacred object, it defines her largely in terms of her continent sexuality.

Thus while PJ promotes a praiseworthy image of Mary, it also advances a decidedly androcentric portrayal of the virgin. As Schaberg notes, "although Proto-James focuses on female characters, male interests predominate. There is no clear evidence of . . . interest in female apart from the male (including the male God). . . ."[20] Whereas the narrative's concern for its female characters may be welcome, feminist readers may yet resist the interests and categories by which these characters are defined and delimited. Despite its encomiastic purposes, the *genesis Marias,* that is, the virgin's "coming into being," does not come without a cost. She is indeed deemed worthy of praise, but she is drawn in great contrast to the Lucan virgin, who not only speaks but utters a powerful and programmatic hymn of praise (Lk 1.46–55). Here the Holy Spirit imparts no prophetic *dynamis.* The apocryphal "virgin of the Lord" loses her prophetic voice even as she gains praise for, and vindication of, her unequivocal holiness.

Reading Luke-Acts and the Protevangelium of James, we see that the notion of Mary as a virgin is no simple matter. Each narrative manipulates the meanings and images of virginity in different ways. Rather than imposing a single valence for *parthenos* and *parthenia* upon his text, Luke allows a range of meanings to echo throughout Mary's portrayal. Indeed, by presenting Mary in the context of several relationships (including those with Joseph, her elder kinswoman, the deity, and Israel), Luke-Acts utilizes multiple images of virginity. Together they enrich Mary's characterization. Luke's readers need not limit themselves to a single image of the virgin. As a virgin, Mary functions as an object of social exchange, a figure of nubility, an instrument of God, a symbol of her people, and a model of right behavior. The virgin as young woman need eclipse neither the virgin as prophet nor the model of faith. As a *parthenos,* Mary is multidimensional. Sounding a full chord, rather than a single note, virginity lends fullness to Mary's portrayal.

The Mary of the Protevangelium of James is also a *parthenos.* Yet although PJ retains Mary as its protagonist and chronicles a greater portion of her life, it presents a more unifocal picture of the virgin than does its predecessor. Mary is, above all else, the virgin of the Lord. Everything in Mary's portrayal, including mention of her physical and sexual maturation, her family background, and her environment, underscores her purity and holi-

ness. Within this context, virginity functions as the most concrete and objectifying indication of Mary's holiness. By retaining
her virginity *ante partum, in partu,* and *post partum,* Mary is
transformed from being a *parthenos* in the cult to being a cult
object. She embodies a purity that is absolute, untouchable, and
unique. Not only is the portrayal of Mary more uniform in this
narrative than in Luke-Acts, the nature and significance of her
sexual status is absolute.

This study was motivated by my desire to gain a better understanding of the significance of virginity for the construction
of Mary in two early Christian narratives. What has emerged
over the course of my investigation is a better sense not only of
the differences that distinguish these portrayals of Mary but of
the degree to which the narratives exploit, interpret, and reinter-
pret cultural connotations of virginity. To speak of Mary as a
virgin is to engage a host of competing but not necessarily exclusive valences. As readers reflecting on the virgin as both a
religious symbol and a literary character, we have two choices:
either we can sacrifice ambiguity for certitude or we can find
meaning in multiplicity.

Notes

1. Which Virgin? What Virginity?

1. For detailed discussion of the christological significance of Mary's virginal conception of Jesus, see the monumental work of Raymond E. Brown, *The Birth of the Messiah: A Commentary on the Infancy Narratives in the Gospels of Matthew and Luke*, 2nd ed., Anchor Bible Reference Library (New York: Doubleday, 1993).

2. Jaroslav Pelikan, *Mary through the Centuries: Her Place in the History of Culture* (New Haven, Conn.: Yale University Press, 1996), 8. John Kaltner underscores Mary's significance in Muslim tradition in *Ishmael Instructs Isaac: An Introduction to the Qur'an for Bible Readers* (Collegeville, Minn.: Liturgical Press, 1999).

3. Cf. Els Maeckelberghe, *Desperately Seeking Mary: A Feminist Interpretation of a Traditional Religious Symbol* (Kampen: Kok Pharos, 1991), and "Mary: Maternal Friend or Virgin Mother?" in *Concilium: Motherhood: Experience, Institution, Theology*, ed. Anne Carr and Elisabeth Schüssler Fiorenza (Edinburgh: T. and T. Clark, 1989), 120–27; Elizabeth Johnson, "The Marian Tradition and the Reality of Women," *Horizon*, January 1985, 116–35, and "The Symbolic Character of Theological Statements about Mary," *Journal of Ecumenical Studies*, Spring 1985, 312–35; Rosemary Radford Ruether, *Mary: The Feminine Face of the Church* (Philadelphia: Westminster, 1977), and *Sexism and God-Talk: Toward a Feminist Theology* (Boston: Beacon Press,

1983); and Mary Jo Weaver, *New Catholic Women: A Contemporary Challenge to Traditional Religious Authority* (San Francisco: Harper and Row, 1985), 201.

4. See the work of Kate Cooper, *The Virgin and the Bride: Idealized Womanhood in Late Antiquity* (Cambridge, Mass.: Harvard University Press, 1996); Gillian Cloke, *This Female Man of God: Women and Spiritual Power in the Patristic Age, A.D. 350–450* (London: Routledge, 1995); and Susanna Elm, *Virgins of God: The Making of Asceticism in Late Antiquity* (New York: Oxford University Press, 1994).

5. A majority of interpreters considers Luke-Acts to be a two-volume work. Cogent arguments for such unity, noting the consistent language, style, and thought evidenced in the two books, appeared in German and American scholarship during the first half of this century. See especially Henry J. Cadbury, *The Making of Luke-Acts* (London: SPCK, 1927; reprint, 1958), *The Style and Literary Method of Luke-Acts,* Harvard Theological Studies, vol. 6 (Cambridge, Mass.: Harvard University Press, 1920), and *The Book of Acts in History* (London: A. and C. Black, 1955). Cf. Martin Dibelius, *From Tradition to Gospel,* trans. Bertram Lee (New York: Scribner, 1935), and *Studies in the Acts of the Apostles,* trans. Mary Ling (New York: SCM Press, 1956); Charles H. Talbert, *Literary Patterns, Theological Themes, and the Genre of Luke-Acts,* SBLMS 20 (Missoula: Scholars Press, 1971). The minority view that sees Luke and Acts as distinct compositions focuses on the problem of genre, not authorship (Richard I. Pervo and Mikeal Parsons, *Rethinking the Unity of Luke-Acts* [Minneapolis: Fortress, 1993]).

6. For a review of the issues concerning Luke and the virginal conception of Mary, see Raymond E. Brown, *Birth of the Messiah,* 697–712, and *The Virginal Conception and Bodily Resurrection of Jesus* (New York: Paulist Press, 1973).

7. F. W. Burnett, "Characterization and Reader Construction of Characters in the Gospels," *Semeia* 63 (1993): 3–28.

8. Ibid.

9. Reference to the "readers" of these early Christian texts includes both readers and hearers of the narratives.

10. Petri Merenlahti, "Characters in the Making: Individuality and Ideology in the Gospels," in *Characterization in the Gospels: Reconceiving Narrative Criticism,* ed. David Rhoads and Kari Syreeni, JSNT Supplement Series 184 (Sheffield: Sheffield Academic Press, 1999), 49.

11. As Mieke Bal notes, "in the course of the long history of western criticism and poetics, characters have never been described in a satisfactory way theoretically" (*Lethal Love: Feminist Literary Readings of Biblical Love Stories* [Bloomington: Indiana University Press, 1987], 105).

12. See Baruch Hochman, *Character in Literature* (Ithaca, N.Y.: Cornell University Press, 1985), and Seymour Chatman, *Story and Dis-*

course: Narrative Structure in Fiction and Film (Ithaca, N.Y.: Cornell University Press, 1978).

13. John A. Darr, *On Character Building: The Reader and the Rhetoric of Characterization in Luke-Acts* (Louisville: Westminster/John Knox Press, 1992).

14. Beverly Roberts Gaventa asks, "What does Mary say and do? How do other characters speak to and about her? What actions do they take that have significance for her? How is Mary described in comparison and contrast with other characters? In what ways, if any, does Mary change as the narrative develops? What role or roles does Mary play in the development of the plot? What place does Mary have in the 'governing principle' of the work itself?" (*Mary: Glimpses of the Mother of Jesus* [Columbia: University of South Carolina Press, 1995], 23).

15. For example, Aristotle delineates "goods external to virtue and those actually inherent in virtue" (*ta exo tes aretes agatha kai ta en aute te arete onta*) as *topoi* appropriate for eulogy (*Rhetorica ad Alexandrum* 35.1440b.14–20, 26–29). To the first category belong topics such as "high birth, strength, beauty (*kallos*) and wealth." To the latter belong the fourfold manifestations of virtue: "wisdom, justice, courage, and creditable habits." Emotion (*pathos*), action (*pragma*), speech (*logos*), and possession (*ktema*) are to be praised explicitly in terms of the virtue that they exhibit. In his discussion of epideictic, Cicero also lists praiseworthy *topoi* whose opposites are subject to censure (*Rhetorica ad Herennium* 3.6.10). External circumstances subject to praise include, but are not limited to, "descent, education, wealth, kinds of power, titles to fame, citizenship, friendships." Praiseworthy physical attributes include "agility, strength, beauty, health." Admirable qualities of character "rest upon our judgement and thought: wisdom, justice, courage, temperance." Actions are expressly evaluated in terms of these virtues of character. Since ancient writers used epideictic rhetoric to lend witness to virtue, certain *topoi* served as markers of *ethos* or *animus*. Although their catalogues are neither identical nor intended to be exclusive, together they demonstrate that persons were portrayed in terms of markers similar to those that modern interpreters refer to as character indicators. Moreover, *synkrisis* (comparison) is a significant feature of epideictic rhetoric (Arist. *Rh. Al.* 35.1441a.9).

16. For example, the style and appropriateness of presentation valued by ancient theorists is repeatedly evidenced in Luke-Acts, particularly in the numerous speeches that occur throughout the two-volume narrative. In the *Poetics,* Aristotle addresses characterization in terms of *mimesis* and argues that persons should be portrayed in a manner that is appropriate, consistent, inevitable, or probable (15.1–10). Lucian pleads for historical writing that employs language appropriate for its characters and subject (*How to Write History,* 58). Dionysius of Halicarnassus notes, "It is generally agreed that appropriateness is that

treatment which is fitting for the actors and the actions concerned . . . the good poet or orator should be ready to imitate the things which he is describing in words, not only in the choice of the word but also in the composition" (*On Literary Composition,* 20).

17. Robert Scholes and Robert Kellogg, *The Nature of Narrative* (Oxford: Oxford University Press, 1966), 164.

18. David Gowler writes that characters in Greek tragedy "run the gamut of complexity from type-character (e.g., a watchman) to an extremely complex character (e.g., Sophocles' Antigone)" (*Host, Guest, Enemy and Friend: Portraits of the Pharisees in Luke and Acts,* Emory Studies in Early Christianity [New York: Peter Lang, 1991], 173–74). Likewise, Burnett argues that New Testament critics need to recognize "degrees of characterization" in the Gospels, such that "even characters who are typical can become round momentarily during the reading process" ("Characterization and Reader Construction"). That modern literary conventions can impose blinders upon our reading of ancient texts is evidenced by Robert Alter's question: "all the indicators of nuanced individuality to which the Western literary tradition has accustomed us . . . would appear to be absent from the Bible. In what way, then, is one to explain how, from these laconic texts, figures like Rebekah . . . emerge (as) characters, who, beyond any archetypal role they may play as bearers of a divine mandate, have been etched as indelibly vivid individuals in the imagination of a hundred generations?" (*The Art of Biblical Narrative* [New York: Basic Books, 1981]). See also Erich Auerbach's influential work, *Mimesis: The Representation of Reality in Western Literature,* trans. Willard Trask (Princeton, N.J.: Princeton University Press, 1968), 3–23.

19. See especially Darr, *Character Building.* Wolfgang Iser devotes significant attention to the interaction between texts and readers and insists that texts yield multiple meanings and resonate differently for a variety of readers and in relation to varying extratextual environments. See Iser, *The Implied Reader: Patterns of Communication in Prose Fiction from Bunyan to Beckett* (Baltimore: Johns Hopkins University Press, 1974), and *The Act of Reading: A Theory of Aesthetic Response* (Baltimore: Johns Hopkins University Press, 1978). See also Meier Sternberg, *The Poetics of Biblical Narrative: Ideological Literature and the Drama of Reading* (Bloomington: Indiana University Press, 1985). For a recent theoretical review and discussion of the reader's role in generating biblical characters, see Rhoads and Syreeni, eds., *Characterization in the Gospels.*

20. Here Iser develops Ingarden's concept of "Unbestimmtheitsstellen" ("spots of indeterminacy") to expose the dynamic nature of the reading process. Gaps are perceived when patterns of reading require completion, or "filling in," by the reader. Blanks are the "unseen joints" with which readers connect patterns of reading (cf. *Act of Reading,* 183).

A familiar example of such a narrative gap and blank occurs in Mark 14.51–52. Who is the *neaniskos* who loses his clothes in the garden? Readers "fill in" this gap when they ascribe this figure a particular identity; they complete a "blank" when they adjoin "him" to narrative patterns of discipleship in Mark. Iser maintains that textual gaps do not direct reading: "The most that can be said of the indeterminacies is that they may *stimulate*, but not that they *demand* completion from our existing store of knowledge" (*Act of Reading*, 177; cf. *Implied Reader*, 226–27). Cf. Sternberg's discussion of temporary and permanent gaps in reading. Calling the latter "blanks," Sternberg argues that permanent gaps can be "disregarded without loss, indeed must be disregarded to keep the narrative in focus" (*Poetics of Biblical Narrative*, 236). For discussion of gaps in Luke's narrative, see Darr, *Character Building*, and William Kurz, *Reading Luke-Acts: Dynamics of Biblical Narrative* (Louisville: Westminster John Knox Press, 1993).

21. Darr, *Character Building*, 29.

22. Iser, *Act of Reading*, 118.

23. Iser, *Implied Reader*, 280.

24. Vernon K. Robbins, "The Reversed Contextualization of Psalm 22 in the Markan Crucifixion: A Socio-Rhetorical Analysis," in *The Four Gospels: 1992—In Honour of Frans Neirynck*, ed. J. Delobel et al. (Leuven: University Press, 1992), 1161–86.

25. Among his many writings on Paul, see especially Abraham J. Malherbe, *Paul and the Popular Philosophers* (Minneapolis: Augsburg Fortress, 1989).

26. Frank Kermode, *The Genesis of Secrecy: On the Interpretation of Narrative* (Cambridge, Mass.: Harvard University Press, 1979), 78.

27. See Gowler, *Host, Guest, Enemy, and Friend*, and Darr, *Character Building*, 61.

Although study of Lucan characterization has remained largely in what Darr calls "the embryonic stage" (174), fairly recent treatments of characterization in Luke-Acts include Gaventa, *Mary;* William H. Shepherd Jr., *The Narrative Function of the Holy Spirit as a Character in Luke-Acts*, SBL Dissertation Series (Atlanta: Scholars Press, 1994); J. M. Dawsey, *The Lukan Voice: Confusion and Irony in the Gospel of Luke* (Macon, Ga.: Mercer University, 1986, and "What's in a Name? Characterization in Luke," *Biblical Theology Bulletin* 16 (1986): 143–47; Gowler, *Host, Guest, Enemy and Friend;* and Robert Tannehill, *The Narrative Unity of Luke-Acts*, 2 vols. (Philadelphia: Fortress, 1986 and 1990).

28. For general discussion of the echoes of Jewish and Hellenistic themes in PJ, see Ronald F. Hock, *The Infancy Gospels of James and Thomas: Introduction, Greek Text, English Translation, and Notes* (Santa Rosa, Calif.: Polebridge Press, 1995), and Oscar Cullman, "Infancy Gospels," in *New Testament Apocrypha*, vol. 1: *Gospels and Related Writ-*

ings, ed. Edgar Hennecke, Wilhelm Schneemelcher, and R. McL.Wilson (Philadelphia: Westminster, 1963), 363–69.

29. For discussion of New Historicist biblical interpretation, see Mary Ann Tolbert, "The Gospel in Greco-Roman Culture," in *The Book and the Text: The Bible and Literary Theory,* ed. Regina Schwartz (Oxford: Basil Blackwell, 1990), 258–75; A. K. M. Adam, *What Is Postmodern Biblical Criticism?* Guides to Biblical Scholarship, New Testament Series (Minneapolis: Fortress Press, 1995); and John R. Donahue, "The Literary Turn and New Testament Theology: Detour or New Direction?" *Journal of Religion* 76 (1996): 250–75.

30. Harold C. Washington, "Violence and the Construction of Gender in the Hebrew Bible: A New Historicist Approach," *Biblical Interpretation* 5, no. 4 (1997): 327.

31. For discussion of both "cultural intertexture" and the "inner texture" of texts, see Vernon K. Robbins, *Exploring the Texture of Texts: A Guide to Socio-Rhetorical Interpretation* (Valley Forge: Trinity Press, 1996). Cf. idem, *The Tapestry of Early Christian Discourse: Rhetoric, Society, and Ideology* (London: Routledge, 1996).

32. Joseph B. Tyson reviews the range of terms by which Luke 1–2 has been characterized in "The Birth Narratives and the Beginning of Luke's Gospel," *Semeia* 52 (1990): 103–20.

33. Since the character of Mary figures more prominently in the infancy narrative than in the remainder of the Lucan corpus, the integrity of the Lucan infancy narrative is particularly significant for this study. In the history of modern scholarship, this issue has been debated on several different fronts. See Raymond E. Brown, *Birth of the Messiah,* 239–53 for a review of the issues. Late-nineteenth-century theories concerning semitic sources for Luke 1–2 eventually yielded to the argument that the chapters were composed in an intentionally Septuagintal style and penned by a writer whose skill in *prosopopoiia* is evidenced throughout Luke and Acts. See Cadbury, *The Making of Luke-Acts,* for seminal arguments concerning both the unity of Luke-Acts and the author's compositional skill.

On a very different front, the ideational and theological integrity of the Lucan infancy narrative also came under fire by postwar redaction critics of Luke 1–2. Hans Conzelmann essentially dismissed Luke's opening chapters as "a special problem" (*The Theology of St. Luke* [Philadelphia: Fortress, 1982], 172). Subsequent interpreters began to remark upon the "structural-literary propensities" that lend coherence to Luke's narrative. See Paul Schubert, "The Structure and Significance of Luke 24," in *Neutestamentliche Studien für Rudolf Bultmann* (Berlin: Alfred Topelmann, 1954), 165–86, and Paul S. Minear, "Luke's Use of the Birth Stories," in *Studies in Luke-Acts,* ed. L. Keck and J. L. Martyn (Philadelphia: Fortress Press, 1966), 111–30. With a well-founded argument for unity in place, the integrity of the infancy narrative reappeared on the horizon of scholarly analysis. Attention to the language, style, themes, and interests that characterize the Gospel narrative as a whole revealed the consistency and "homogeneity" of the infancy narrative that finally came to be judged as "thoroughly Lucan" (Minear, "Luke's Use," 112).

34. Among such readings are: Luke T. Johnson, *The Literary Function of Possessions in Luke-Acts,* SBL Dissertation Series 39 (Missoula: Scholars Press, 1977); Dawsey, *Lukan Voice;* Tannehill, *Narrative Unity;* Jack Dean Kingsbury, *Conflict in Luke: Jesus, Authorities, Disciples* (Minneapolis: Fortress Press, 1991); Gowler, *Host, Guest, Enemy, and Friend;* Darr, *Character Building;* Kurz, *Reading Luke-Acts;* Shepherd, *Narrative Function of the Holy Spirit;* and Vernon K. Robbins, "Socio-Rhetorical Criticism: Mary, Elizabeth, and the Magnificat as a Test Case," in *The New Literary Criticism and the New Testament,* ed. Elizabeth Struthers Malbon and Edgar V. McKnight, JSNT Supplement Series 109 (Sheffield: Sheffield Academic Press, 1994), 164–209. Most relevant for this project, Gaventa's study of Mary in Luke is clearly founded on arguments for Lucan unity and the integrity of the infancy narrative (*Mary*).

35. See note 5.

36. Hochman, *Character in Literature,* 8. As indicated previously, this study presupposes a degree of narrative incompleteness and instability. However, while one ought to refrain from overstating the unity of any New Testament narrative, with Merenlahti and Raimo Hakola I agree that "[o]n a very basic level, the Gospels might probably be considered unified enough to meet the goal-oriented and genre-specific standards of their time" ("Reconceiving Narrative Criticism," in *Characterization in the Gospels,* ed. Rhoads and Syreeni, 32).

37. One hundred sixty-seven extant witnesses to the Greek tradition of the Protevangelium, as well as numerous translations and paraphrases of the Greek text in Latin, Syriac, Coptic, Armenian, Ethiopic, Arabic, and Georgian, are known. This attests to the widespread popularity, but not the provenance, of the Protevangelium of James.

38. The first being that of J. C. Thilo in 1832 (*Codex apocryphus Novi Testamenti,* ed. J. C. Thilo, [Leipzig: Vogel, 1832], 159–273), and the most influential being the 1853 edition of C. von Tischendorf (*Evangelia Apocrypha,* 2nd ed. [Leipzig: Avenarius and Mendelssohn, 1853], 1–50). Study of PJ was significantly advanced by M. Testuz's 1958 publication of the newly discovered Papyrus Bodmer V (*Papyrus Bodmer V: Nativité de Marie*) and E. de Strycker's 1961 critical text representing a reworking of Tischendorf's manuscript in relation to Papyrus Bodmer V (*La Forme la plus ancienne du Protevangile de Jacques: Recherches sur le Papyrus Bodmer 5, avec une edition critique du texte grec et une traduction annotee,* Subsidia Hagiographa 33 (Brussels: Societé des Bollandistes, 1961). Together with Papyrus Bodmer V, the critical

editions of Tischendorf and de Strycker remain the primary texts for interpreting the Protevangelium of James, with de Strycker's text often serving as the standard.

39. See Hock, *Infancy Gospels*. Hock makes primary use of de Strycker, noting both where his predecessor departs from Tischendorf and where he himself disagrees with de Strycker.

40. As in the case of Lucan interpretation, the late nineteenth century witnessed the proposal of various source theories for PJ. Some scholars continue to view the text as a disjointed, composite work (Wilhelm Michaelis, *Die Apokryphen Schriften zum Neuen Testament*. [1956], 62–95; Oscar Cullman, "The Protevangelium of James," in *New Testament Apocrypha*, vol. 1, ed. Hennecke, Schneemelcher, and Wilson, 421–38; Helmut Köster, "Uberlieferung und Geschichte der früchristlichen Evangelienliteratur," *Aufstieg und Niedergang der römischen Welt* 2.25.2 [1984]: 1463–542; and Walter Pratscher, *Der Herrenbruder Jakobus und die Jakobustradition*, FRLANT 139 [Göttingen: Vandenhoeck and Ruprecht, 1987]). Others have argued that the narrative's unity is evidenced by its rhetorical technique and its consistent syntax, vocabulary, style, and themes. In "The Suspension of Time in Chapter 18 of Protevangelium Jacobi" (in *The Future of Early Christianity*, ed. Birger A. Pearson [Minneapolis: Fortress Press, 1991]), François Bovon argues that seemingly disjointed shifts in the narrative are evidence not of different source materials, but of a common ancient rhetorical strategy. H. R. Smid argues for the coherence of the composition and contends that the writer of the Protevangelium alternates third and first person narration in order to create "the fiction of an eye-witness report" (*Protevangelium Jacobi: A Commentary*, Apocrypha Novi Testamenti, vol. 1. [Assen: Van Gorcum, 1965], 177). Finally, de Strycker notes the consistent vocabulary and syntax that point to the unity of the Protevangelium (*La Forme la plus ancienne*, 6–13).

41. In studies that depend in part on the unity of the Protevangelium, Gaventa (*Mary*) and Hock (*Infancy Gospels*) both investigate specific narratological dimensions of the text.

42. See Jane Schaberg, *The Illegitimacy of Jesus: A Feminist Theological Interpretation of the Infancy Narratives* (San Francisco: Harper and Row, 1987), 178–92.

43. Cf. Aloys Grillmeier, *Christ in Christian Tradition*, vol. 1: *From the Apostolic Age to Chalcedon 451*, 2nd ed., trans. John Bowden (Atlanta: John Knox Press, 1975), and Richard Norris, *The Christological Controversy* (Philadelphia: Fortress, 1980).

44. Gaventa, *Mary*, 73.

45. Renee Laurentin speculates that Mary is cognizant of Jesus' divine identity ever since the annunciation, *Jésus au Temple: Mystère de Paques et foi de Marie en Luc 2.48–50* (Paris: Gabalda, 1966), 180, 184. Whereas he sees Mary as a theologian who puts together (*symballein*)

the meaning of the events unfolding in her midst (*Structure et theologie de Luc 1–2* [Paris: Gabalda, 1957], 97, 100, 116–19), Brown et al. take *symballein, synterein,* and *diaterein* as evidence of Mary's puzzlement (Raymond E. Brown, Karl P. Donfried, Joseph A. Fitzmyer, and John R. Reumann, eds., *Mary in the New Testament: A Collaborative Assessment by Protestant and Roman Catholic Scholars* [Philadelphia: Fortress Press; New York: Ramsey; Toronto: Paulist Press, 1978], 149–50).

46. Gaventa, *Mary,* 75.

47. Heikki Räisänen, *Die Mutter Jesu im Neuen Testament* (Helsinki: Suomalainen Tiedeakatemia, 1969), 104–106.

48. Raymond E. Brown, *Birth of the Messiah,* 462; Joseph A. Fitzmyer, *The Gospel According to Luke,* 2 vols., Anchor Bible 28 (Garden City, N.Y.: Doubleday, 1981), 429.

49. Gaventa, *Mary,* 64–66. Cf. Räisänen, *Mutter,* 133. Gaventa notes that "in the long history of reflection on Mary, this saying has understandably aroused a variety of interpretations, some of which are quite fanciful. For example, Origen understood the sword as a reference to Mary's doubt about Jesus' identity during the time of his passion and death" (64).

50. Gaventa writes that Mary is "first and foremost a disciple of Jesus" (*Mary,* 73). Cf. Charles Talbert, *Reading Luke* (New York: Crossroad, 1982), 22–26; P. J. Bearsley, "Mary the Perfect Disciple: A Paradigm for Mariology," *Theological Studies* 41 (1980): 461–504; Fitzmyer, *Luke,* 341.

51. Because it was as God's "favored one" that Mary was chosen to bear Jesus, her "motherhood serve[s] the Lucan picture of Christian discipleship" (Fitzmyer, *Luke,* 341).

52. Raymond E. Brown et al., *Mary in the New Testament,* 151 (cf. Talbert, *Reading Luke,* 23).

53. Raymond E. Brown et al., *Mary in the New Testament,* 177. The writers assert that by drawing upon Acts 1.14, readers may assume that Mary is present in Acts 2.1 (Pentecost).

54. For arguments in favor of Mary as the Daughter of Zion, see Stanislaus Lyonnet, S.J., "Chaire Kecharitome," *Biblica* 20 (1939): 131–41; Harald Sahlin, *Der Messias und das Gottesvolk. Studien zur protolukanischen Theologie* ASNU 12 (Uppsala: Almqvist and Wiksells, 1945); Arthur Gabriel Hebert, "The Virgin Mary as the Daughter of Zion," *Theology* 53 (1950): 403–10; John McHugh, *The Mother of Jesus in the New Testament* (Garden City, N.Y.: Doubleday, 1975), 50–52; and G. A. F. Knight, "The Virgin and the Old Testament," *Reformed Theological Review* 12 (1953): 1–13. Laurentin includes a detailed discussion of this interpretation (*Structure et Theologie,* 148–61). Against these, see the arguments of Raymond E. Brown et al., *Mary in the NT,* 132; and Räisänen, *Mutter,* 154. Some who see a relationship between Mary and the Daughter of Zion also posit her connection with the Ark

of the Covenant. See Lyonnet, "Chaire Kecharitome"; Sahlin, *Der Messias;* Hebert, "The Virgin Mary"; Laurentin, *Structure et Theologie;* and McHugh, *Mother.* The authors of *Mary in the New Testament* note that "the symbolism of Mary as the Tabernacle runs into particular difficulty, depending on how one interprets Luke's attitude toward Stephen's speech in Acts 7.44–49. Stephen says that the Most High does not dwell in houses made with hands." One must decide whether Acts 7.44–49 precludes the association of Mary and the tabernacle or presents readers with a different kind of dwelling place for the divine.

55. F. Danker, *Jesus and the New Age: A Commentary on St. Luke's Gospel,* 2nd ed. (Philadelphia: Fortress, 1988). Mary has been revered as a model of servanthood and obedience since the Patristic era. Cf. Talbert, *Reading Luke,* 22–26; and Joel Green, "The Social Status of Mary in Luke 1.5–2.52: A Plea for Methodological Integration," *Biblica* 4, no. 73 (1992): 468.

56. Danker, *Jesus and the New Age.*

57. Schaberg, *Illegitimacy of Jesus,* 137–38.

58. For discussion of the attribution of the hymn to either Mary or Elizabeth, see Stephen Benko, "The Magnificat: A History of the Controversy," *Journal of Biblical Literature* 89 (1967): 263–75. For the suggestion that the Magnificat was originally a Jewish, rather than Jewish-Christian, composition, see, among others, Hermann Günkel, "Die Lieder in der Kindheitsgeschichte Jesu bei Lukas," in *Festgabe von Fachgenossen und Freuden A. Von Harnack zum siebzigsten Geburtstag dargebracht* (Göttingen: Vanderhoech and Ruprecht, 1921), 43–60; F. Spitta, "Das Magnificat ein Psalm der Maria und nicht der Elisabeth," *Theologische Anhandlungen, eine Festgabe zum 17 Mai 1902 für Heinrich Julius Holtzmann* (Tübingen: J. C. B. Mohr [Paul Siebeck], 1902), 61–94, and "Die chronologischen Notizen und die Hymnen in Lc 1 u.2," *Zeitschrift für die Neutestamentliche Wissenschaft* 7 (1906): 281–317; and Paul Winter, "Magnificat and Benedictus—Maccabean Psalms?" *Bulletin of the John Rylands Library of the University of Manchester* 37 (1954): 328–47, who argues that the Magnificat first served as a Maccabean battle hymn and later became part of a larger document circulating among followers of John the Baptist. Arguments that Luke attributed the hymn to Elizabeth have a long history. As Benko notes, the problem was raised in Tischendorf's 8th edition of the Greek New Testament, which cited Latin variants attributing the Magnificat to Elizabeth. For early arguments, see, among others, Alfred Loisy, "L'origin du Magnificat," *Revue d'histoire et de littérature religieuse* 2 (1897): 424–32, and Adolf von Harnack, "Das Magnificat der Elisabet (Luc 1, 46–55) nebst einigen Bemerkungen zu Luc. 1 und 2," *Sitzungberichte der Königlichen Preussischen Akademie der Wissenschaften zu Berlin* 27 (1900): 538–66. J. G. Davies ("The Ascription of the Magnificat to Mary," *Journal of Theological Studies* 15 [1964]: 307–308) later argued that the attribution

to Mary resulted from readers' mistaken association of the *doule* Mary (Lk 1.38) with the *doule* Hannah (1 Sam 1.11). Arguments for original Lucan attribution of the Magnificat to Mary include Spitta (see above) and Laurentin, *Structure et théologie.*

59. Schaberg declares Mary an "evangelist and prophet" (*Illegitimacy of Jesus,* 128–32); Gaventa ascribes to Mary a prophetic role as she utters the Magnificat (*Mary,* 58). For a detailed discussion of the proper rendering of the aorist verbs in the Magnificat, see Raymond E. Brown, *Birth of the Messiah,* 355–65. Cf. Tannehill, "The Magnificat."

60. The portrayal of Simeon functions similarly. See the programmatic speech attributed to Simeon in Luke 2.34–35.

61. See Shepherd, *The Holy Spirit as Character,* 245.

62. In 1897 Loisy ("L'origin du Magnificat") developed the connection between the activity of the Holy Spirit and the prophetic nature of the Magnificat when he argued that the Magnificat was originally attributed to Elizabeth (cf. Lk 1.41). In 1922, Hans Leisegang posited a positive connection between Mary's prophetic speech and Jesus' extraordinary conception by the Holy Spirit (*Pneuma Hagion, Der Ursprung des Geistbegriffs der synoptischen Evangelien aus der griechischen Mystik,* cited in J. G. Machen, *The Virgin Birth of Christ* [London: Marshall, Morgan, and Scott, 1930], 363).

63. Turid Karlsen Seim, *The Double Message: Patterns of Gender in Luke-Acts* (Nashville: Abingdon Press, 1994), 175.

64. See Raymond E. Brown, *Birth of the Messiah,* 350. He adds, "There is considerable scholarly debate about the pre-exilic origins of the Anawim, and about the extent to which they constituted a class or community, and not merely an attitude of mind" (350–51). Brown finds in Ps 149.4; Isa 49.13, 66.32; and 1QH ii 34–35, v 13–14, xviii 14; 1QM xi 9; and 4QpPs 37 evidence of a community who considered themselves not only "the Poor," but also the faithful remnant community of Israel.

65. On the theme of reversal in the Magnificat, see Jacques Dupont, "Le Magnificat comme discours sur Dieu," *Nouvelle Revue Théologique* 102 (1980): 321–43. See also Robert Tannehill, "The Magnificat as Mary's Poem," *Journal of Biblical Literature* 93 (1974): 263–75, and *Narrative Unity,* 26–32; John Drury, *Tradition and Design in Luke's Gospel* (Atlanta: John Knox Press, 1977), 50.

66. See Gail O'Day's comparison of Mary with Miriam and Hannah, women in the biblical tradition who, in "defiance and thanksgiving," sing of God's liberation ("Singing Woman's Song: A Hermeneutic of Liberation," *Currents in Theology and Mission* 12 [1985]: 203–10). By placing Mary within this tradition, O'Day is able to claim that Mary's encounter with God "is part of the larger experience of Israel's knowledge of God" (207). Likewise, I. Goma Civit calls Mary the "Virgin of Liberation" in *The Song of Salvation: The Magnificat*

(Middlegreen, UK: St. Paul, 1986). And, in his reading of the Magnificat, R. Horsley (*The Liberation of Christmas: The Infancy Narratives in Social Context* [New York: Crossroad, 1989]) situates Mary in the traditions of Deborah and Judith. He concludes that Mary's hymn reflects not an eschatological worldview, but an ideology of revolution (107–14).

67. In Dialogue 67.1, Trypho argues that Justin and his fellow Christians have been misled by a faulty translation of Isaiah 7.14, a text that prophesies that a young girl, rather than a virgin, will conceive and bear a son.

68. For discussion of the translation of *parthenos*, see G. Delling, "*Parthenos*," *The Dictionary of the New Testament*, vol. 5, ed. Gerhard Kittel and Gerhard Friedrich (Grand Rapids, Mich.: Eerdmans, 1967), 826–37; J. Massingberde Ford, "The Meaning of 'Virgin,'" *New Testament Studies* 12, no. 3 (1966): 293–99; and C. H. Dodd, "New Testament Translation Problems I," *Bible Translator* 27 (1976): 301–11.

69. Sternberg's concept of the "echoing interrogative," wherein a question attributed to a character deepens the reader's sense of mystery, is operative here. Mary's question confirms both her virginity and the oddity of the annunciation itself. See *Poetics of Biblical Narrative*, 240–41.

70. This was also the case among early Christian writers. For example, Origen maintained that it was Mary's perpetual virginity that evidenced the purity of soul that qualified her to become the mother of Jesus. Here Mary became established as an exemplar for all women who would hope to give birth to Jesus within their own souls: "Jesus is born only in the one who is chaste and He grows all the more if the individual is a virgin" (Henri Crouzel, *Origen: The Life and Thought of the First Great Theologian*, trans. A. S. Worrall [San Francisco: Harper and Row, 1989], 143).

71. J. Fitzmyer initially argued along this line ("The Virginal Conception of Jesus in the New Testament," *Theological Studies* 34 [1973]: 567–70) but later conceded, in agreement with Brown, that the step parallelism evidenced in Luke 1–2 points to the virginal conception of Jesus (*Gospel According to Luke*).

72. Schaberg, *Illegitimacy*. In support of her interpretation of Luke's annunciation scene, Schaberg argues that biblical traditions that recount the sexual humiliation (*tapeinosis*) of virgins in Israel (i.e., 2 Sam 13; Gen 34) provide the Lucan infancy account its intertextual context, such that the tradition of Jesus' illegitimacy is rendered by Luke as the story of a virgin's restoration. Schaberg's argument is innovative insofar as it engages the intertextual dimensions of Luke's references to Mary's virginity (see also Robbins, "Mary, Elizabeth, and the Magnificat"). Although her analysis ultimately exceeds the textual evidence provided in Luke 1.26–38, it does remind us of the difficulty that

Mary's reference to *tapeinosis* (Lk 1.48) has caused for previous interpreters. For the untenable position that virginity is itself cause for shame, see Heshmat Keroloss, "Virginity in the Early Church: The Meaning and the Motives of Sexual Renunciation in the First Four Centuries" (Ph.D. diss., Fordham University, 1996), 80. While some have argued that the Magnificat was originally attributed to the lips of the once-infertile Elizabeth (see Benko, "The Magnificat"), one of our tasks here is to understand the reference as it appears in the final form of the text. Thus I am interested in uncovering those contexts in which virginity and *tapeinosis* are juxtaposed.

73. Among others, see Stanislaus Lyonnet, S.J., "Le récit de l'Annunciation et la maternité divine de la Sainte Vierge," *Ami du Clergé* 66 (1956): 33–48 (partially in English, "St. Luke's Infancy Narrative," in *Word and Mystery,* ed. L. J. O'Donovan [New York: Newman, 1968], 143–54); Raymond E. Brown, "Luke's Description of the Virginal Conception," *Theological Studies* 35 (1974): 360–62, and *Birth of the Messiah;* J. Fitzmyer, *Luke;* Janice Capel Anderson, "Mary's Difference: Gender and Patriarchy in the Birth Narratives," *Journal of Religion* 2 (1987): 183–202. Step parallelism in Luke 1–2 implicitly subordinates the remarkable origin and destiny of John the Baptist to the unsurpassed virginal conception and unique identity of Jesus. For discussion of the narrative logic of Mary's exchange with Gabriel, see David Landry, "Narrative Logic in the Annunciation to Mary (Lk 1.26–38)," *Journal of Biblical Literature* 114 (1995): 65–79.

74. Some fourth-century church fathers (Gregory of Nyssa, Augustine) took Mary's question in Luke 1.34 as evidence of her lifelong commitment to virginity. The influence of such readings can still be detected in a few modern writers: R. Laurentin, *Structure et Theologie;* Geoffrey Graystone, "Virgin of All Virgins: The Interpretation of Lk. 1.34" (Ph.D. dissertation, Pontica Instituto Biblico, Rome, 1968); and A. Plummer, *A Critical and Exegetical Commentary on the Gospel According to St. Luke,* International Critical Commentary, 5th ed. (New York: Scribner's Sons, 1922). Most interpreters, however, now read Mary's question as a Lucan literary device that advances the narrative. For an early argument in this direction, see J. M. Creed, *The Gospel According to St. Luke* (London: Macmillan, 1930).

75. Raymond E. Brown, *Birth of the Messiah,* 340–41.

76. Among others, see M. Dibelius, "Jungfrauensohn und Krippenkind: Untersuchungen zur Geburtsgeschichte Jesu im Lukas-Evangelium," in *Botschaft und Geschichte: Gesammelte Aufsätze von Martin Dibelius,* vol. 1 (Tübingen: Mohr, 1953, orig. 1932), 1–78; T. Boslooper, "Jesus' Virgin Birth and Non-Christian Parallels," *Religion in Life* 26 (1956–57): 87–97, and *The Virgin Birth* (Philadelphia: Westminster Press, 1962), 135–86; and Beverly Ann Bow, "The Story of Jesus' Birth: A Pagan and Jewish Affair" (Ph.D. diss., University of

Iowa, 1995). Cf. Charles H. Talbert, "Prophecies of Future Greatness: The Contribution of Greco-Roman Biographies to an Understanding of Luke 1.5–4.15," in *The Divine Helmsman: Studies on God's Control of Human Events, Presented to Lou H. Silberman*, ed. James L. Crenshaw and Samuel Sandmel (New York: KTAV Publishing House, 1980).

77. See the early work of G. H. Box, "The Gospel Narratives of the Nativity and the Alleged Influence of Heathen Ideas," *Zeitschrift für die Neutestamentliche Wissenschaft* 6 (1905): 80–101; and the more recent work of Janice Capel Anderson, "Mary's Difference," 186; and Schaberg, *Illegitimacy of Jesus*, 122. J. G. Machen (*Virgin Birth of Christ*, 380) and John Nolland (*Luke 1–9.10*, Word Biblical Commentary, vol. 35A [Dallas: Word, 1989], 43–48) assert that the Jewish milieu of the Gospel not only disallows the presence of any sexual (pagan) overtones whatsoever, but makes the historicity of the virgin conception the only valid explanation of the tradition. Note that while Raymond E. Brown et al. hold that Luke does not intend to portray a *hieros gamos*, the authors do allow that "of course, some Greek readers of pagan background may have interpreted the Lucan scene in this way" (*Mary in the NT,* 121 n. 263).

78. Raymond E. Brown et al., *Mary in the NT,* 132. Räisänen also opposes the identification of Mary as the Daughter of Zion (*Mutter,* 154).

79. Schaberg, *Illegitimacy,* 119. She also notes that she finds "no clear indication that the Christian annunciation tradition had any implication of (Mary's) disobedience or infidelity" (119).

80. Raymond E. Brown, *Birth of the Messiah,* 467 n. 68.

81. Peter Brown, *The Body and Society: Men, Women, and Sexual Renunciation in Early Christianity* (New York: Columbia University Press, 1988), 67.

82. Seim, *Double Message,* 180, cf. 256.

83. De Strycker, *La Forme la plus ancienne,* 424; Smid, *Commentary,* 10–12.

84. Hock, *Infancy Gospels,* 15–20.

85. Emile Amann, *Le Protevangile de Jacques et ses remaniements latins* (Paris: Letouzey, 1910), 31.

86. PJ contains several pieces of information that answer the kinds of charges against Mary evidenced in Celsus's *True Doctrine.* As van Stempvoort argues, PJ implicitly refutes the claims that Mary is of little status, that she had to earn a living by spinning, and that she was found guilty of adultery ("The Protevangelium Jacobi: The Sources of Its Theme and Style and Their Bearing on Its Date," in *Studia Evangelica 3*, ed. F. Cross, TU 88 [Berlin: Akademie-Verlag, 1964], 412–23). For others who hold that PJ is primarily apologetic in aim, see Smid, *Commentary*; J. K. Elliott, ed., *The Apocryphal New Testament: A Collection of Apocryphal Christian Literature in an English Transla-*

tion (Oxford: Clarendon Press, 1993); Pratscher, *Herrenbruder Jakobus;* E. Cothenet, "Le Protévangile de Jacques: origine, genre et signification d'un premier midrash chrétien sur la Nativité de Marie," *Aufstieg und Niedergang der römischen Welt* 2.25.6 (1988): 4252–69; J. Allen, "The Protevangelium of James as an 'Historia': The Insufficiency of the 'Infancy Gospel' Category," in *Society of Biblical Literature Seminar Papers,* ed. Eugene Lovering (Atlanta: Scholars Press, 1991), 508–17. Schaberg notes the correspondence between PJ and the story of Melchizedek's conception in 2 Enoch 23 and concludes: "The Christian author of the *Protevangelium of James* may be attempting to show that Jewish claims concerning the fatherless conception of Melchizedek were not unique. Once the conception of Jesus was regarded as miraculous, it had to be a *virginal* conception" (*Illegitimacy of Jesus,* 190).

87. Hock, *Infancy Gospels,* 15–20.

88. Ibid., 15.

89. Gaventa, *Mary,* 183; Hock, *Infancy Gospels,* 19.

90. Gaventa's remark (*Mary,* 183) is reminiscent of the debate over the primacy of plot over character that was first introduced by Aristotle in his discussion of character in the *Poetics.* As Darr notes, "Character and plot are interdependent, and both are essentials of narrative. Audiences 'actualize' plot in terms of character and character in terms of plot. Where the interpretive evidence falls depends largely on the varying interests of critics, readers, and authors" (*Character Building,* 38–39). Because this project is particularly interested in the way in which *parthenos/parthenia* can function in the portrayal of Mary, our focus will remain largely upon the discursive constituents with which readers construct her character.

91. For a discussion of the symbolic meaning of the temple in Judaism, see Jerome H. Neyrey, "The Symbolic Universe of Luke-Acts: 'They Turned the World Upside Down,'" in *The Social World of Luke-Acts: Models for Interpretation,* ed. Jerome H. Neyrey (Peabody: Hendrickson, 1991), 271–304.

2. Bodies and Selves

1. Michael L. Satlow, *Tasting the Dish: Rabbinic Rhetorics of Sexuality,* Brown Judaic Studies 303 (Atlanta: Scholars Press, 1995), 1–2. In addition to Satlow, Peter Brown (*Body and Society*); David Biale (*Eros and the Jews: From Biblical Israel to Contemporary America* [New York: Basic Books, 1992]); Howard Eilberg-Schartz (*The Savage in Judaism: An Anthropology of Israelite Religion and Ancient Judaism* [Bloomington: Indiana University Press, 1990], *People of the Body: Jews and Judaism from an Embodied Perspective,* SUNY Series, The Body in Culture, History and Religion [Albany: SUNY Press, 1992], and *God's*

Phallus and Other Problems for Men and Monotheism [Boston: Beacon
Press, 1994]); Daniel Boyarin (*Carnal Israel: Reading Sex in Talmudic
Culture* [Berkeley and Los Angeles: University of California Press,
1993]); and Judith Romney Wegner (*Chattel or Person? The Status of
Women in the Mishnah* [Oxford: Oxford University Press, 1988]) are
among those addressing sexuality in Jewish and Christian discourse.
Satlow reviews how recent studies of sexuality in ancient and rabbinic
Judaism differ markedly from the apologetical and legally oriented
writings of earlier interpreters such as Julius Preuss (*Biblisch-talmudische
Medizin: Beiträge zur Geschichte der Heilkunde und der Kultur überhaupt*
[Berlin: S. Karger, 1921], Eng. trans. by Fred Rosner, *Biblical and Tal-
mudic Medicine* [New York: Sanhedrin Press, 1978]); and Louis M. Ep-
stein (*Marriage Laws in the Bible and the Talmud* [Cambridge, Mass.:
Harvard University Press, 1942], and *Sex Laws and Customs in Judaism*
[New York: Bloch, 1948]).

   2. See Michel Foucault, *An Introduction,* vol. 1 of *The History of
Sexuality,* trans. Robert Hurley (New York: Random House, 1980), *The
Use of Pleasure,* vol. 2 of *The History of Sexuality,* trans. Robert Hurley
(New York: Viking, 1985), and *The Care of the Self,* vol. 3 of *The History
of Sexuality,* trans. Robert Hurley (New York: Pantheon Books, 1986).
Studies that follow Foucault's lead include David Halperin, ed., *One
Hundred Years of Homosexuality* (New York: Routledge, 1990); David
Halperin, John J. Winkler, and Froma I. Zeitlin, eds., *Before Sexuality:
The Construction of Erotic Experience in the Ancient Greek World* (Prince-
ton, N.J.: Princeton University Press, 1990); John J. Winkler, *The Constraints of Desire* (New York: Routledge, 1990); Thomas Laqueur, *Making Sex: Body and Gender from the Greeks to Freud* (Cambridge, Mass.:
Harvard University Press, 1990); David Cohen, "Sex, Gender, and
Sexuality in Ancient Greece," *Classical Philology* 87 (1992): 145–60;
and Amy Richlin, ed., *Pornography and Representation in Greece and
Rome* (Oxford: Oxford University Press, 1992). As Laqueur notes, it
was Foucault who "rendered problematic the nature of human sexuality
in relation to the body. Sexuality is not, he argues, an inherent quality
of the flesh that various societies extol or repress—not, as Freud would
seem to have it, a biological drive. . . . It is instead a way of fashion-
ing the self 'in the experience of the flesh,' which itself is 'constituted
from and around certain forms of behavior'" (13). Satlow (*Tasting the
Dish,* 1) rightly shows that Foucault himself built upon the work of
Kenneth James Dover (*Greek Homosexuality* [London: Gerald Duckworth, 1978]). See also Aline Rousselle, *Porneia: On Desire and the Body
in Antiquity,* trans. Felicia Pheasant (reprint, New York: Basil Blackwell, 1988; reprint, 1993).

   3. Foucault, *Care of the Self,* 39.
   4. Ibid.

5. Chapter 3 underscores the inadequacy of Foucault's treatment of ancient narrative sources.

6. Cooper, *Virgin and the Bride*.

7. While the focus of such discussion has remained on *parthenos* as a reference to female sexual status, the term does on occasion refer to a chaste man (cf. Rev 14.4; JosAs 4.7). The latter usage, though decidedly rare, is evidenced in the survey that follows.

8. See Giulia Sissa, *Greek Virginity*, trans. Arthur Goldhammer (Cambridge, Mass.: Harvard University Press, 1990), 76–88.

9. Ibid. Sissa argues against interpreters who have aimed to define *parthenos* apart from virginity: Henri Jeanmaire, *Couroi et couretes* (Lille: Bibliotheque Universitaire, 1939); Angelo Brelich, *Paides e parthenoi* (Roma: Edizioni dell'Ateneo, 1969); Claude Calame, *Les Choeurs des jeunes filles en Grece archaique*, vol. 1 (Rome: Edizioni dell'Ateneo and Bizzarri, 1977); and Pierre Grimal, "Vierges et virginité," in *La Première Fois* (Paris: 1981).

10. Sissa, *Greek Virginity*, 77.

11. Ibid., 83. Sissa cites Herodotus 4.180.

12. Sissa, *Greek Virginity*.

13. Ibid., 91.

14. Ibid., 86.

15. Mieke Bal, *Death and Dissymmetry: The Politics of Coherence in the Book of Judges* (Chicago: University of Chicago Press, 1988), 69–93.

16. The term coined by Laqueur, *Making Sex*, 28. Both Lesley Dean-Jones (*Women's Bodies in Classical Greek Science* [Oxford: Clarendon Press, 1994]) and Helen King (*Hippocrates' Woman: Reading the Female Body in Ancient Greece* [London: Routledge, 1998]) observe that the Hippocratic corpus at times presumes a second model of the female body that differs from what one finds in Aristotle and those who follow him. According to this alternative model, woman is not simply an incomplete male. Rather, she is radically different from her male superior. Despite such differences, Aristotle and the Hippocratics hold in common that it is menstruation that expresses the difference between men and women: "Menstrual blood is the linchpin of both the Hippocratic and the Aristotelian theories on how women differed from men. Whether a woman was healthy, diseased, pregnant, or nursing, in Classical Greece her body was defined in terms of blood-hydraulics" (*Women's Bodies*, 225). Dean-Jones cites the degree to which menstruation defines woman's difference as a possible explanation for why menstruation is not of cultic concern (cf. Robert Parker, *Miasma: Pollution and Purification in Early Greek Religion* [Oxford: Oxford University Press, 1983]). Since it is the physiology of menstruation that renders woman "different," the specific time during which she bleeds is insignificant (*Women's Bodies*, 234).

17. Dean-Jones, *Women's Bodies.* Laqueur cites Galen, *On the Usefulness of the Parts of the Body,* trans. Margaret Tallmadge May, 2 vols. (Ithaca, N.Y.: Cornell University Press, 1968), 2.630.

18. Soranus cites Aristotle and Zenon the Epicurean to argue both that "the female is imperfect, the male, however, perfect" and that "[o]nly as far as particulars and specific variations are concerned does the female show conditions peculiarly her own . . . [t]herefore she is subject to treatment generically the same" (*Gynecology,* trans. Owsei Temkin [Baltimore: Johns Hopkins University Press, 1956], 3.5).

19. Ancient medicine is the focus of several recent studies, including Dean-Jones, *Women's Bodies;* Ann Ellis Hanson, "The Medical Writer's Woman," in *Before Sexuality,* ed. Halperin et al., 309–37; and Aline Rousselle, "Observation Féminine et Idéologie Masculine, Le Corps de la Femme d'après les Médecins Grecs," *Annales: Économies, Sociétés, Civilisations* 35 (1980): 1089–115.

20. Aristotle, *Generation of Animals,* trans. A. L. Peck, LCL (Cambridge, Mass.: Harvard University Press, 1942), 1.17–21.

21. Laqueur, *Making Sex,* 30.

22. Aristotle's discussion responds, in part, to Hippocratics who believed that females also produce sperm. The Hippocratic corpus, a collection of anonymous medical writings written during the fifth and fourth centuries B.C.E., remained influential in the early centuries of the common era. For further discussion of Aristotle and the more popular two-seed theory, see Guilia Sissa, "Sexual Philosophies of Plato and Aristotle," in *A History of Women in the West,* vol. 1: *From Ancient Goddesses to Christian Saints,* ed. Pauline Schmitt Pantel (Cambridge, Mass.: Belknap, 1992), 46–81, and Laqueur, *Making Sex,* 38–43.

23. While Galen suggests that women do produce sperm, he also indicates that female seed is, by nature, weaker than that of the male (*On the Usefulness of the Parts of the Body* 2.631). Soranus resists crediting female seed with any reproductive role (*Gyn.*). The Hippocratic corpus allows for the generation of strong and weak sperm by both men and women in reproduction, but posits that females are produced either by sperm weak by nature or by stronger sperm being outnumbered by the weaker (*On Generation* 1.1; 6.2; 8.1). Cf. Laqueur, *Making Sex,* 39–40. Furthermore, Laqueur argues that "if pushed on the point, the Hippocratic writer would have to admit that there was something uniquely powerful about male seed, the fluid that comes from an actual male, because otherwise he would have no answer to the question with which two-seed theorists were plagued for millennia: if the female has such powerful seed, then why can she not engender within herself alone; who needs men?" (40).

24. Dale Martin emphasizes the materiality of *pneuma:* "In both scientific theory and popular thought, then, pneuma was the life-giving

material for the members of the body, nourishing the body through a complex interaction of elements. It was commonly believed that the arteries carried pneuma, either alone or mixed with blood" (*The Corinthian Body* [New Haven, Conn.: Yale University Press, 1995], 22). Aristotle, Galen, and Soranus are among those medical writers who identify the dangers of an immoderate loss of semen. Such concern is also exhibited in the Hippocratic corpus.

25. Laqueur, *Making Sex,* 21.

26. Ibid., 33. Laqueur cites Aristotle, *History of Animals,* 3.1.510b13; 10.5.637a23–25.

27. Galen, *On the Usefulness of the Parts of the Body,* 2.

28. Soranus, *Gynecology,* 14–15. The translator, Temkin, notes that *kaulos* ("neck") is second-century nomenclature for penis (10 n.6).

29. Ibid., 9; Galen, *De uteri dissectione,* 4; Aristotle, *Gen. An.,* 1.12.720a.

30. Rousselle, *Porneia,* 26.

31. Laqueur, *Making Sex,* 36; Sissa, *Greek Virginity,* 5, 53–66, 70, 166–68; Dale Martin, *Corinthian Body,* 237–38.

32. Aristotle, *Hist. an.* 9(7).3, 10.2–5; 10.5.637a18–19; Galen, *De uteri dissectione,* 7.

33. Soranus, *Gynecology,* 134–35.

34. Laqueur, *Making Sex,* 36.

35. Ann Ellis Hanson and David Armstrong, "The Virgin's Voice and Neck: Aeschylus, *Agememnon* 245, and Other Texts," *British Institute of Classical Studies* 33 (1986): 97–100.

36. Aristotle, *Hist. an.* 10.3.635b19–14; Soranus, *Gynecology,* 34; Hippocrates *Mul.* 1.11.

37. Galen, *On the Usefulness of the Parts of the Body,* 15.3. Laqueur takes this "nymph" to be a reference to the female clitoris (*Making Sex,* 37). Cf. Sor. *Gyn.* 1.3.18. See Sissa, *Greek Virginity,* 112, and Temkin in *Gynecology,* 16 n. 32.

38. Sissa, *Greek Virginity,* 65–66. Sissa draws upon Emile Benveniste, "Termes greco-latins d'anatomie," *Revue de philologie,* 2nd ser. 39 (1965): 8.

39. Hanson and Armstrong, "Virgin's Voice and Neck," 97–100.

40. Hanson, "Medical Writers' Woman," 320.

41. Soranus, *Gynecology,* 13, 25–27, 30–32.

42. Dale Martin, *Corinthian Body,* 224.

43. Rufus, "Regimen for Virgins," in Oribasius, *Libri Incerti* 18.17, 19. Cited in Dale Martin, *Corinthian Body,* 225.

44. Hanson, "Medical Writers' Woman," 327.

45. Sissa, *Greek Virginity,* 115. Sissa argues further that Hippocratic theory posits a normal network of blood vessels along the passage leading out from the uterus that either facilitates or restrains the evacuation of blood collected in the uterus. It is the dilation of these blood

vessels that first intercourse and childbirth encourages. Against Sissa, Hanson takes the imagery of a broken seal and an upside-down jug as indication of belief in the existence of a hymen ("Medical Writer's Woman"). Dean-Jones considers both perspectives and argues that the Hippocratic notion of defloration, wherein the *stoma* is so loosened that bleeding occurs, need not presume the existence of a hymen. For hymeneal blood may be similar to the menstrual blood that is only allowed to begin flowing freely upon first intercourse (*Women's Bodies,* 52–53).

46. Soranus, *Gynecology,* 15. Sissa notes that this is the earliest extant reference to belief in the normal presence of a hymen ("Maidenhood," 355).

47. Ibid., 15. Cf. the debate between Sissa, Hanson, and Dean-Jones (note 45).

48. Ibid. Soranus notes, "if this membrane, bursting in defloration, were the cause of pain, then in virgins before defloration excessive pain ought necessarily to follow upon the appearance of menstruation and no more in defloration."

49. For example, Sissa argues that Soranus's discussion of female genitalia posits the entire vagina as a membrane akin to that of the intestine (*Greek Virginity,* 113). Laqueur understands Soranus to be drawing a direct parallel between the female genitalia and the male penis, such that "the vagina and external structures are imagined as one giant foreskin of the female interior penis whose glans is the dome-like apex of the 'neck of the womb'" (*Making Sex,* 34).

50. Hippocrates *Virg.* 8.466–70. Such symptoms included madness and suicidal ideation brought about by pressure on the vital organs. Plutarch testifies to this condition in his account of suicidal virgins at Miletus (*Moralia,* trans. Frank Cole Babbitt et al., 15 vols., LCL [Cambridge, Mass.: Harvard University Press, 1927–1972], 249b–d).

51. Hippocrates *Mul.* 1.1–2. The Hippocratic notion of a wandering womb was rejected by both Soranus (*Gynecology,* 153) and Galen (*On the Affected Parts,* trans. Rudolph E. Siegal [Basel and London: Karger, 1976], 6.5).

52. Gal. *De loc. aff.* 6.5.

53. Rufus, "Regimen for Virgins," in Oribasius, *Libri Incerti,* 18.1–2, 25. Cited in Dale Martin, *Corinthian Body,* 225.

54. Soranus, *Gynecology,* 29; cf. 30–32.

55. See Dale Martin's extended discussion in *Corinthian Body,* 219–28.

56. Soranus, *Gynecology,* 31.

57. Anne Carson, "Putting Her in Her Place: Women, Dirt, and Desire," in *Before Sexuality,* ed. Halperin et al., 138–39. Cited in Dale Martin, *Corinthian Body,* 221.

58. George Luck, *Arcana Mundi: Magic and the Occult in the Greek and Roman Worlds* (Baltimore: Johns Hopkins University Press, 1985), 230. David E. Aune argues that the etymological relationship between *mantis* and the terms *mania* and *mainesthai* "contributes little or nothing to our knowledge of the role of most diviners in the Greco-Roman period" (*Prophecy in Early Christianity and the Ancient Mediterranean World* [Grand Rapids, Mich.: William B. Eerdmans, 1983], 35).

59. For a concise discussion of *divinatio, manteia, mantis,* and *prophetes,* see Luck, *Arcana Mundi,* 229–30.

60. See Cicero, *De divinatione, De senectute, De amicitia,* LCL (Cambridge, Mass., and London: Harvard University Press and Heinemann, 1964], 2.57.117, 118; Plutarch, *De defectu oraculorum;* Pausanias, *Description of Greece,* trans. W. H. S. Jones, 5 vols., LCL (Cambridge, Mass.: Harvard University Press, 1964–1965), 1, 9.

61. Cic. *Div.,* 1.125.

62. Robert R. Wilson, *Prophecy and Society in Ancient Israel* (Philadelphia: Fortress Press, 1980), 162; cf. Thomas W. Overholt, *Channels of Prophecy: The Social Dynamics of Prophetic Activity* (Minneapolis: Augsburg Fortress, 1989). Luke reflects a similar bias when he associates the enthusiasm of the slave girl in Acts 16.16 with *manteia.*

63. Aune, *Prophecy in Early Christianity.*

64. Peter Brown, *Body and Society,* 67.

65. *Philo,* trans. F. H. Colson and the Rev. G. H. Whitaker, vol. 6, LCL (Cambridge, Mass., and London: Harvard University Press and Heinemann, 1935), 483. Cf. Philo, *Life of Moses,* 2.68–69.

66. Peter Brown, *Body and Society,* 67 n. 8. Here Brown cites Irenaeus, *Against Heresies,* 1.13.2.

67. Dale Martin, *Corinthian Body,* 239.

68. See Plutarch, *De E apud Delphos, De Pythiae oraculis,* and *De def. or.* Cf. Herodotus 1.51, 1.66, 1.67, 5.42–43, 5.62–63, 5.91, 6.52, 6.57, 6.66, 6.76, 6.86, 7.220, 7.239, 8.114, 8.141; Thucydides 2.7.55, 3.11.92, 4.13.118, 5.15.17.

69. Lucan, *The Civil War,* trans. J. D. Duff (London and New York: Heinemann and G. P. Putnam's Sons, 1928), 5.160–97.

70. Paus. *Description of Greece* 10.5.8–9; 10.5.12.

71. Aune, *Prophecy in Early Christianity,* 354 n. 121. Aune cites P. Amandry's argument that Lucan's account is dependent upon a good deal of literary invention; see P. Amandry, *La mantique Apollinienne à Delphes, essai sur le fonctionnement de l'Oracle* (Paris: E. de Boccard, 1950), 20ff., 234–35; cited in Aune, 33–34.

72. Aune, *Prophecy in Early Christianity,* 355 n. 130.

73. Plut. *De def. or.* 436F.

74. Ibid., 437D; cf. 438C.

75. Ibid., 438B, C.

76. Dale Martin, *Corinthian Body,* 241. For early observation of the sexuality connoted by the Pythian oracle, cf. E. Fehrle, *Die Kultische Keuschheit im Altertum* (Giessen: A. Topelmann, 1910), 75–89.

77. Plutarch uses the term *pneuma* to refer to the exhalations that inspired the Pythia's utterance (*De def. or.* 438). For the combination of *pneuma* and *dynamis* in sperm, see Galen *On Semen* 1.1, 3.10, 5.13–15, 6.1–2.

78. Dale Martin, *Corinthian Body,* 242.

79. Plut. *De def. or.* 414. For woman as the mouthpiece of a god, cf. Paus. *Description of Greece* 10.12.

80. Diodorus of Sicily, *The Library of History,* trans. W. H. S. Jones (vols. 1, 3, 4); W. H. S. Jones and H. A. Ormerod (vol. 2); R. E. Wycherley (vol. 5); C. H. Oldfather (vols. 6–12), 12 vols., LCL (Harvard University Press, 1970–1989), 16.26.2–6.

81. Plut. *De Pyth. or.* 405C, D.

82. Though it is often translated in the general sense as "nature," see the discussion of *physis* as genitalia in Winkler, "Appendix Two: *Physis* and *Natura* Meaning 'Genitals,'" in *Constraints of Desire,* 217–20.

83. Sissa, *Greek Virginity,* 168.

84. Hippocrates *Aphorisms* 5.51.

85. Peter Brown, *Body and Society,* 69.

86. Sissa, *Greek Virginity,* 122–23.

87. In *Contra Celsum,* Origen rails against the indecent manner by which the demonic spirit would enter the Pythian priestess ([Cambridge: Cambridge University Press, 1953], 7.3).

88. Mary Beard, "Re-reading (Vestal) Virginity," in *Women in Antiquity: A New Assessment,* ed. Richard Hawley and Barbara Levick (London: Routledge, 1995), 166–77. Cf. Mary Beard, "The Sexual Status of Vestal Virgins," *Journal of Roman Studies* 70 (1980): 12–27.

89. Beard, "Re-reading (Vestal) Virginity," 172.

90. Dionysius of Halicarnassus, *The Roman Antiquities,* trans. Earnest Cary, 12 vols., LCL (Cambridge, Mass.: Harvard University Press, 1937–1950), 2.67.1–5; 2.68.4; 2.69.2.

91. Ibid., 2.67.1–5.

92. Plut. *Vit.* 10.9.

93. The quote is taken from Mary Beard, "Vestal Virginity," 172. This study assumes the historicity of neither Seneca's accounts nor the laws cited in them, but only the ideological significance of the arguments contained within them. Note M. Winterbottom's observation that "[t]he themes of the declamations were later much derided; and even those in Seneca's collection often seem to stray far from reality." Yet he adds that some of the laws may have a better historical grounding than others: "S. F. Bonner has argued in an important study that genuine parallels in Roman law exist for many of the laws on which the themes are based" (*The Elder Seneca: Declamations in Two Volumes,* trans.

M. Winterbottom, LCL [Cambridge, Mass., and London: Harvard University Press and Heinemann, 1974], xii–xiii; cf. S. F. Bonner, *Roman Declamation in the Late Republic and Early Empire* [Berkeley and Los Angeles: University of California Press, 1949]).

94. Aulus Gellius, *Attic Nights,* LCL (London and New York: Heinemann and G. P. Putnam's Sons, 1927), 1.12.

95. Suet. *Aug.* 34; cf. Dio Cassius, *History of Rome,* trans. E. Cary, LCL (London and New York: Heinemann and Macmillan, 1914–1927), 54.16.1–2. Legally, full Roman marriage was limited to citizen men and women and those who received *connubium,* that is, the right to contract a legal marriage.

96. Elaine Fantham et al., *Women in the Classical World: Image and Text* (New York: Oxford University Press, 1994), 314–55.

97. Ibid., 322–23. The authors cite the examples of the erotic imagery depicted on clay objects and Horace's description of a wife who, with her husband's knowledge, commits adultery at a dinner party (*Odes* 3.6). Cf. the court gossip of Suet. *Vit.*

98. Ross Shepard Kraemer, *Her Share of the Blessings* (New York: Oxford University Press, 1992), 55.

99. Justinian, *Digest of Justinian,* 48.5.35(34)–48.5.35(34)1, ed. Theodor Mommsen and Paul Krueger, trans. Alan Watson, 4 vols. (Philadelphia: University of Pennsylvania Press, 1985).

100. Among others, see Ephraim E. Urbach, *The Sages: Their Concepts and Beliefs* (Cambridge, Mass.: Harvard University Press, 1987); Eilberg-Schwartz, ed., *People of the Body;* Boyarin, *Carnal Israel.*

101. Elaine Pagels, *Adam, Eve, and the Serpent* (New York: Random House, 1988); Gary Anderson, "Celibacy or Consummation in the Garden: Reflections on Early Jewish and Christian Interpretations of the Garden of Eden," *Harvard Theological Review* 82, no. 2 (1989): 21–48, and "The Garden of Eden and Sexuality in Early Judaism," in *People of the Body,* ed. Eilberg-Schwartz, 47–68; Boyarin, *Carnal Israel.* See especially Pagels's chapter 3, "Different Eves: Myths of Female Origins and the Discourse of Married Sex," 77–106.

102. The difficulty of differentiating and defining rabbinic and Hellenistic Judaism has been the subject of numerous studies. As Wayne Meeks states, "The conventional categories suffer from vagueness, anachronism, and inappropriate definition. Vagueness is most obvious in the case of 'Hellenistic Judaism.' Does this mean all Jews who spoke Greek in the Hellenistic and Roman periods? Or does it mean people who shared other aspects of Greek urban culture, including certain metaphysical beliefs, some standards of literary and artistic style, a certain ethos? 'Rabbinic Judaism' is the category most affected by anachronism. . . . We will do well to avoid using the term *rabbi* or *rabbinic* of any phenomenon earlier than the academy founded at Yavneh (Jamnia) by Yohanan ben Zakkai, and we will be on safer ground to

restrict these terms to second-century and later developments" (*The First Urban Christians* [New Haven, Conn.: Yale University Press, 1983], 33). Neither does this study wish to give the impression that rabbinic culture is monolithic. For the purposes of this project, the designation "rabbinic" refers to rabbinic *texts*. Because the era under investigation terminates with the close of the second century, the Mishnah, produced by *tannaim* of the second century, is the primary rabbinic text with which we are concerned. Due to similarities in content, occasional references are also made to the Tosefta, whose composition and redaction postdate that of the Mishnah.

103. Boyarin, *Carnal Israel*, 168. However, this is not to suggest that the Mishnah, as a whole, necessarily reflects actual Jewish practice. For example, despite the destruction of the temple in 70 C.E., more than half of the Mishnah is dedicated to the temple cult. The laws handed down in the Mishnah have ideological value, whether or not they were actually practiced.

104. Peter Brown, "Late Antiquity" in *A History of Private Life*, ed. Philippe Ariès and George Duby, vol. 1: *From Pagan Rome to Byzantium*, ed. Paul Veyne and trans. Arthur Goldhammer (Cambridge, Mass.: Belknap Press of Harvard University Press, 1987), 267. For a detailed discussion of rabbinic discourse on sexuality, see Satlow, *Tasting the Dish*. For a discussion of women and sexuality in the Mishnah, see Wegner, *Chattel or Person?*

105. Eilberg-Schwartz, "The Problem of the Body for the People of the Book," in *People of the Body*, 20.

106. Ibid., 22.

107. Here we may observe that the Hebrew *betulim*, appearing in both the Masoretic Text and the Mishnah, refers to the bride's requisite "tokens of virginity." In the Septuagint, reference is made to the bride's *parthenia*. The translation of *betulah* has long been debated, especially in regard to Deuteronomy 22.13–21. In his well-known article "'Betulah' A Girl of Marriageable Age" (*Vetus Testamentum* 22:326–41), Gordon Wenham argues that *betulah* (v. 19) and *betulim* (vv. 14, 15, 17, 20) consistently refer to a female's age, rather than to her sexual experience. He translates *betulim* as "tokens of adolescence," implying signs of menstruation, and concludes that the husband's complaint refers to the absence of his wife's menstrual period and his concurrent suspicion that she entered into marriage having already become pregnant by another man. However, Wenham's thesis fails to account for the distinction between *naarah* and *betulah*, both of which occur in Deuteronomy 22.13–21. Even without *betulim*, a *naarah*, a "girl of a marriageble age" remains as such. Wenham briefly considers the possibility that the husband's complaint is that his wife has not yet begun to menstruate and is pre-nubile. This seems highly unlikely since no evidence exists to view such a situation as cause for the kind of slander and punishment alluded

to in Deuteronomy 22.13–21. Coincidently, the much later Tosefta, which once (out of a number of discussions of virginity) defines virginity in terms of the absence of menstrual (rather than hymeneal) blood, offers no reason for such a condition to invite ridicule (T. Nid. 1.6; cf. M. Nid. 1.4). In contrast to Wenham, Clemens Locher finds evidence in several Akkadian texts that *batultu* is best rendered "virgin" within a semantic field that often retains the meaning "young woman." He also demonstrates that several Mesopotamian legal texts posit virginity as a significant legal notion and concludes that in Hebrew texts, legal codes especially support the translation of *betulah* as "virgin" (*Die Ehre einer Frau in Israel* [Freiburg: Universitätsverlag; Göttingen: Vandenhoech and Ruprecht, 1986], 117–237).

108. A custom without parallel in the Roman exchange of dowries, this code may reflect the idealizing tendency of the text.

109. Wegner, *Chattel or Person?* 22. (Cf. M. Nid. 5.4 A, I, "A girl three years and one day old is betrothed by intercourse . . . (if) she is younger than that, (it) is like putting a finger in her eye.") Satlow adds that it is at three years and one day that females become legally recognized as sexual beings (*Tasting the Dish,* 136).

110. Wegner, *Chattel or Person?* 23.

111. Translated by Jacob Neusner in *A History of the Mishnaic Law of Purities,* part 16: *Niddah: Literary and Historical Problems* (Leiden: E. J. Brill, 1977). This is developed even further in the Tosefta, which explains that here the virgin is defined not "in respect to the tokens of virginity" but "in respect to menstrual blood" (T. Nid. 1.6, ibid.).

112. Wegner, *Chattel or Person?* 21.

113. Satlow notes that rabbinic discussion of non-marital sex is preoccupied with the control of female sexuality: "Adultery represents more to the rabbis than a breach of God's command; it is also the 'theft' of a woman's reproductive potential from her husband. Similarly premarital sex reflects poorly on the father, who is expected by the rabbis and his society to control his daughter's sexuality" (*Tasting the Dish,* 119). Neusner also emphasizes how the Mishnah's "system of women" focuses on the proper control of woman as she is transferred from the jurisdiction of one man to another ("From Scripture to Mishna: The Origins of Mishnah's Division of Women," *Journal of Jewish Studies* 30 [1979]: 138–53). Wegner's thesis pivots on the distinctive status of the minor daughter in the Mishnah. She finds that when a female's biological function falls within the responsibility of a particular man (e.g., the minor daughter's reproductive function falls under the jurisdiction of her father) and when a situation arises that threatens his control, the female is regarded not as a person endowed with rights, but as chattel (*Chattel or Person?* vi, 8, 14–15, 19, 178). Wegner's discussion is limited to the arena of legal "rights"; although her schematization of "chattel vs. person" and "other vs. self" is not synonymous with the categories I em-

ploy, her observations do resonate with the notion that the virgin is constructed in terms of body and agency.

114. Mieke Bal examines the danger to women and the threat to male control posed by the liminal status of the *betulah* in the Book of Judges. Liminality, or suspension, characterizes virginity: "The negative formulation it receives is due to the temporally impossible suspension it entails. This suspension can only be understood as a transition between one state, or stage, and another, a transition that receives the excessively patriarchal flavor of the inacceptability of female autonomy. . . . Virgins are to be given away, in order to bring their disturbingly ambiguous state to an end as quickly as possible" (*Death and Dissymmetry,* 42). Helen King also cites the problem of liminality in relation to young Greek women negotiating the same transition ("Bound to Bleed: Artemis and Greek Women," in *Images of Women in Antiquity,* ed. Averil Cameron and Amelie Kuhrt [Detroit: Wayne State University Press, 1983], 109–27).

115. Wegner, *Chattel or Person?* 32.

116. Wayne Meeks, *Origins of Christian Morality* (New Haven, Conn.: Yale University Press, 1993), concurs with Dale Martin's reading of 1 Corinthians 7.36–38. For the latter's most recent and extensive treatment of this text, see Dale Martin, *Corinthian Body,* 219–28.

117. Dale Martin, *Corinthian Body,* 226. Cf. Luke Johnson's argument that the growing sensual desire of young widows is the presenting problem in 1 Timothy 5.11 (*Letters to Paul's Delegates* [Valley Forge: Trinity Press International, 1997], 181, 186). Ben Witherington III has recently argued that the claim that Paul is addressing the phenomenon of spiritual marriage is ill-founded and anachronistic (*Women in The Earliest Churches* [New York: Cambridge University Press, 1991], 37). For a review of various interpretations of 1 Corinthians 7.36, see Roland H. A. Seboldt, "Spiritual Marriage in the Early Church: A Suggested Interpretation of 1 Cor. 7.36–38," *Concordia Theological Monthly* 30 (1959): 103–19, 176–89; and John J. O'Rourke, "Hypotheses Regarding 1 Corinthians 7:36–38," *Catholic Biblical Quarterly* 20 (1958): 292–98.

118. Bow, *Jesus' Birth.*

119. Ovid, *Metamorphoses,* trans. Frank Justus Miller, 2 vols., LCL (London and New York: Heinemann and G. P. Putnam's Sons, 1916), 2.443–446. Cf. the two versions of Romulus's birth in Plutarch: in the first story, an oracle prophesies the union of a *parthenos* and a *phasma daimonion* (*Vit.* 2.4); in the second, a Vestal Virgin conceives twins fathered by the god Ares (*Vit.* 4.2).

120. Satlow, *Tasting the Dish,* 130.

121. See "The Guardianship of Women" and "Marriage," in J. F. Gardner, *Women in Roman Law and Society* (Bloomington: Indiana University Press, 1991), 5–65.

122. Even those virgins who entered the Vestal priesthood had to do so while they were yet under their father's power. They left their fathers' jurisdiction only as they were handed over to the *pontifices* (Gell. *NA* 1.12).

123. Legally, he could go so far as to have his daughter put to death, as long as the adulterer received the same punishment. Husbands, in contrast, were denied the right to kill an adulterous wife.

124. The view of women that shaped such custom is reflected in one later writer's observations: "Guardians are appointed for males as well as for females, but only for males under puberty, on account of their infirmity of age; for females, however, both under and over puberty, on account of weakness of their sex as well as their ignorance of legal matters" (Ulp. *Rules* 11.1, cited in Mary R. Lefkowitz and Maureen B. Fant, *Women's Life in Greece and Rome: A Sourcebook in Translation*, 2nd ed. [Baltimore: Johns Hopkins University Press, 1992], 101). With Augustus's legislation, citizen women were eligible to become free of guardianship once they had given birth to three children. Freedwomen could be released from tutelage if they bore four children. Women with greater wealth and influence were also able to secure the privilege without bearing the requisite number of children (Gardner, "Guardianship of Women," 20).

125. Justinian *Digest* 23.2.36; 48.5.7

126. Justinian *Codex* 9.10.1, cited in Lefkowitz and Fant, *Women's Life in Greece and Rome*, 100.

127. *Controv.* 1.5 and 7.8. Bonner (*Roman Declamation*, 89–90) cites parallels in actual Greek and Roman practice.

128. See Fantham et al., *Women in the Classical World*, 322–23 (cf. Ovid, *Art of Love and Other Poems*, trans. J. H. Mozley, LCL [Cambridge, Mass., and London: Harvard University Press and Heinemann, 1967], 1.673–80, and Soranus, *Gynecology*, 36), and Christopher A. Faraone, *Ancient Greek Love Magic* (Cambridge, Mass.: Harvard University Press, 1999), 78–95.

129. Cf. Ann Michele Tapp, "An Ideology of Expendability: Virgin Daughter Sacrifice in Genesis 19.1–11, Judges 11.30–39 and 19.22–26," in *Anti-Covenant: Counter-Reading Women's Lives in the Hebrew Bible*, ed. Mieke Bal (Sheffield: Almond Press, 1989), 157–74.

130. Meeks, *Origins of Christian Morality*, 134.

131. Cited in Eilberg-Schwartz, *God's Phallus*, 111.

132. Ibid., 113.

133. Ibid. For detailed consideration of the female imagery for Jerusalem in Ezekiel, see Julie Galambush, *Jerusalem in the Book of Ezekiel: The City as Yahweh's Wife*, SBL Dissertation Series 130 (Atlanta: Scholars Press, 1992).

134. Dion. Hal. *Ant. Rom.* 2.67.5.

135. Ibid., 2.68.4. For another example of how women's bod-

ies represent the Roman body politic, see Sandra Joshel's observations of how "Livy's narrative of Rome's political transformation revolves around chaste, innocent women raped and killed for the sake of preserving the virtue of the body female and the body politic" ("The Body Female and the Body Politic: Livy's Lucretia and Verginia," in *Pornography and Representation,* ed. Richlin, 117).

136. Ariadne Staples, *From Good Goddess to Vestal Virgins: Sex and Category in Roman Religion* (London: Routledge, 1998), 135.

137. Ibid., 137.

138. Gell. *NA,* 1.12.

139. Ibid.

140. *The Shepherd of Hermas,* Vis. 4.2.1–2.

141. Sen. *Controv.* 1.2.5.

142. Clem. Al. *Instructor* 1.5, p. 214.

143. Peter Brown, "Late Antiquity," 266.

144. Philo *Contemplative Life* 68.

145. Bruce J. Malina and Richard L. Rohrbaugh note that "[i]t is . . . important not to misunderstand the notion of 'shame.' One can 'be shamed,' and this refers to the state of publicly known loss of honor. This is negative shame. But to 'have shame' means to have concern about one's honor" (*Social-Science Commentary on the Synoptic Gospels* [Minneapolis: Augsburg Fortress Press, 1992], 77).

146. Ov. *Met.* 14.129–154.

147. Sen. *Controv.* 1.2.4–5

148. Plut. *Vit.* 10.1–7.

149. Peter Brown, *Body and Society,* 29.

150. Dion. Hal. *Ant. Rom.* 2.67.5–69.3.

151. Sen. *Controv.* 1.3; Valerius Maximus 3.7.9; 6.8.1; Livy 4.44. 11–12; Dio Cass. 26, fr. 87; Plut. *Quaest. Rom.* 284.

152. Karl Kerényi, *Athene: Virgin and Mother: A Study of Pallas Athene,* trans. Murray Stein (Zurich: Spring Publications, 1978), 21.

153. Christine Downing, *The Goddess: Mythological Images of the Feminine* (New York: Crossroad, 1981), 118.

154. Ibid.

155. Jean-Pierre Vernant, *Mortals and Immortals: Collected Essays,* ed. Froma I. Zeitlin (Princeton, N.J.: Princeton University Press, 1991), 196.

156. Rick Strelan, *Paul, Artemis, and the Jews in Ephesus.* Beihefte zur Zeitschrift für die neutestamentliche Wissenschaft und die Kunde der älteren Kirche. Herausgegeben von Erich Grässer, Band 80 (Berlin: Walter de Gruyter, 1996), 49, 89–90.

157. Helen King, "Bound to Bleed."

158. Vernant, *Mortals,* 198.

159. Ibid., 202.

160. Suet. *Aug.* 44.5–7 (cf. 31.4); Plut. *Vit.* 10.1–7.

161. Plut. *Vit.* 10.3.

162. Gell. *NA* 1.12. In other words, she will serve "with all a Vestal's entitlements." (See L. Holford-Strevens, *Aulus Gellius* [London, 1988], 221 n. 38. Cited in Lefkowitz and Fant, *Women's Life in Greece and Rome,* 355 n. 41.)

163. Mary R. Lefkowitz, *Women in Greek Myth* (Baltimore: Johns Hopkins University Press, 1986), 31.

164. Cf. Plut. *Vit.* 10.4–7, and Gell. *NA* 1.12.

165. Lefkowitz, *Women in Greek Myth,* 36.

166. Parker, *Miasma,* 92.

167. Ibid., 94.

168. Ibid., 91.

169. Philo *Life of Moses* 2.68–69.

170. Parker, *Miasma,* 87.

171. Satlow, *Tasting the Dish,* 136.

172. Satlow notes: "The term 'defilement,' as referring to a woman who has had non-marital intercourse, is used infrequently in rabbinic literature, and then almost only as an appropriation of the biblical terminology of the *sotah.* Even in these quotations, it is clear that 'defilement' means 'sin,' rather than actual ritual impurity" (ibid.).

173. Parker, *Miasma,* 300–301.

174. Peter Brown, *Body and Society,* 80.

175. Ibid.

176. Tert. *On the Veiling of Virgins* 10. Cf. *An Exhortation to Chastity* 1, wherein Tertullian discusses degrees of sanctification and identifies "a life of virginity from the time of one's birth" as the first degree. Such a life is "one of blessedness, because you have no experience whatever of that from which you will wish later to be free."

177. This is Clement of Alexandria's understanding of the views held by Marcion, Cassian, and Valentine (*Misc.* 3.17.102). As Peter Brown notes, "Such views are tacitly combatted by later Jewish exegesis: it was Adam and Eve who taught the animals how to have intercourse by initiating the act" (*Body and Society,* 94 n. 43).

178. Peter Brown, *Body and Society,* 86.

179. Clem. Al. *Misc.* 3.6.45. Here Clement quotes the *Gospel according to the Egyptians.*

180. Irenaeus *Against Heresies* 1.28; Cf. Clem. Al. *Misc.* 3.6.49. On the development of the practice of "spiritual marriage," a practice most associated with Encratite Christian circles, see Hans Achelis, *Virgines Subintroductae: Ein Beitrag zum VII Kapitel des I Korinthersbriefe* (Leipzig: J. C. Hinrichs, 1902), and "Agapetae," in *Encyclopedia of Religion and Ethics,* ed. James Hasting, vol. 1 (New York: Scribner's, 1926), 177; Derrick Sherwin Bailey, *Sexual Relations in Christian Thought*

(New York: Harper and Row, 1959); and Elizabeth A. Clark, "John Chrysostom and the *Subintroductae*," in *Ascetic Piety and Women's Faith: Essays in Late Ancient Christianity* (New York: Edwin Mellen Press, 1986), 265–90. Arthur Vööbus notes that the translation of Luke 2.36 in the Persian Diatessaron thus portrays the prophetess Anna's marriage: "She remained a virgin with her husband seven years" (*Celibacy: A Requirement for Admission to Baptism in the Early Syrian Church*, Papers of the Estonian Theological Society in Exile 1 [Stockholm: Etse, 1951], 19).

181. Peter Brown, *Body and Society*, 92.
182. See Clem. Al. *Misc.* 3.7.57–58.
183. Peter Brown, *Body and Society*, 159.

3. Constraining the Virgin

1. Tomas Hägg, *The Novel in Antiquity* (Berkeley and Los Angeles: University of California Press, 1983), 3.
2. Bryan P. Reardon, *The Form of Greek Romance* (Princeton, N.J.: Princeton University Press, 1991), 50.
3. The five extant novels are, in chronological order: Chariton, *Chaereas and Callirhoè*; Xenophon of Ephesus, *Ephesiaca* (*An Ephesian Tale*); Achilles Tatius, *Leucippe and Clitophon*; Longus, *Daphnis and Chloe*; Heliodorus, *Ethiopica* (*An Ethiopian Tale*). Although the plot of Heliodorus's novel does revolve around a virgin, the narrative remains beyond the focus of this study because it originates from the third, perhaps even the fourth, century C.E.
4. Hägg, *Novel in Antiquity*, 3.
5. In 1876, Erwin Rohde pioneered such inquiry, tracing the novel's origins to travel narratives and erotic poetry (*Der griesche roman und seine Vorlaüfer* [Hildesheim: Georg Olms, 1960]). Following Rohde's lead, investigation into the novel's origins has focused more on the literary parentage of these compositions than on the social or cultural impetus behind them. J. R. Morgan suggests that it was probably "within historiography . . . that the contract of fictional complicity was first extended to narrative prose" ("Make-Believe and Make Believe: The Fictionality of the Greek Novels," in *Lies and Fiction in the Ancient World*, ed. Christopher Gill and T. P. Wiseman [Exeter: University of Exeter Press, 1993], 175–229, p. 187). He notes that several of the novels have historiographical titles (e.g., *Aethiopica*, *Ephesiaca*) and that all five of the extant novels open with realism, that is, with historically and geographically concrete references (197–98). Likewise, H. Kuch discusses the novel's origins in terms of genre theory ("Die Herausbildung des antiken Romans als Literaturgattung," in H. Kuch, ed., *Der antike Roman* [Berlin: Akademie-Verlag, 1989], 11–51). For an excellent re-

view of the history of scholarship, see Richard I. Pervo, *Profit with Delight: The Literary Genre of the Acts of the Apostles* (Philadelphia: Fortress Press, 1987), 86–114.

6. Morgan, "Make-Believe," 222.

7. Pervo, *Profit with Delight*, 101. Pervo remarks that at the 1976 international conference marking the centenary of Rohde's publication, "The entire subject of origins was ignored. (Graham) Anderson summarized the situation by saying, 'We are all eclectics now'" (100).

8. Brigitte Maria Egger ("Women in the Greek Novel: Constructing the Feminine" [Ph.D. diss., University of California, Irvine, 1990]) reviews the evolution of the classification of the novels as popular reading. While interpreters following Rohde viewed the romances as *Trivialliteratur*, that is, "literature for the masses," more recent scholarship has concluded that "their intended audience must have been largely 'bourgeois' or middle-to-leisure class, and that the social borders of this main circle of recipients may be assumed to have been open more on the upper than on the lower fringe" (10–11). Thus we may think of such "popular" literature as the ancient equivalent of what we call "light" reading today.

9. Morgan, "Make-Believe," 178.

10. Ibid. Likewise, modern interpreters, including Rohde, have read the novels with similar ambivalence, demonstrating a certain disdain for their literary inferiority even as they show great interest in their evolution.

11. Ibid., 182–83. Among Rohde and others, see B. E. Perry, *The Ancient Romances: A Literary Historical Account of Their Origins* (Berkeley and Los Angeles: University of California Press, 1967), and Graham Anderson, *Ancient Fiction: The Novel in the Greco-Roman World* (Totowa, N.J.: Barnes and Noble, 1984).

12. For example, Karl Kerényi (*Die griechisch-orientalische Romanliteratur in religionsgeschichtlicher Beleuchtung* [Darmstadt: Wissenschaftliche Buchgesellschaft, 1962]) de-emphasized the significance of form and explored the religious and mythic origins of the stories conveyed in the novels. B. E. Perry (*The Ancient Romances*) and Bryan P. Reardon (*Courants littéraires grecs des IIe et IIIe siècles*, Ann Litt Univ. Nantes 3 [Paris: Les Belles Lettres, 1971]) consider the broader cultural interests and phenomena reflected in the novels. For a review of this line of inquiry, see again Pervo, *Profit with Delight*, 86–114.

13. Reardon, *Form of Greek Romance*, 164.

14. Pervo, *Profit with Delight*, 112.

15. Ibid., 111.

16. Thus Morgan ("Make-Believe") examines ancient fiction's function of encouraging readers/hearers to believe that certain ideals, views, and hopes could indeed be realized.

17. Reardon, *Form of Greek Romance*, 81. In comparison with

tragedy, Reardon adds that *pathos* in the romance is "less grim." What distinguishes romance from tragedy is how the elements "do not add up to the same effect. . . . In tragedy, *peripeteia* and *anagnorisis* are crucial in the operation of the irony which constitutes the tragedy, they are its very means: the unforeseen reversals that take Oedipus and Achilles to their fate, the understanding that floods into Oedipus and Achilles when they recognize where they are in life as a result of them. . . . In romance, reversal is not irreversible, it is merely vicissitude. Recognition involves no radical change of spiritual condition; it merely evokes from the hero another despairing cry of 'What do I do *now?*' as the screw is turned yet tighter."

18. Egger, *Women in the Greek Novel,* and Cooper, *Virgin and the Bride.* See also Judith Perkins, *The Suffering Self: Pain and Narrative Representation in the Early Christian Era* (London: Routledge, 1995).

19. Simon Goldhill, *Foucault's Virginity: Ancient Erotic Fiction and the History of Sexuality* (Cambridge: Cambridge University Press, 1995), 93.

20. Ibid.

21. Ibid., 110.

22. Reardon, *Form of Greek Romances,* 5.

23. See Egger, *Women in the Greek Novel,* 47–66.

24. Ibid., 232.

25. Ibid., 39–42.

26. Ibid., 57.

27. Ibid., 59. As Egger notes, "However, for the male hero, virginity or erotic fidelity is not as basic a requirement as for the female protagonists" (188). This is especially clear in Longus and Achilles Tatius.

28. Ibid.

29. As Christoph Burchard ("The Importance of Joseph and Asenath for the Study of the New Testament: A General Survey and a Fresh Look at the Lord's Supper," *New Testament Studies* 33 [1987]: 102–24) notes, it was Friedrich Düsterdieck who first called attention to the relevance of JosAs for interpretation of the New Testament (102). Commenting on Revelation 14.4, Düsterdieck cited the reference to male virginity in JosAs as the only such instance outside the New Testament. The issue is examined later in this chapter.

30. Originally written in Greek during the second century C.E., the Acts are contemporaries of the two novels in view. Although the virgins in these stories do not occupy center stage of the action, they do figure as central characters in particular scenes that serve as the focus of our reading.

JosAs is most often identified as an early- to mid-second-century C.E. composition (see Burchard, *Untersuchungen zu Joseph und Asenath,* WUNT 8 ([Tübingen: Mohr, 1965], and Marc Philonenko, *Joseph et Asénath: Introduction, Texte, Critique, Traduction et Notes,* SPB 13 [Leiden: E. J. Brill, 1968]), and a general consensus has held that the text dates to anywhere from the late second/early first century B.C.E. to the middle of the second century C.E. Recently, Ross Shepard Kraemer has suggested that JosAs is either a Jewish or Christian composition that "there is no compelling evidence . . . for dating . . . any earlier than the fourth century C.E." (*When Asenath Met Joseph: A Late Antique Tale of the Biblical Patriarch and His Egyptian Wife Reconsidered* [New York: Oxford University Press, 1998], 5). Yet Kraemer's arguments for locating the composition in late antiquity, though interesting and at times plausible, fail to provide compelling evidence for not dating JosAs any earlier. As investigation into JosAs's origins continues, together these readings remind us that the narrative contains popular literary motifs that can be traced across a range of ancient literature. A consensus view holds that the narrative was originally written in Greek and that it demonstrates some dependence on the Septuagint (ibid.; see also G. Delling's discussion of the relationship between JosAs and the Septuagint, "Einwirkungen der Sprache der Septuaginta in 'Joseph und Asenath,'" *Journal for the Study of Judaism in the Persian, Hellenistic and Roman Period* 9 (1978): 29–56.

Although JosAs is regularly regarded as a novel, the nature of its identity as such remains under debate. Noting that JosAs has been grouped with the Jewish Ruth, Esther, Jonah, Judith, Tobit, and Daniel 1–6 on the one hand, and with the erotic Greek novels and the Christian Apocryphal Acts on the other, Burchard correctly cautions that "[w]ith full acknowledgement of the merits that all these approaches have it must be observed that neither of them does full justice to the three main features combined in JosAs, love, conversion, and dangerous adventure" ("The Present State of Research on Joseph and Asenath," in *New Perspectives on Ancient Judaism,* ed. Jacob Neusner et al., vol. 2 [Lanham, N.Y.: University Press of America, 1987], 36–37). Despite the questions that remain concerning its specific genre, we can nevertheless appreciate the novelistic tendencies of JosAs.

31. See Ernst von Dobschütz's early article, "Der Roman in der altchristlichen Literatur," *Deutsche Rundschau* 111 (1902): 87–106, and the recent contributions of Ronald Hock ("Why New Testament Scholars Should Read Ancient Novels"), Melissa Aubin ("Reversing Romance? *The Acts of Thecla* and the Ancient Novel"), and Christine M. Thomas ("Stories without Texts and without Authors: The Problem of Fluidity in Ancient Novelistic Texts and Early Christian Literature"), in *Ancient Fiction and Early Christian Narrative,* ed. Ronald F. Hock, J. Bradley Chance, and Judith Perkins, SBL Symposium Series 6 (Atlanta: Society of Biblical Literature, 1998).

32. Von Dobschütz, 91.

33. Reardon, *Form of Greek Romance,* 164–65. During the inter-

val between von Dobschütz and Reardon, numerous interpreters have explored the relationship between the novels and Acts. See especially Rosa Söder, *Die apokryphen Apostelgeschichten und die romanhafte Literatur der Antike* (Stuttgart: W. Kohlhammer Verlag, 1932; reprint, Darmstadt: Wissenschaftliche Buchgesellschaft, 1969); Philipp Vielhauer, "Apokryphe Apostelgeschichten," in *Geschichte der urchristlichen Literatur* (New York: Walter de Gruyter, 1975); and Jean-Daniel Kaestli, "Les principales orientations de la recherche sur les Acts apocryphes des Apotres," in *Les Actes apocryphes des Apotres*, ed. François Bovon (Geneva: Labor et fides, 1981), 49–67. In contrast, Richard Reitzenstein identified the genre of the Acts within the framework of miracle stories (see *Hellenistische Wundererzählungen* [Leipzig: B. G. Teubner, 1906]). Yet as Pervo has argued, aretalogy is not really "genre-specific" (*Profit with Delight*, 122). For a good review of research into the origins of the Acts, see again Pervo, *Profit with Delight*, 86–114, 121–31; and Virginia Burrus, *Chastity as Autonomy: Women in the Stories of the Apocryphal Acts*, Studies in Women and Religion, vol. 23 (Lewiston and Queenston: Edwin Mellen Press, 1987), 7–30.

Söder's argument that the Acts cannot be identified with any single novelistic genre casts doubt upon the value of making exclusive claims about their form (*Die apokryphen Apostelgeschichten*, 183–86). Her conclusion resonates with Pervo's comments about the novels and Burchard's observations about JosAs. All of these narratives demonstrate a fair degree of literary eclecticism. Taking note of the critical difference between form and origin, Virginia Burrus departs from the ongoing investigation of the literary genre of the Acts. Instead she focuses on the origins of the chastity stories, arguing that the Acts are rooted in folklore. Burrus (*Chastity as Autonomy*) suggests that in contrast to literature created out of whole literary cloth, the narratives reflect oral traditions that predate their composition. As she indicates, Burrus follows the lead of previous interpreters who sought to identify the origins of the traditions contained in the Acts. Burrus cites especially Ludwig Rademacher, "Hippolytos und Thekla. Studien zur Geschichte von Legende und Kultus," *Sitzungsberichte, Kaiserliche Akademie der Wissenschaft in Wien, Philosophisch-historische Klasse* 182, no. 3 (1916); Kerényi, *Die griechisch-orientalische Romanliteratur;* and Dennis R. MacDonald, *The Legend and the Apostle: The Battle for Paul in Story and Canon* (Philadelphia: Westminster Press, 1983).

34. Pervo, *Profit with Delight*, 90. As in the case of the novels, the popular quality of the Acts has given some interpreters cause to regard them as both literarily and theologically inferior.

35. References are to Ebbe Vilborg's edition of the Greek text (*Achilles Tatius: Leucippe and Clitophon*, 2 vols. [Stockholm: Almquist and Wiksell, 1971]), and John J. Winkler's English translation ("Achilles Tatius: Leucippe and Clitophon," in *Collected Ancient Greek*

Novels, ed. B. P. Reardon [Berkeley and Los Angeles: University of California Press, 1989]), which is based upon Vilborg.

36. Cf. Hägg, *Novel in Antiquity,* 48; Goldhill, *Foucault's Virginity,* 70; and Shadi Bartsch, *Decoding the Ancient Novel* (Princeton, N.J.: Princeton University Press, 1989), 49, 53–54.

37. Vilborg, *Achilles Tatius,* 6 n. 2.

38. Egger, *Women in the Greek Novels,* 52, 52 n.1.

39. Goldhill, *Foucault's Virginity,* 74. Goldhill adds: "For Cleitophon's reaction is placed under the aegis of a schooling in *sophrosyne,* that dominant *askesis* of Greek philosophies of *eros;* but it is a schooling that slips in the face of *erotikoi logoi,* as the lure of imitating an exemplum proves too strong, especially when the example is provided by *tou kreittonos,* 'one of the greater ones' . . . Cleitophon takes a god as his paradigm—but of slippage" (73).

40. That virgins must be protected while outdoors is confirmed when Kalligone is kidnapped during a holiday excursion. The male kidnappers were able to infiltrate the festivities only because they shaved their beards and dressed as women (2.18).

41. Male attempts to possess the virgin come full circle in this scene, for it was the jealousy and desire of yet another male suitor that first triggered the events leading to Leucippe's supposed beheading.

42. Cf. chapter 2.

43. Several episodes in the narrative demonstrate Artemis's role as the advocate of virgins. When Leucippe's virginity is tested at the cave of the syrinx, Clitophon, fearful that Pan will assault Leucippe in the cave, implores the god to "[l]et Leucippe come back to us a virgin. *You have made an agreement with Artemis.* Do not play this virgin false!" (8.13; emphasis added). Likewise, Leucippe appeals to Artemis's protection of virgins when she is threatened with rape: "Tell me, aren't you afraid of your goddess Artemis? You rape a virgin in the virgin's own city? Lady goddess, where are your arrows?" (6.21). When Clitophon recounts the story of Rhodopis in order to explain how the Styx came to be used as a means for testing the virginity of young women, he underscores Artemis's special relationship with virgins. Artemis turned her beloved Rhodopis into a fount at the very place where her virginity had been taken (*entha ten parthenian elyse,* 8.12).

44. Bartsch, *Decoding the Ancient Novel,* 53. Cf. A. R. Littlewood, "Romantic Paradises: The Role of the Garden in the Byzantine Romance," *Byzantine and Modern Greek Studies* 5 (1979): 95–114.

45. Goldhill, *Foucault's Virginity,* 91.

46. Ibid., 116.

47. Unless otherwise noted, references are to the Greek text of Michael D. Reeve, *Longus: Daphnis et Chloe* (Leipzig: Teubner Verlagsgesellschaft, 1982), and the English translation based on Reeve's edition, Christopher Gill, "Longus: Daphnis and Chloe," in Reardon, ed.,

Collected Ancient Greek Novels. See also the well-known edition of J. M. Edmonds, ed., *Longus: Daphnis and Chloe*, with a revised translation by George Thornley, LCL (London and New York: William Heinemann and G. P. Putnam's Sons, 1924).

As interpreters have long noted, *Daphnis and Chloe* is distinctive among the novels in several ways. First, the travel motif that characterizes the other romances is absent—the entire story takes place in Lesbos. Second, the novel introduces the protagonists when they are yet infants and follows their maturation. Third, and most important for this study, the narrative presents Chloe as the more sexually aware of the two characters. It is this last element that proves most significant for our consideration. For discussion of Longus's text as a mid- to late-second-century product of the Second Sophistic, see R. L. Hunter, *A Study of Daphnis and Chloe* (Cambridge: Cambridge University Press, 1983).

48. Froma I. Zeitlin, "The Poetics of *Eros:* Nature, Art, and Imitation in Longus' *Daphnis and Chloe*," in *Before Sexuality: The Construction of Erotic Experience in the Ancient Greek World*, ed. David M. Halperin et al. (Princeton, N.J.: Princeton University Press, 1990), 417–64.

49. Ibid., 432 n. 45.

50. Ibid., 439.

51. J. J. Winkler, "The Education of Chloe: Hidden Injuries of Sex," in *The Constraints of Desire*, ed. J. J. Winkler (New York: Routledge, 1990), 103.

52. Egger, *Women in the Greek Novels*, 312–13.

53. Ibid., 313.

54. Ibid.; cf. Goldhill, *Foucault's Virginity*, 35.

55. Goldhill, *Foucault's Virginity*, 35. Alternatively, he also underscores the potential humor of Daphnis's response to Lycaenion's teaching: "The male who is afraid to penetrate his loved female because of her physical feelings is as much a (comic) figure of Greek patriarchal normative imagination as the *kinaidos*, or the parasitic man of uncontrolled appetites" (39).

56. Winkler, "Education of Chloe," 124.

57. Ibid., 40.

58. Cooper, *Virgin and the Bride*, 24.

59. An authoritative critical edition of JosAs has not yet been established. Whereas Philonenko's edition of JosAs, based on the shorter recension of "family d," has been most accessible, Burchard's preliminary edition, based on the longer recension of "family b," has received the most critical attention. For a review of such text critical scholarship, see Randall Davis Chesnutt, "Conversion in Joseph and Asenath: Its Nature, Function, and Relation to Contemporaneous Paradigms of Conversion and Initiation" (Ph.D. diss. Duke University, 1986). See as well Kraemer's recent text critical work in *When Asenath Met Joseph*.

Here, references to JosAs are based on Christoph Burchard's preliminary edition of JosAs ("Ein vorläufiger griechischer Text von Joseph und Asenath," *Dielheimer Blätter zum Alten Testament* 14 [1979]: 2–53; supplemented in "Verbesserungen zum vorläufigen Text von Joseph und Asenath," *Dielheimer Blätter zum Alten Testament* 16 [1982]: 37–39) and his English translation ("Joseph and Asenath" in *The Old Testament Pseudepigrapha,* ed. James H. Charlesworth, vol. 2 [Garden City: Doubleday, 1985], 177–247).

60. As Burchard ("Joseph and Asenath," 182) notes, "Joseph and Asenath falls into two parts, which could almost stand by themselves. Part I (chs. 1–21) is suspended between two allusions to the Story of Joseph (Gen 37–50). Chapter 1.1 echoes Genesis 41.46 to tell that Pharaoh sent Joseph around Egypt to gather up the corn of the seven years of plenty, followed in 1.2 by a remark about Joseph's arrival in Heliopolis. Chapter 21.9 notes the birth of Ephraim and Manasseh in accordance with Genesis 41.50–52. . . . Part II (chs. 22–29) opens in 22.1f with a summary of Genesis 41.53f. and 45.26–46.7; 47.27: Jacob and his kin come to Egypt and settle in Goshen. Joseph and Asenath go to visit them (ch. 22 is an exposition)."

61. JosAs's unqualified reference to Joseph as a *parthenos* is unusual (4.7). As Burchard, among others, has observed, it is probably the first reference to a male *parthenos* that either predates or is contemporary with Revelation 14.4 (as noted earlier, some have debated the gender reference of 1 Cor 7.25). As with Achilles Tatius, the reference here may only undergird the degree to which *parthenos* is understood as a female condition: "The fact that Joseph is *parthenos hos sy semeron* may indicate that *parthenos* is still so fundamentally feminine that its use for males is a comparison rather than a predication" ("Importance of JosAs for the Study of the NT," 128 n. 5).

62. Ibid., 203 n. 2a.

63. Ibid.

64. For extended discussion of the foreign/strange woman motif, see Kraemer, *When Asenath Met Joseph,* 24–25; see also Kraemer's examination of the imagery that links Woman Wisdom/Metanoia/City of Refuge and Asenath throughout the narrative (ibid., 26, 61, 68, 72).

65. Ibid., 98. Noting the scene in which Asenath is suddenly encircled by bees who do not sting her, Kraemer examines how bees symbolized, among other things, the expressly female virtues of "chastity, purity, and diligence" (168).

66. Here Kraemer likens Asenath to Moses, whose face shone after his encounter with the deity (ibid., 40).

67. References are to the Greek edition of Lipsius-Bonnet (Richard Adelbert Lipsius and Maximillian Bonnet, eds., *Acta apostolorum apocrypha,* 3 vols. [Leipzig: Hermann Mendelssohn, 1891–1903;

reprint, Darmstadt: Wissenschaftliche Buchgesellschaft, 1959)], and to J. K. Elliott's English translation ("The Acts of Paul and Thecla," in *Apocryphal New Testament,* 350–89).

68. Margaret Miles, *Carnal Knowing: Female Nakedness and Religious Meaning in the Christian West* (Boston: Beacon, 1989), 58. Aubin also cites Miles ("Reversing Romance?" 231).

69. The underlying erotic dimension of the sequence that leads to Thecla's appearance in the arena is heightened in later antiquity. In his treatise *On Virgins,* Ambrose tells of Thecla being thrown before a lion. As Boyarin notes: "Male sexuality is figured as a devouring of the woman, and the lion represents the rapacity of a husband, as well as that of the Empire . . . , the text draws an explicit analogy between the hunger of the male lion to eat the virgin's flesh and the lust of her husband to consummate the marriage" (*Dying for God: Martyrdom and the Making of Christianity and Judaism* [Stanford: Stanford University Press, 1999], 74).

70. See Cooper's argument that Christian *enkrateia* does not realize, but rather subverts, the Greco-Roman notion of *sophrosyne* (*Virgin and the Bride,* 55–56, 65–66). See also Perkins, *The Suffering Self,* and Aubin's exploration of the narrative-rhetorical strategies that the *Acts of Paul and Thecla* employs in its subversion of the romance's ideological agenda ("Reversing Romance?").

71. Aubin, "Reversing Romance?" 271.

72. Söder, *Die apokryphen Apostelgeschichten,* 148.

73. For an extended treatment of the autonomy of the female protagonists in the Apocyrphal Acts, see Burrus, *Chastity as Autonomy.*

74. Since no Greek witnesses to the relevant portions of the Acts have survived, references are to the English translation of "The Acts of Peter" in Elliott, *Apocryphal New Testament,* 390–426.

4. The Virgin Speaks

1. Robbins, *Exploring the Texture of Texts,* 40.
2. Gowler, *Host, Guest, Enemy and Friend,* 72.
3. Hochman, *Character,* 63.
4. Luke Timothy Johnson, *The Gospel of Luke* (Sacra Pagina. Collegeville, Minn.: Liturgical Press, 1993), 50. Cf. Acts 2.43; 4.16, 22, 30; 5.12; 6.8; 8.6, 13; 14.3; 15.2. Seeing how the phrase is associated with the Septuagintal portrayal of Moses as a prophet, Johnson argues "that Luke exploits this tradition is clear from his application of it to Moses in 7.31, and immediately to Jesus in 2.22."
5. Green, "The Social Status of Mary," 464.
6. Raymond E. Brown, *Birth of the Messiah,* 343.

7. *Kecharitomene* occurs only once in the Septuagint; Sirach 18.17 refers to the "gracious man" who possesses a word (*logos*) whose value surpasses even that of a good gift.

8. Janice Capel Anderson observes the marginalization of Joseph in "Mary's Difference," 188.

9. Fred Horton notes how in contrast to Matthew, who uses Mary's virginity as a means for grounding the events of the birth narrative in Septuagintal prophecy, Luke poses Mary's virginity as a challenge to the divine plan that Gabriel reveals. See "Parenthetical Pregnancy: The Conception and Birth of Jesus in Mt 1.18–25," *Society of Biblical Literature Seminar Papers* 26 (1987): 175–89.

10. Landry, "Narrative Logic," 76.

11. Although Schaberg repeatedly asserts that the angel sidesteps Mary's question of how his message is to be fulfilled, she fails to demonstrate why Luke 1.35 cannot be properly understood as his answer. See Landry, "Narrative Logic," again.

12. She claims instead that Luke 1.35 refers to the empowerment that Mary will receive from the Holy Spirit after she is sexually violated and impregnated (Schaberg, *Illegitimacy of Jesus,* 112–17).

13. Ibid. Schaberg cross-references Gen 42.21; Lev 14.43;. Judg 9.57; 1 Kings 30.23; 2 Kings 19.7, 22.1; Job 21.17; etc.

14. References to *pneuma* and *dynamis* are repeated elsewhere in the Gospel and Acts: John will go before the Lord in the *pneuma* and *dynamis* of Elijah (Lk 1.17); Jesus returns *en te dynamei tou pneumatos* into Galilee at the beginning of his ministry (Lk 4.14); the risen Jesus tells his apostles, *alla lempsesthe dynamin epelthontos tou hagiou pneumatos eph' hymas* (Acts 1.8); and Peter teaches, *Iesoun ton apo Nazareth hos echrisen auton ho theos pneumati hagio kai dynamei* (Acts 10.38). Luke clearly assumes a special relationship between *pneuma* and *dynamis.* See Shepherd, *Narrative Function of the Holy Spirit,* 133; C. K. Barrett, *The Holy Spirit and the Gospel Tradition* (London: SPCK, 1947), 76–77; Robert P. Menzies, *The Development of Early Christian Pneumatology with Special Reference to Luke-Acts* (Sheffield: JSOT Press, 1991), 125–28.

15. Among many, cf. Raymond E. Brown, *Birth of the Messiah,* 340; Schaberg, *Illegitimacy of Jesus,* 122, 144. Dibelius argued that while *episkiaszo* does not refer to a sexual act, it does point to an extraordinary conception ("Jungfrauensohn," 19–20).

16. Bow, *Jesus' Birth,* 9.

17. Ibid., 167.

18. Schaberg argues that the allusion to Deuteronomy 22.23–24 is direct and intentional (*Illegitimacy,* 91–92).

19. See Robert Alter, "How Conventions Help Us Read: The Case of the Bible's Annunciation Type-Scene," *Prooftexts* 3 (May

1982): 118, and Fitzmyer, *Luke,* 318. Cf. Gen 16.7–13, 17.1–21, 18.1–15; Judg 13.2–7; 1 Sam 1.1–20.

20. Robbins ("Socio-Rhetorical Criticism," 175) notes the significance of Mary's perspective in this scene. She is the character who experiences the announcement of favor as troubling (v. 29), raises the issue of virginity as a problem (v. 34), and identifies herself as God's servant (v. 38).

21. Schaberg, *Illegitimacy of Jesus,* 131. For comparison with cinematic representation of the male ego as voyeur/object and the female ego as exhibitionist/object, see Laura Mulvey, *Visual and Other Pleasures* (Houndsmill: Macmillan, 1989).

22. In 1 Corinthians 7.32–34, virginity expresses singleness of heart in one's devotion to God.

23. Schaberg, *Illegitimacy of Jesus,* 129–31.

24. The meaning here may also be causative: "for/because there will be fulfillment of what was spoken to her from the Lord." In either case, Elizabeth emphasizes Mary's faith in the divine word.

25. The triangle of maternity, faithfulness, and blessing reoccurs in Luke 11.27–28, where faithfulness is valued even above maternity. Later, in Luke 23.29, the connection is radically severed when Jesus tells the women who mourn for him, *hoti idou erchontai hemerai en hais erousin, makariai hai steirai kai hai koiliai hai ouk egennesan kai mastoi hoi ouk ethrepsan.* In stark contrast to the promise and blessing of maternity with which Luke opens (1.7), it is the barren who will be blessed in the aftermath of the people's rejection of Jesus. The consequences of faithlessness and disobedience nullify the blessings of maternity.

26. Robbins, "Socio-Rhetorical Criticism," 197, and Seim, *Double Message,* 199–200.

27. Robbins focuses on the *tapeinosis* of pregnancy outside of marriage ("Socio-Rhetorical Criticism," 182–84).

28. Schaberg herself writes, "I readily admit that the fact that we cannot prove that any early Christians read the Infancy Narratives of Matthew and Luke in the way I have proposed their authors intended is a major objection against my interpretation. Could these authors have failed so completely in their efforts to communicate the tradition to their early readers?" (*Illegitimacy of Jesus,* 193).

29. Nolland (*Luke,* 69) and Gaventa (*Mary,* 56) identify Mary's speech as a "response" to Elizabeth.

30. A narrative gap is detected here. Who are all these generations of whom Mary speaks? Are they her descendants? all Israel?

31. Robbins (ibid., 175–76) notes the resonance between the following verses: 1.14, 47; 1.25, 48a; 1.45, 48b; 1.35, 49; and 1.32–33, 54. In a manner that tropes the theme of fulfillment, Mary's language reconfigures that uttered by the angel and Elizabeth.

32. As Horsley notes, "In biblical, particularly psalmic language . . . 'the poor/humble/lowly' (*tapeinoi/anawim*) in verse 52 is a clear reference to the people of Israel, usually in conditions of domination, oppression, and affliction (e.g. see Deut 26.7; Ps 136.23, including the contexts). . . . Mary, in her 'low estate,' or humility (Lk 1.48), is thus a representation of the people, 'the lowly,' generally" (*Liberation of Christmas*, 111).

33. The vindication of a violated virgin is the theological focus of Schaberg's reading (*Illegitimacy of Jesus*).

34. See Raymond E. Brown, *Birth of the Messiah*, 357–60.

35. Gaventa (*Mary*, 57–59, 73) and Seim (*Double Message*, 175–76), among others.

36. Raymond E. Brown, *Birth of the Messiah*, 355–65; cf. Schaberg, *Illegitimacy of Jesus*, 92–95.

37. Schubert, "The Structure and Significance of Luke 24." See also the following examinations of the theological and narrative significance of prophecy in Luke-Acts: Minear, "Luke's Use of the Birth Stories," and *To Heal and to Reveal: The Prophetic Vocation According to Luke* (New York: Crossroad, 1976); Nils A. Dahl, "The Story of Abraham in Luke-Acts," in Leander E. Keck and J. Louis Martyn, eds., *Studies in Luke-Acts* (Philadelphia: Fortress Press, 1980), 139–58; Luke Timothy Johnson, *The Literary Function of Possessions in Luke-Acts* and *Luke;* and David P. Moessner, *Lord of the Banquet: The Literary and Theological Significance of the Lukan Travel Narrative* (Minneapolis: Fortress Press, 1989).

38. Luke Timothy Johnson, *Luke,* 16–17. Three forms of prophecy permeate the Lucan narrative: literary prophecy, programmatic prophecy, and speech-narrative prophecy. Literary prophecy is speech that is attributed to a character and comes to fulfillment later in the narrative (cf. Lk 9.21, 44; 18.32–33; 24.6–8, 44). Programmatic prophecy concerns prophetic utterances that provide the interpretive key to subsequent plot developments (cf. Lk 2.24, 24.49; Acts 2.1–4). Finally, speech-narrative prophecy involves the sequential organization of speech and narrative. As the plot unfolds, a narrative unit fulfills an immediately preceding speech (Lk 4.16–30). See also Moessner, *Lord of the Banquet.*

39. Phyllis Trible, "Eve and Miriam: From the Margins to the Center," in *Feminist Approaches to the Bible,* ed. Hershel Shanks (Washington, D.C.: Biblical Archaeology Society, 1995), 22.

40. Whereas some, like Mary Rose D'Angelo ("[Re]presentations of Women in the Gospel of Matthew and Luke-Acts," in *Women and Christian Origins,* ed. Ross Shepard Kraemer and Mary Rose D'Angelo [New York: Oxford University Press, 1999]), resist identifying Mary as a prophet because the text does not directly assign her that role, I see

the characterization of Mary as a prophet similar to that of Simeon. Though never identified as a prophet, per se, Simeon nevertheless utters prophetic speech that figures programmatically in Luke-Acts (Lk 2.29–32, 35–35).

41. Gaventa, *Mary,* 58.

42. John H. Elliott, "Temple versus Household in Luke-Acts: A Contrast in Social Institutions," in *The Social World of Luke-Acts: Models for Interpretation,* ed. Jerome H. Neyrey (Peabody: Hendrickson, 1991), 226; cf. 215–16.

43. Ibid., 194.

44. In contrast, Mary's condition in Luke 1.46–56 is ambiguous. Although Elizabeth refers to Mary as the "mother of my Lord" (1.43) and to Jesus as "the fruit" of her womb, the narrative does not indicate that Mary is already pregnant. Since Elizabeth is speaking prophetically, she may well be alluding to the fulfillment of what is sure to come. Whereas direct reference is made to the baby in Elizabeth's womb (1.41), no such reference is made to Mary's pregnancy.

45. Gaventa, *Mary,* 70–71.

46. Ibid., 65. She cites as examples: Seneca, *To Helvia on Consolation* 3.1, "Of all the wounds that have ever gone deep into your body, this latest one, I admit, is the most serious; it has not merely torn the outer skin, but pierced your very breast and vitals"; Seneca, *To Marcia on Consolation* 1.5, "that you may know that even this deep-cut wound will surely heal, I have shown you the scar of an old wound that was no less severe"; Pliny's description of a mother who refrained from telling her ill husband of their son's death in *Letters* 3.16, "When she found she could no longer restrain her grief, but her tears were gushing out, she would leave the room, and having given vent to her passion, return again with dry eyes and a serene countenance, as if she had dismissed every pang of bereavement at her entrance. The action was, no doubt, truly noble, when drawing the dagger she plunged it into her breast, and then presented it to her husband with that ever-memorable, I had almost said that divine expression, 'It does not hurt, my Paetus' . . . was it not something much greater . . . to hide her tears, to conceal her grief, and cheerfully play the mother when she was one no more?"

47. Luke Timothy Johnson, *Luke,* 57. Cf. McHugh, *Mother,* 110–11; P. Benoit, "'Et toi-meme, un glaive te transpercera l'ame!' (Luc 2, 35): Ezek 14, 7," *Catholic Biblical Quarterly* 25 (1963): 251–61; reprinted in *Exégèse et théologie* (Paris: Cerf, 1968) 216–27.

48. Seim concurs (*Double Message,* 164–65).

49. Ibid., 180.

50. F. Scott Spencer, "Out of Mind, Out of Voice: Slave-Girls and Prophetic Daughters in Luke-Acts," *Biblical Interpretation* 7, no. 2 (1999): 133–55.

5. Defying Nature

1. Bow, *Jesus' Birth*, 204.

2. In both verses some MSS read that Anna is pregnant already, while others retain the future tense *(lempsetai, lempsomai)*. De Strycker and Hock favor the past tense, while Tischendorf favors the future. While de Strycker's reading may have the advantage of subtly introducing the theme of purity into the narrative, each reading portrays Anna's pregnancy as miraculous. Cf. C. Michel, "Protévangile de Jacques," in *Évangiles Aprocryphes*, ed. H. Hemmer and P. Lejay (Paris: Auguste Picard, 1924), 10–11.

3. Hock, *Infancy Gospels*, 17.

4. Ibid., 18. Citing Hermogenes, *Progymnasmata*, and Aphthonius, *Progymnasmata*, in particular, Hock lists the *topoi* common to *egkomion:* race *(genos)*, nationality *(ethnos)*, region *(patris)*, ancestors *(progonoi)*, parents *(pateres)*, upbringing *(anatrophe)*, and the presentation of virtuous deeds. As Hock observes, the latter is detailed in PJ 13–16.

5. Saul Olyan, *Rites and Rank: Hierarchy in Biblical Representations of Cult* (Princeton, N.J.: Princeton University Press, 2000), 39. Cf. Neyrey, "Symbolic Universe," 271–304.

6. Olyan, *Rites and Rank*, 121.

7. Dean-Jones argues that in Greek medical literature, puberty is signaled by age, and menarche represents not its commencement, but its completion *(Women's Bodies*, 50). In PJ, expectation of Mary's menarche follows immediately upon recognition of her age.

8. For a discussion of how blurred definitions and unclear boundaries are especially threatening to purity systems, see Neyrey's application of Mary Douglas's discussion of purity in "Symbolic Universe," 281.

9. Hock, *Infancy Gospels*, 18. Mary weaves not to earn a living, but as a religious duty (cf. the 16 women of Elis who weave the robe for Hera in Paus. 2.14.9, LCL 2.153).

10. Hock, *Infancy Gospels*, 53.

11. Smid notes that PJ 11.5 has been read as an early trace of *logos* Christology. He cites an Armenian variant that places the occurrence of Mary's miraculous conception in her ear *(Commentary*, 84).

12. For ignorance of one's pregnancy, cf. 2 Enoch 71.1–8.

13. Cf. note 4 for the significance of Mary's virtue in encomiastic rhetoric.

14. For example, the LCL edition of Diodorus translates *physis* as "innocence" *(Library of History* 16.26.2–6), and Hock *(Infancy Gospels)* altogether refrains from a direct translation, "and Salome inserted her finger into Mary" (20.2; cf. 19.19). See again chapter 2, note 82.

15. Cf. de Strycker, 157. For discussion of the cross-cultural imagery of light as a sign of divine presence, see Smid, *Commentary*, 135–57.

16. See Hock, *Infancy Gospels*, 19.

17. Olyan, *Rites and Rank*, 65.

18. Beard, "Re-Reading (Vestal) Virginity," 169.

19. Ibid.

20. Jane Schaberg, "Infancy of Mary of Nazareth," in *Searching the Scriptures*, ed. Elisabeth Schüssler Fiorenza with the assistance of Shelley Matthews, 2 vols. (New York: Crossroad, 1993–94), 718.

Bibliography

Texts and Translations

Achilles Tatius. *Leucippe and Clitophon.* Ed. Ebbe Vilborg. 2 vols. Stockholm: Almquist and Wiksell, 1971.

The Ante-Nicene Fathers. Rev. and ed. A. Cleveland Coxe. Grand Rapids, Mich.: William B. Eerdmans, 1979–1982.

The Apostolic Fathers. Vol. 2. Trans. Kirsopp Lake. LCL. Cambridge, Mass., and London: Harvard University Press and Heinemann, 1913.

Aristotle. *Generation of Animals.* Trans. A. L. Peck. LCL. Cambridge, Mass.: Harvard University Press, 1942.

———. *Rhetorica ad Alexandrum.* Trans. H. Rackham. LCL. Cambridge, Mass.: Harvard University Press, 1937.

Aulus Gellius. *Attic Nights.* LCL. London and New York: Heinemann and G. P. Putnam's Sons, 1927.

Blackman, Philip. *Mishnayoth.* 6 vols. 3rd ed. New York: Judaica Press, 1965.

Burchard, Christoph. "Ein vorläufiger griechischer Text von Joseph und Asenath." *Dielheimer Blätter zum Alten Testament* 14 (1979): 2–53.

———. "Verbesserungen zum vorläufigen Text von Joseph und Asenath." *Dielheimer Blätter zum Alten Testament* 16 (1982): 37–39.

Cicero. *De divinatione, De senectute, De amicitia.* LCL. Cambridge,

Mass., and London: Harvard University Press and Heinemann, 1964.

———. *Rhetorica ad Herennium.* LCL. Cambridge, Mass.: Harvard University Press, 1981.

de Strycker, Émile. "Die griechischen Handschriften des Protevangeliums Iacobi." In *Griechische Kodikologie und Textüberlieferung,* ed. D. Harlfinger. Darmstadt:Wissenschaftliche Buchgesellschaft, 1980.

———. *La Forme la plus ancienne du Protevangile de Jacques: Recherches sur le Papyrus Bodmer 5, avec une edition critique du texte grec et une traduction annotee.* Subsidia Hagiographa 33. Brussels: Sociéte des Bollandistes, 1961.

Dio Cassius. *History of Rome.* Trans. E. Cary. LCL. London and New York: Heinemann and Macmillan, 1914–1927.

Diodorus of Sicily. *The Library of History.* 12 vols. Trans. W. H. S. Jones (vols. 1, 3, 4); W. H. S. Jones and H. A. Ormerod (vol. 2); R. E. Wycherley (vol. 5); C. H. Oldfather (vols. 6–12). LCL. Cambridge, Mass.: Harvard University Press, 1970–1989.

Dionysius of Halicarnassus. *The Roman Antiquities.* 7 vols. Trans. Earnest Cary. LCL. Cambridge, Mass.: Harvard University Press, 1937–1950.

Elliott, J. K., ed. *The Apocryphal New Testament: A Collection of Apocryphal Christian Literature in an English Translation.* Oxford: Clarendon Press, 1993.

Fabricus, J., ed. *Codex apocryphus Novi Testamenti,* 1.66–125. 2 vols. Hamburg: Schiller, 1703.

Galen. *On the Affected Parts.* Trans. Rudolph E. Siegal. Basel: Karger, 1976.

———. *On the Usefulness of the Parts of the Body.* 2 vols. Trans. Margaret Tallmadge May. Ithaca, N.Y.: Cornell University Press, 1968.

Hippocrates. *Oeuvres complètes d'Hippocrate.* 10 vols. Ed. Émile Littré. Paris: J. B. Bailliere, 1839–1861; repr. Amsterdam: M. Hakkert, 1961–1962.

Hock, Ronald F. *The Infancy Gospels of James and Thomas: Introduction, Greek Text, English Translation, and Notes.* Scholars Bible. Santa Rosa: Polebridge Press, 1995.

Horace. *Odes and Epodes.* Trans. C. E. Bennett. LCL. Cambridge, Mass., and London: Harvard University Press and Heinemann, 1924.

Justinian. *Digest of Justinian.* Ed. Theodor Mommsen and Paul Krueger. Trans. Alan Watson. 4 vols. Philadelphia: University of Pennsylvania Press, 1985.

Kraemer, Ross Shepard. *Maenads, Martyrs, Matrins, Monastics: A Sourcebook on Women's Religions in the Greco-Roman World.* Philadelphia: Fortress Press, 1988.

Lefkowitz, Mary R., and Maureen B. Fant. *Women's Life in Greece and Rome: A Sourcebook for Translation.* 2nd ed. Baltimore: Johns Hopkins University Press, 1992.

Lipsius, Richard Adelbert, and Maximillian Bonnet, eds. *Acta apostolorum apocrypha.* 3 vols. Leipzig: Hermann Mendelssohn, 1891–1903; reprint, Darmstadt: Wissenschaftliche Buchgesellschaft, 1959.

Longus. *Daphnis and Chloe.* Ed. Michael D. Reeve. Leipzig: Tuebner Verlagsgesellschaft, 1982.

———. *Daphnis and Chloe.* Ed. J. M. Edmonds. Revised translation by George Thornley. LCL. London and New York: Wm. Heinemann and G. P. Putnam's Sons, 1924.

Lucan. *The Civil War.* Trans. J. D. Duff. London and New York: Heinemann and G. P. Putnam's Sons, 1928.

Lucian. *Lucian.* 8 vols. Trans. A. M. Harmon. LCL. Cambridge, Mass.: Harvard University Press, 1968–1979.

Migne, J. P., ed. *Patrologiae cursus completus, seu bibliotheca universalis, integra, uniformis, commoda, oeconomica, omnium SS. Patrum, doctorum scriptorumque ecclesiasticorum.* Series Graeca. 165 vols. Paris: Migne, 1857–1866.

Neander, M., ed. *Catechesis Martini Lutheri parva graeco-latina.* Basel: Ioannis Oporinum, 1564.

Neusner, Jacob. *The Mishnah: A New Translation.* New Haven, Conn.: Yale University Press, 1988.

Origen. *Contra Celsum.* Trans. Henry Chadwick. Cambridge: Cambridge University Press, 1953.

Ovid. *Art of Love and Other Poems.* Trans. J. H. Mozley. LCL. Cambridge, Mass., and London: Harvard University Press and Heinemann, 1967.

———. *Metamorphoses.* 2 vols. Trans. Frank Justus Miller. LCL. London and New York: Heinemann and G. P. Putnam's Sons, 1916.

Pausanias. *Description of Greece.* 5 vols. Trans. W. H. S. Jones. LCL. Cambridge, Mass.: Harvard University Press, 1964–1965.

Philo. *Philo.* 10 vols. Trans. F. H. Colson and the Rev. G. H. Whitaker. LCL. Cambridge, Mass., and London: Harvard University Press and Heinemann, 1935.

Philonenko, Marc. *Joseph et Asénath: Introduction, Texte, Critique, Traduction et Notes.* SPB 13. Leiden: E. J. Brill, 1968.

Pliny. *Letters.* 2 vols. Trans. William Melmoth. LCL. Cambridge, Mass., and London: Harvard University Press and Heinemann, 1915.

Plutarch. *Lives.* 11 vols. Trans. Bernadotte Perrin. LCL. Cambridge, Mass.: Harvard University Press, 1914–1921.

———. *Moralia.* 15 vols. Trans. Frank Cole Babbitt et al. LCL. Cambridge, Mass.: Harvard University Press, 1927–1972.

Reardon, Bryan P., ed. *Collected Ancient Greek Novels.* Berkeley and Los Angeles: University of California Press, 1989.

Roberts, Alexander, and James Donaldson, eds. *Ante-Nicene Fathers.* Vol. 4: *Tertullian, Part Fourth; Minucius Felix; Commodian; Origen, Parts First and Second.* Peabody: Hendrickson, 1995.

Schneemelcher, Wilhelm, ed. *New Testament Apocrypha.* 2 vols. Rev., ed., and trans. R. McL. Wilson. Louisville: Westminster/John Knox Press, 1991–1992.

Seneca. *Moral Essays.* 3 vols. Trans. John W. Basore. LCL. London: Heinemann, 1928.

Seneca (the Elder). *The Elder Seneca: Declamations in Two Volumes.* Trans. M. Winterbottom. LCL. Cambridge, Mass., and London: Harvard University Press and Heinemann, 1974.

Soranus. *Gynecology.* Trans. Owsei Temkin. Baltimore: Johns Hopkins University Press, 1956.

Suetonius. *Lives of the Caesars.* 2 vols. Trans. J. C. Rolfe. LCL. London and New York: Heinemann and G. P. Putnam's Sons, 1914.

Tertullian. *Treatises on Marriage and Remarriage.* Translated and annotated by William P. Le Saint. New York: Newman Press, 1956.

Testuz, M., ed. and trans. *Papyrus Bodmer V: Nativité de Marie.* Cologny-Genève: Bibliotheca Bodmeriana, 1958.

Thilo, J. C., ed. *Codex apocryphus Novi Testamenti.* Leipzig: Vogel, 1832.

Tischendorf, Constantin von, ed. *Evangelia Apocrypha.* 2nd ed. Leipzig: Avenarius and Mendelssohn, 1853.

Secondary Sources

Achelis, Hans. *Virgines Subintroductae: Ein Beitrag zum VII Kapitel des I Korinthersbriefe.* Leipzig: J. C. Hinrichs, 1902.

Adam, A. K. M. *What Is Postmodern Biblical Criticism?* Guides to Biblical Scholarship, New Testament Series. Minneapolis: Fortress Press, 1995.

Allen, J. "The Protevangelium of James as an 'Historia': The Insufficiency of the 'Infancy Gospel' Category." In *Society of Biblical Literature Seminar Papers,* ed. Eugene Lovering. Atlanta: Scholars Press, 1991.

Alter, Robert. *The Art of Biblical Narrative.* New York: Basic Books, 1981.

———. "How Conventions Help Us Read: The Case of the Bible's Annunciation Type-Scene." *Prooftexts* 3 (May 1982): 115–30.

Amandry, P. *La mantique Apollinienne à Delphes, essai sur le fonctionnement de l'Oracle.* Paris: E. de Boccard, 1950.

Amann, Emile. *Le Protevangile de Jacques et ses remaniements latins.* Paris: Letouzey, 1910.

Anderson, Gary. "Celibacy or Consummation in the Garden: Reflections on Early Jewish and Christian Interpretations of the Garden of Eden." *Harvard Theological Review* 82, no. 2 (1989): 121–48.

——. "The Garden of Eden and Sexuality in Early Judaism." In *People of the Body: Jews and Judaism from an Embodied Perspective,* ed. Howard Eilberg-Schwartz. SUNY Series, The Body in Culture, History and Religion. Albany: State University of New York Press, 1992.

Anderson, Graham. *Ancient Fiction: The Novel in the Greco-Roman World.* Totowa, N.J.: Barnes and Noble, 1984.

Anderson, Janice Capel. "Mary's Difference. Gender and Patriarchy in the Birth Narratives." *Journal of Religion* 2 (1987): 183–202.

Aubin, Melissa. "Reversing Romance? *The Acts of Thecla* and the Ancient Novel." In *Ancient Fiction and Early Christian Narrative,* ed. Ronald F. Hock, J. Bradley Chance, and Judith Perkins. SBL Symposium Series 6. Atlanta: Society of Biblical Literature, 1998.

Auerbach, Erich. *Mimesis: The Representation of Reality in Western Literature.* Trans. Williard Trask. Princeton, N.J.: Princeton University Press, 1968.

Aune, David E. *Prophecy in Early Christianity and the Ancient Mediterranean World.* Grand Rapids, Mich.: William B. Eerdmans, 1983.

Bal, Mieke. *Death and Dissymmetry: The Politics of Coherence in the Book of Judges.* Chicago: University of Chicago Press, 1988.

——. *Lethal Love: Feminist Literary Readings of Biblical Love Stories.* Bloomington: Indiana University Press, 1987.

Barrett, C. K. *The Holy Spirit and the Gospel Tradition.* London: SPCK, 1947.

Bartsch, Shadi. *Decoding the Ancient Novel.* Princeton, N.J.: Princeton University Press, 1989.

Beard, Mary. "Re-reading (Vestal) Virginity." In *Women in Antiquity: A New Assessment,* ed. Richard Hawley and Barbara Levick. London: Routledge, 1995.

——. "The Sexual Status of Vestal Virgins." *Journal of Roman Studies* 70 (1980): 12–27.

Bearsley, P. J. "Mary the Perfect Disciple: A Paradigm for Mariology," *Theological Studies* 41 (1980): 461–504.

Benko, Stephen. "The Magnificat: A History of the Controversy." *Journal of Biblical Literature* 89 (1967): 263–75.

——. *The Virgin Goddess: Studies in the Pagan and Christian Roots of Mariology.* New York: E. J. Brill, 1993.

Benoit, P. "Et toi-meme, un glaive te transpercera l'ame! (Luc 2, 35): Ezek 14, 7." *Catholic Biblical Quarterly* 25 (1963): 251–61. Reprinted in *Exégèse et théologie* (Paris: Cerf, 1968), 216–27.

Benveniste, Emile. "Termes greco-latins d'anatomie." *Revue de philologie,* 2nd series 39 (1965): 8.

Biale, David. *Eros and the Jews: From Biblical Israel to Contemporary America.* New York: Basic Books, 1992.

Bible and Cultural Collective. *The Postmodern Bible.* New Haven, Conn.: Yale University Press, 1995.

Bonner, S. F. *Roman Declamation in the Late Republic and Early Empire.* Berkeley and Los Angeles: University of California Press, 1949.

Boslooper, Thomas. "Jesus' Virgin Birth and Non-Christian Parallels." *Religion in Life* 26 (1956–57): 87–97.

———. *The Virgin Birth.* Philadelphia: Westminster Press, 1962.

Bovon, François. "The Suspension of Time in Chapter 18 of Protevangelium Jacobi." In *The Future of Early Christianity,* ed. Birger A. Pearson. Minneapolis: Fortress Press, 1991.

Bow, Beverly Ann. "The Story of Jesus' Birth: A Pagan and Jewish Affair." Ph.D. diss., University of Iowa, 1995.

Box, G. H. "The Gospel Narratives of the Nativity and the Alleged Influence of Heathen Ideas." *Zeitschrift für die Neutestamentliche Wissenschaft* 6 (1905): 80–101.

Boyarin, Daniel. *Carnal Israel: Reading Sex in Talmudic Culture.* Berkeley and Los Angeles: University of California Press, 1993.

———. *Dying for God: Martyrdom and the Making of Christianity and Judaism.* Stanford: Stanford University Press, 1999.

Brown, Peter. *The Body and Society: Men, Women, and Sexual Renunciation in Early Christianity.* New York: Columbia University Press, 1988.

———. "Late Antiquity." In *A History of Private Life.* Vol. 1: *From Pagan Rome to Byzantium,* ed. Paul Veyne and trans. Arthur Goldhammer. Cambridge, Mass.: Belknap Press of Harvard University Press, 1987.

Brown, Raymond E. *The Birth of the Messiah: A Commentary on the Infancy Narratives in the Gospels of Matthew and Luke.* 2nd ed. Anchor Bible Reference Library. New York: Doubleday, 1993.

———. "Luke's Description of the Virginal Conception," *Theological Studies* 35 (1974): 360–62.

———. *The Virginal Conception and Bodily Resurrection of Jesus.* New York: Paulist Press, 1973.

Brown, Raymond E., Karl P. Donfried, Joseph A. Fitzmyer, and John R. Reumann, eds. *Mary in the New Testament: A Collaborative Assessment by Protestant and Roman Catholic Scholars.* Philadelphia: Fortress Press; New York, Ramsey; and Toronto: Paulist Press, 1978.

Burchard, Christoph. "The Importance of Joseph and Asenath for the Study of the New Testament: A General Survey and a Fresh Look at the Lord's Supper." *New Testament Studies* 33 (1987): 102–24.

———. "Joseph and Asenath." In *The Old Testament Pseudepigrapha*. Vol. 2, ed. James H. Charlesworth. Garden City: Doubleday, 1985.

———. "The Present State of Research on Joseph and Asenath." In *New Perspectives on Ancient Judaism*. Vol. 2, ed. Jacob Neusner et al. Lanham, N.Y.: University Press of America, 1987.

———. *Untersuchungen zu Joseph und Asenath*. WUNT 8. Tübingen: Mohr, 1965.

Burnett, Fred. "Characterization and Reader Construction of Characters in the Gospels." *Semeia* 63 (1993): 1–28.

Burrows, E. *The Gospel of the Infancy and Other Biblical Essays*. London: Burns, Oats, and Washbourne, 1940.

Burrus, Virginia. *Chastity as Autonomy: Women in the Stories of the Apocryphal Acts*. Studies in Women and Religion, vol. 23. Lewiston and Queenston: Edwin Mellen Press, 1987.

Cadbury, Henry J. *The Book of Acts in History*. London: A. and C. Black, 1955.

———. *The Making of Luke-Acts*. 2nd ed. London: SPCK, 1958.

———. *The Style and Literary Method of Luke-Acts*. Harvard Theological Studies, vol. 6. Cambridge, Mass.: Harvard University Press, 1920.

Cantarella, Eva. *Pandora's Daughters: The Role and Status of Women in Greek and Roman Antiquity*. Trans. Maureen B. Fant. Baltimore: Johns Hopkins University Press, 1987.

Cantinat, Jean C. M. *Marie dans la Bible*. Le Puy-Lyon: Éditions Xavier Mappus, 1963.

Carroll, Michael. *The Cult of the Virgin Mary: Psychological Origins*. Princeton, N.J.: Princeton University Press, 1986.

Carson, Anne. "Putting Her in Her Place: Women, Dirt, and Desire." In *Before Sexuality: The Construction of Erotic Experience in the Ancient Greek World*, ed. David M. Halperin et al. Princeton, N.J.: Princeton University Press, 1990.

Chatman, Seymour. *Story and Discourse. Narrative Structure in Fiction and Film*. Ithaca, N.Y.: Cornell University Press, 1978.

Chesnutt, Randall Davis. "Conversion in Joseph and Asenath: Its Nature, Function, and Relation to Contemporaneous Paradigms of Conversion and Initiation." Ph.D. diss., Duke University, 1986.

———. "The Social Setting and Purpose of Joseph and Asenath." *Journal for the Study of Pseudepigrapha* 2 (1988): 21–48.

Clark, Elizabeth A. "John Chrysostom and the *Subintroductae*." In *Ascetic Piety and Women's Faith: Essays in Late Ancient Christianity*, ed. Elizabeth A. Clark. New York: Edwin Mellen Press, 1986.

Cloke, Gillian. *This Female Man of God: Women and Spiritual Power in the Patristic Age, A.D. 350–450*. London: Routledge, 1995.

Cohen, David. "Sex, Gender, and Sexuality in Ancient Greece." *Classical Philology* 87 (1992): 145–60.

Conrady, L. *Quelle der kanonischen Kindheitgeschichte Jesu.* Göttingen: Vandenhoeck und Ruprecht, 1900.

Conzelmann, Hans. *The Theology of St. Luke.* Trans. Geoffrey Buswell. New York: Harper and Row, 1961; Philadelphia: Fortress Press, 1982.

Cooper, Kate. *The Virgin and the Bride: Idealized Womanhood in Late Antiquity.* Cambridge, Mass.: Harvard University Press, 1996.

Cothenet, E. "Le Protévangile de Jacques: origine, genre et signification d'un premier midrash chrétien sur la Nativité de Marie," *Aufstieg und Niedergang der römischen Welt* 2.25.6 (1988): 4252–69.

Craddock, Fred. *Luke.* Interpretation. Louisville: John Knox Press, 1990.

Creed, J. M. *The Gospel According to St. Luke.* London: Macmillan, 1930.

Crouzel, Henri. *Origen: The Life and Thought of the First Great Theologian.* Trans. A. S. Worrall. San Francisco: Harper and Row, 1989.

Cullmann, Oscar. "Infancy Gospels." In *New Testament Apocrypha.* Vol. 1: *Gospels and Related Writings,* ed. Edgar Hennecke, Wilhelm Schneemelcher, and R. McL. Wilson. Philadelphia: Westminster Press, 1963.

———. "The Protevangelium of James." In *New Testament Apocrypha.* Vol. 1: *Gospels and Related Writings,* ed. Edgar Hennecke, Wilhelm Schneemelcher, and R. McL. Wilson. Philadelphia: Westminster Press, 1963.

D'Angelo, Mary Rose. "(Re)Presentations of Women in the Gospel of Matthew and Luke-Acts." In *Women and Christian Origins,* ed. Ross Shepard Kraemer and Mary Rose D'Angelo. New York: Oxford University Press, 1999.

Daniels, B. L. "The Greek Manuscript Tradition of the Protevangelium Jacobi." Ph.D. diss., Duke University, 1956.

Danker, F. *Jesus and the New Age: A Commentary on St. Luke's Gospel.* 2nd ed. Philadelphia: Fortress Press, 1988.

Darr, John A. *On Character Building: The Reader and the Rhetoric of Characterization in Luke-Acts.* Louisville: Westminster/John Knox Press, 1992.

Davies, J. G. "The Ascription of the Magnificat to Mary." *Journal of Theological Studies* 15 (1964): 307–308.

Dawsey, J. M. *The Lukan Voice: Confusion and Irony in the Gospel of Luke.* Macon, Ga.: Mercer University, 1986.

———. "What's in a Name? Characterization in Luke." *Biblical Theology Bulletin* 16 (1986): 143–47.

Dean-Jones, Lesley. *Women's Bodies in Classical Greek Science.* Oxford: Clarendon Press, 1994.

Deiss, Lucien. *Mary, Daughter of Zion.* Collegeville, Minn.: Liturgical Press, 1972.

Delling, G. "Einwirkungen der Sprache der Septuaginta in 'Joseph und Asenath.'" *Journal for the Study of Judaism in the Persian, Hellenistic and Roman Period* 9 (1978): 29–56.

———. "*Parthenos.*" In *The Dictionary of the New Testament.* Vol. 5, ed. Gerhard Kittel and Gerhard Friedrich. Grand Rapids, Mich.: William B. Eerdmans, 1967.

Dibelius, Martin. *From Tradition to Gospel.* Trans. Bertram Lee. New York: Scribner, 1935.

———. "Jungfrauensohn und Krippenkind: Untersuchungen zur Geburtsgeschichte Jesu im Lukas-Evangelium." In *Botschaft und Geschichte: Gesammelte Aufsätze von Martin Dibelius.* Vol. 1. Tübingen: Mohr, 1953; orig. 1932.

———. *Studies in the Acts of the Apostles.* Trans. Mary Ling. New York: SCM Press, 1956.

Dobschütz, Ernst von. "Der Roman in der altchristlichen Literatur." *Deutsche Rundschau* 111 (1902): 87–106.

Docherty, Thomas. *Reading (Absent) Character: Towards a Theory of Characterization in Fiction.* Oxford: Clarendon Press, 1983.

Dodd, C. H. "New Testament Translation Problems I." *Bible Translator* 27 (1976): 301–11.

Donahue, John R. "The Literary Turn and New Testament Theology: Detour or New Direction?" *Journal of Religion* 76 (1996): 250–75.

Dover, Kenneth James. *Greek Homosexuality.* London: Gerald Duckworth, 1978.

Downing, Christine. *The Goddess: Mythological Images of the Feminine.* New York: Crossroad, 1981.

Drury, John. *Tradition and Design in Luke's Gospel.* Atlanta: John Knox Press, 1977.

Dupont, Jacques. "Le Magnificat comme discours sur Dieu," *Nouvelle Revue Théologique* 102 (1980): 321–43.

Egger, Brigitte Maria. "Women in the Greek Novel: Constructing the Feminine." Ph.D. diss., University of California, Irvine, 1990.

Eilberg-Schwartz, Howard. *God's Phallus and Other Problems for Men and Monotheism.* Boston: Beacon Press, 1994.

———. *The Savage in Judaism: An Anthropology of Israelite Religion and Ancient Judaism.* Bloomington: Indiana University Press, 1990.

Eilberg-Schwartz, Howard, ed. *People of the Body: Jews and Judaism from an Embodied Perspective.* SUNY Series, The Body in Culture, History and Religion. Albany: SUNY Press, 1992.

Elliott, John H. "Temple versus Household in Luke-Acts. A Contrast in Social Institutions." In *The Social World of Luke-Acts: Models for Interpretation,* ed. Jerome H. Neyrey. Peabody: Hendrickson, 1991.

Elm, Susanna. *Virgins of God: The Making of Asceticism in Late Antiquity.* New York: Oxford University Press, 1994.

Epstein, Louis M. *Marriage Laws in the Bible and Talmud.* Cambridge, Mass.: Harvard University Press, 1942.

———. *Sex Laws and Customs in Judaism.* New York: Bloch, 1948.

Fantham, Elaine, et al. *Women in the Classical World: Image and Text.* New York: Oxford University Press, 1994.

Faraone, Christopher A. *Ancient Greek Love Magic.* Cambridge, Mass.: Harvard University Press, 1999.

Fehrle, Eugene. *Die Kultische Keuschheit in Altertum.* Giessen: A. Topelmann, 1910.

Feuillet, André. *Jésus et sa Mère.* Paris: J. Gabalda et Cie, 1974.

Fitzmyer, Joseph A. *The Gospel According to Luke.* 2 vols. Anchor Bible 28. Garden City, N.Y.: Doubleday, 1981.

———. "The Virginal Conception of Jesus in the New Testament." *Theological Studies* 34 (1973): 567–70.

Ford, J. Massingberde. "The Meaning of 'Virgin.'" *New Testament Studies* 12, no. 3 (1966): 293–99.

Forster, E. M. *Aspects of the Novel.* New York: Harcourt, Brace and World, 1927.

Foucault, Michel. *The History of Sexuality.* Trans. Robert Hurley. Vol. 1: *An Introduction.* New York: Random House, 1980.

———. Vol. 2: *The Use of Pleasure.* New York: Viking, 1985.

———. Vol. 3: *The Care of the Self.* New York: Pantheon Books, 1986.

Friedrich, J. *Der Lukasevangelium und die Apostelgeschichte Werke desselben Verfassers.* Halle: C. A. Kaemmerer, 1890.

Gächter, P. *Light on Mary's Life.* London: Burns and Oats, 1966.

Galambush, Julie. *Jerusalem in the Book of Ezekiel: The City as Yahweh's Wife.* SBL Dissertation Series 130. Atlanta: Scholars Press, 1992.

Gardner, J. F. *Women in Roman Law and Society.* Bloomington: Indiana University Press, 1991.

Gaventa, Beverly Roberts. *Mary: Glimpses of the Mother of Jesus.* Columbia: University of South Carolina Press, 1995.

Godet, Frederick Louis. *A Commentary on the Gospel of St. Luke.* 5th.ed. Trans. E. W. Shalders. Edinburgh: T. and T. Clark, 1870.

Goldhill, Simon. *Foucault's Virginity: Ancient Erotic Fiction and the History of Sexuality.* Cambridge: Cambridge University Press, 1995.

Goma Civit, I. *The Song of Salvation: The Magnificat.* Middlegreen [UK]: St. Paul, 1986.

Gowler, David. *Host, Guest, Enemy, and Friend: Portraits of the Pharisees in Luke and Acts.* Emory Studies in Early Christianity. New York: Peter Lang, 1991.

———. "A Socio-Narratological Character Analysis of the Pharisees in Luke-Acts." Ph.D. diss., Southern Baptist Theological Seminary, 1989.

Grassi, Joseph. *Mary, Mother and Disciple: From the Scriptures to the Council of Ephesus.* Wilmington, Del.: Michael Glazier, 1988.

Graystone, Geoffrey. "Virgin of All Virgins: The Interpretation of Lk. 1.34." Ph.D. diss., Pontificio Instituto Biblico, Rome, 1968.

Green, Joel. "The Social Status of Mary in Luke 1.5–2.52: A Plea for Methodological Integration." *Biblica* 4, no. 73 (1992): 457–72.

Grillmeier, Aloys. *Christ in Christian Tradition.* Vol. 1: *From the Apostolic Age to Chalcedon (451).* 2nd ed. Trans. John Bowden. Atlanta: John Knox Press, 1975.

Günkel, Hermann. "Die Lieder in der Kindheitsgeschichte Jesu bei Lukas." In *Festgabe von Fachgenossen und Freuden A. Von Harnack zum siebzigsten Geburtstag dargebracht.* Göttingen: Vanderhoech and Ruprecht, 1921.

———. *Zum religionsgeschichtlichen Verstandnis des Neuen Testaments.* 2. unveranderte Aufl. Göttingen: Vandenhoeck and Ruprecht, 1910.

Hägg, Tomas. *The Novel in Antiquity.* Berkeley and Los Angeles: University of California Press, 1983.

Halperin, David M., ed. *One Hundred Years of Homosexuality.* New York: Routledge, 1990.

Halperin, David M., John J. Winkler, and Froma I. Zeitlin, eds. *Before Sexuality: The Construction of Erotic Experience in the Ancient Greek World.* Princeton, N.J.: Princeton University Press, 1990.

Hanson, Ann Ellis. "Conception, Gestation and the Origin of Female Nature in the *Corpus Hippocraticum.*" *Helios* 19 (1992): 31–71.

———. "Hippocrates: Diseases of Women I." *Signs* 1 (1975): 567–84.

———. "The Medical Writer's Woman." In *Before Sexuality: The Construction of Erotic Experience in the Ancient Greek World,* ed. David M. Halperin et al. Princeton, N.J.: Princeton University Press, 1990.

Hanson, Ann Ellis, and David Armstrong. "The Virgin's Voice and Neck: Aeschylus, *Agememnon* 245, and Other Texts." *British Institute of Classical Studies* 33 (1986): 97–100.

Harnack, Adolf von. "Das Magnificat der Elisabet (Luc 1, 46–55) nebst einigen Bemerkungen zu Luc.1 und 2." *Sitzungberichte der königlichen preussischen Akademie der Wissenschaften zu Berlin* (1900): 538–58.

———. *Die Chronologie der altchristlichen Literatur bis Eusebius.* 2 vols. Leipzig: J. C. Hinrichs, 1897–1904.

———. *Luke the Physician.* London and New York: Williams, and Norgate, G. P. Putnam's Sons, 1907.

Hasting, James, ed. *Encyclopedia of Religion and Ethics.* New York: Scribners, 1924–1927.

Hawkins, John Caesar. *Horae Synopticae: Contributions to the Study of the Synoptic Problem.* 2nd ed. Oxford: Clarendon Press, 1909.

Hebert, Arthur Gabriel. "The Virgin Mary as the Daughter of Zion." *Theology* 53 (1950): 403–10.

Hochman, Baruch. *Character in Literature.* Ithaca, N.Y.: Cornell University Press, 1985.

Hock, Ronald F. "Why New Testament Scholars Should Read Ancient Novels." In *Ancient Fiction and Early Christian Narrative,* ed. Ronald F. Hock, J. Bradley Chance, and Judith Perkins. SBL Symposium Series 6. Atlanta: Society of Biblical Literature, 1998.

Horsley, Richard. *The Liberation of Christmas: The Infancy Narratives in Social Context.* New York: Crossroad, 1989.

Horton, Fred L., Jr. "Parenthetical Pregnancy: The Conception and Birth of Jesus in Mt 1.18–25." *Society of Biblical Literature Seminar Papers* 26 (1987): 175–89.

Hunter, R. L. *A Study of Daphnis and Chloe.* Cambridge: Cambridge University Press, 1983.

Iser, Wolfgang. *The Act of Reading: A Theory of Aesthetic Response.* Baltimore: Johns Hopkins University Press, 1978.

———. *The Implied Reader: Patterns of Communication in Prose Fiction from Bunyan to Beckett.* Baltimore: Johns Hopkins University Press, 1974.

———. "Talk Like Whales: A Reply to Stanley Fish." *Diacritics* 11 (1981): 82–87.

Johnson, Elizabeth. "The Marian Tradition and the Reality of Women." *Horizon,* January 1985: 116–35.

———. "The Symbolic Character of Theological Statements about Mary." *Journal of Ecumenical Studies,* Spring 1985: 312–35.

Johnson, Luke Timothy. *The Acts of the Apostles.* Sacra Pagina. Collegeville, Minn.: Liturgical Press, 1992.

———. *The Gospel of Luke.* Sacra Pagina. Collegeville, Minn.: Liturgical Press, 1993.

———. *Letters to Paul's Delegates.* Valley Forge: Trinity Press International, 1997.

———. *The Literary Function of Possessions in Luke-Acts.* SBL Dissertation Series 39. Missoula: Scholars Press, 1977.

Kaestli, Jean-Daniel. "Les principales orientations de la recherche sur les Acts apocryphes des Apotres." In *Les Actes apocryphes des Apotres,* ed. François Bovon. Geneva: Labor et fides, 1981.

Kaltner, John. *Ishmael Instructs Isaac: An Introduction to the Qur'an for Bible Readers.* Collegeville, Minn.: Liturgical Press, 1999.

Keck, L., and J. L. Martyn, eds. *Studies in Luke-Act.* Philadelphia: Fortress Press, 1966.

Kerényi, Karl. *Athene: Virgin and Mother: A Study of Pallas Athene.* Trans. Murray Stein. Zurich: Spring Publications, 1978.

———. *Die griechisch-orientalische Romanliteratur in religionsgeschicht-*

licher Beleuchtung. Darmstadt: Wissenschaftliche Buchgesellschaft, 1962.

Kermode, Frank. *The Genesis of Secrecy: On the Interpretation of Narrative.* Cambridge, Mass.: Harvard University Press, 1979.

Keroloss, Heshmat. "Virginity in the Early Church: The Meaning and the Motives of Sexual Renunciation in the First Four Centuries." Ph.D. diss., Fordham University, 1996.

King, Helen. "Bound to Bleed: Artemis and Greek Women." In *Images of Women in Antiquity,* ed. Averil Cameron and Amelie Kuhrt. Detroit: Wayne State University Press, 1983.

———. *Hippocrates' Woman: Reading the Female Body in Ancient Greece.* London: Routledge, 1998.

———. "La Femme dans la médecin grecque." *La recherche* 209 (April): 462–69.

Kingsbury, Jack Dean. *Conflict in Luke: Jesus, Authorities, Disciples.* Minneapolis: Fortress Press, 1991.

Knight, G. A. F. "The Virgin and the Old Testament." *Reformed Theological Review* 12 (1953): 1–13.

Köster, Helmut. "Uberlieferung und Geschichte der früchristlichen Evangelienliteratur." *Aufstieg und Niedergang der römischen Welt* 2.25.2 (1984): 1463–1542.

Kraemer, Ross Shepard. *Her Share of the Blessings.* New York: Oxford University Press, 1992.

———. *When Asenath Met Joseph: A Late Antique Tale of the Biblical Patriarch and His Egyptian Wife Reconsidered.* New York: Oxford University Press, 1998.

Kuch, H. *Der antike Roman.* Berlin: Akademie-Verlag, 1989.

Kurz, William. *Reading Luke-Acts: Dynamics of Biblical Narrative.* Louisville: Westminster/John Knox Press, 1993.

Lake, Kirsopp, and Henry J. Cadbury, eds. *The Beginnings of Christianity.* Part I: *The Acts of the Apostles.* London, 1920.

Landry, David. "Narrative Logic in the Annunciation to Mary (Lk 1.26–38)." *Journal of Biblical Literature* 114 (1995): 65–79.

Lanser, Susan. *The Narrative Act: Point of View in Prose Fiction.* Princeton, N.J.: Princeton University Press, 1981.

Laqueur, Thomas. *Making Sex: Body and Gender from the Greeks to Freud.* Cambridge, Mass.: Harvard University Press, 1990.

Laurentin, Renée. *Jésus au Temple: Mystère de Paques et foi de Marie en Luc 2.48–50.* Paris: Gabalda, 1966.

———. *Structure et theologie de Luc 1–2.* Paris: Gabalda, 1957.

Lefkowitz, Mary R. *Women in Greek Myth.* Baltimore: Johns Hopkins University Press, 1986.

Limberis, Vasiliki. *Divine Heiress: The Virgin Mary and the Creation of Christian Constantinople.* London: Routledge, 1994.

Littlewood, A. R. "Romantic Paradises: The Role of the Garden in

Byzantine Romance." *Byzantine and Modern Greek Studies* 5 (1979): 95–114.

Locher, Clemens. *Die Ehre einer Frau in Israel.* Freiburg: Universitätsverlag; Göttingen: Vanderhoech and Ruprecht, 1986.

Loisy, Alfred. "L'origin du Magnificat." *Revue d'histoire et de littérature religieuse* 2 (1897): 424–32.

Lowe, M. "IOYDAIOI of the Apocrypha: A Fresh Approach to the Gospels of James, Pseudo-Thomas, Peter, and Nicodemus." *Novum Testamentum* 23 (1981): 56–90.

Luck, George. *Arcana Mundi: Magic and the Occult in the Greek and Roman Worlds.* Baltimore: Johns Hopkins University Press, 1985.

Lyonnet, Stanislaus, S.J. "Chaire Kecharitome." *Biblica* 20 (1939): 131–41.

———. "Le récit de l'Annunciation et la maternité divine de la Sainte Vierge." *Ami du Clergé* 66 (1956): 33–48. [Partially in English, "St. Luke's Infancy Narrative." In *Word and Mystery,* ed. L. J. O'Donovan. New York: Newman, 1968.]

MacDonald, Dennis R. *The Legend and the Apostle: The Battle for Paul in Story and Canon.* Philadelphia: Westminster Press, 1983.

Machen, J. G. *The Virgin Birth of Christ.* London: Marshall, Morgan, and Scott, 1930.

Macquarrie, John. *Mary for All Christians.* Grand Rapids, Mich.: William B. Eerdmans, 1990.

Maeckelberghe, Els. *Desperately Seeking Mary: A Feminist Interpretation of a Traditional Religious Symbol.* Kampen: Kok Pharos, 1991.

———. "Mary: Maternal Friend or Virgin Mother?" In *Concilium: Motherhood: Experience, Institution, Theology,* ed. Anne Carr and Elisabeth Schüssler Fiorenza. Edinburg: T. and T. Clark, 1989.

Malherbe, Abraham J. *Paul and the Popular Philosophers.* Minneapolis: Augsburg Fortress, 1989.

Malina, Bruce J., and Richard L. Rohrbaugh. *Social-Science Commentary on the Synoptic Gospels.* Minneapolis: Augsburg Fortress, 1992.

Martin, Dale. *The Corinthian Body.* New Haven, Conn.: Yale University Press, 1995.

Martin, R. "Syntactical Evidence of Aramaic Sources in Acts 1–15." *New Testament Studies* 11 (1964–65): 38–59.

Matter, E. Ann. "The Virgin Mary: A Goddess?" In *The Book of the Goddess,* ed. Carl Olson. New York: Crossroad, 1990.

McHugh, John. *The Mother of Jesus in the New Testament.* Garden City, N.Y.: Doubleday, 1975.

Meeks, Wayne. *The First Urban Christians.* New Haven, Conn.: Yale University Press, 1983.

———. *The Origins of Christian Morality.* New Haven, Conn.: Yale University Press, 1993.

Menzies, Robert P. *The Development of Early Christian Pneumatology with Special Reference to Luke-Acts.* Sheffield: JSOT Press, 1991.

Michaelis, Wilhelm. *Die Apokryphen Schriften zum Neuen Testament.* Bremen: C. Schünemann, 1956.

Michel, C. "Protévangile de Jacques." In *Évangiles Aprocryphes,* ed. H. Hemmer and P. Lejay. Paris: Auguste Picard, 1924.

———. *Einleitung in das Neues Testament: Die Entstehung, Sammlung und Veberlieferung der Schriften des Neuen Testaments.* Bern: Buchhandlung der Evangelischen Gesellschaft, 1946.

Miles, Margaret. *Carnal Knowing: Female Nakedness and Religious Meaning in the Christian West.* Boston: Beacon, 1989.

Minear, Paul S. "Luke's Use of the Birth Stories." In *Studies in Luke-Acts,* ed. L. Keck and J. L. Martyn. Philadelphia: Fortress Press, 1966.

———. *To Heal and to Reveal: The Prophetic Vocation According to Luke.* New York: Crossroad, 1976.

Moessner, David P. *Lord of the Banquet: The Literary and Theological Significance of the Lukan Travel Narrative.* Minneapolis: Fortress Press, 1989.

———. "The 'Script' of the Scriptures in the Acts of the Apostles: Suffering as God's 'Plan' (*boule*) for the 'Release of Sins.'" In *History, Literature and Society in the Book of Acts,* ed. Ben Witherington III. Cambridge: Cambridge University Press, 1996.

Moore, Stephen D. *Literary Criticism and the Gospels.* New Haven, Conn.: Yale University Press, 1989.

———. *Poststructuralism and the New Testament.* Philadelphia: Fortress Press, 1994.

Morgan, J. R. "Make-Believe and Make Believe: The Fictionality of Greek Novels." In *Lies and Fiction in the Ancient World,* ed. Christopher Gill and T. P. Wiseman. Exeter: University of Exeter Press, 1993.

Morgenthaler, Robert. *Die lukanische Geschichtsschreibung als Zeugnis: Gestalt und Gehelt der Kunst des Lukas.* 2 vols. Abhandlundlungen zur Theologie des Alten und Neuen Testaments 14–15. Zürich: Zwingli-Verlag, 1949.

———. *Statistik des neutestamentlichen Wortschatzes.* Zürich: Gotthelf-Verlag, 1958.

Mulvey, Laura. *Visual and Other Pleasures.* Houndsmill: Macmillan, 1989.

Neusner, Jacob. *A History of the Mishnaic Law of Purities.* Part 16: *Niddah: Literary and Historical Problems.* Leiden: E. J. Brill, 1977.

———. "From Scripture to Mishnah: The Origins of Mishnah's Division of Women." *Journal of Jewish Studies* 30 (1979): 138–53.

Neyrey, Jerome H. "The Symbolic Universe of Luke-Acts: 'They Turn the World Upside Down.'" In *The Social World of Luke-Acts:*

Models for Interpretation, ed. Jerome H. Neyrey. Peabody: Hendrickson, 1991.

Nolland, John. *Luke 1–9.10.* Word Biblical Commentary vol. 35A. Dallas: Word, 1989.

Norris, Richard. *The Christological Controversy.* Trans. and ed. Richard Norris. Philadelphia: Fortress Press, 1980.

O'Day, Gail. "Singing Woman's Song: A Hermeneutic of Liberation." *Currents in Theology and Mission* 12 (1985): 203–10.

Olyan, Saul. *Rites and Rank: Hierarchy in Biblical Representations of Cult.* Princeton, N.J.: Princeton University Press, 2000.

O'Rourke, John J. "Hypothesis Regarding 1 Corinthians 7:36–38." *Catholic Biblical Quarterly* 20 (1958): 292–98.

Overholt, Thomas W. *Channels of Prophecy: The Social Dynamics of Prophetic Activity.* Minneapolis: Augsburg Fortress, 1989.

Pagels, Elaine. *Adam, Eve, and the Serpent.* New York: Random House, 1988.

Parker, Robert. *Miasma: Pollution and Purification in Early Greek Religion.* Oxford: Oxford University Press, 1983.

Pelikan, Jaroslav. *Mary through the Centuries: Her Place in the History of Culture.* New Haven, Conn.: Yale University Press, 1996.

Perkins, Judith. *The Suffering Self: Pain and Narrative Representation in the Early Christian Era.* London: Routledge, 1995.

Perry, B. E. *The Ancient Romances: A Literary Historical Account of Their Origins.* Berkeley and Los Angeles: University of California Press, 1967.

Pervo, Richard I. *Profit with Delight: The Literary Genre of the Acts of the Apostles.* Philadelphia: Fortress Press, 1987.

Pervo, Richard I., and Mikeal Parsons, *Rethinking the Unity of Luke-Acts.* Minneapolis: Fortress Press, 1993.

Plummer, A. *A Critical and Exegetical Commentary on the Gospel According to St. Luke.* International Critical Commentary. 5th ed. New York: Scribner's Sons, 1922.

Pratscher, W. *Der Herrenbruder Jakobus und die Jakobustradition.* FRLANT 139. Göttingen: Vandenhoeck and Ruprecht, 1987.

Preuss, Julius. *Biblical and Talmudic Medicine.* Trans. Fred Rosner. New York: Sanhedrin Press, 1978.

———. *Biblisch-talmudische Medizin: Beiträge zur Geschichte der Heilkunde und der Kultur überhaupt.* Berlin: S. Karger,1921.

Räisänen, Heikki. *Die Mutter Jesu im Neuen Testament.* Helsinki: Suomalainen Tiedeakatemia, 1969.

Reardon, Bryan P. *Courants littéraires grecs des IIe et IIIe siecles.* Ann Litt Univ. Nantes 3. Paris: Les Belles Lettres, 1971.

———. *The Form of Greek Romance.* Princeton, N.J.: Princeton University Press, 1991.

Rhoads, David, and Kari Syreeni, eds. *Characterization in the Gospels: Reconceiving Narrative Criticism.* JSNT Supplement Series 184. Sheffield: Sheffield Academic Press, 1999.

Richlin, Amy, ed. *Pornography and Representation in Greece and Rome.* Oxford: Oxford University Press, 1992.

Robbins, Vernon K. *Exploring the Texture of Texts: A Guide to Socio-Rhetorical Interpretation.* Valley Forge: Trinity Press, 1996.

———. "The Reversed Contextualization of Psalm 22 in the Markan Crucifixion: A Socio-Rhetorical Analysis." In *The Four Gospels: 1992—In Honour of Frans Neirynck,* ed. J. Delobel et al. Leuven: University Press, 1992.

———. "Socio-Rhetorical Criticism: Mary, Elizabeth, and the Magnificat as a Test Case." In *The New Literary Criticism and the New Testament,* ed. Elizabeth Struthers Malbon and Edgar V. McKnight. JSNT Supplement Series 109. Sheffield: Sheffield Academic Press, 1994.

———. *The Tapestry of Early Christian Discourse: Rhetoric, Society, and Ideology.* London: Routledge, 1996.

Rohde, Erwin. *Der griesche roman und seine Vorlaüfer.* 5 Aufl. Hildesheim: Georg Olms, 1960.

Rousselle, Aline. "Observation Feminine et Idéologie Masculine, Le Corps de la Femme d'après les Médecins Grecs." *Annales: Économies, Sociétes, Civilisations* 35 (1980): 1089–115.

———. *Porneia: On Desire and the Body in Antiquity.* Trans. Felicia Pheasant. New York: Basil Blackwell, 1988; reprint 1993.

Ruether, Rosemary Radford. *Mary: The Feminine Face of the Church.* Philadelphia: Westminster Press, 1977.

———. *Sexism and God-Talk: Toward a Feminist Theology.* Boston: Beacon Press, 1983.

Sahlin, Harald. *Der Messias und das Gottesvolk: Studien zur protolukanischen Theologie.* ASNU 12. Uppsala: Almqvist and Wiksells, 1945.

Satlow, Michael L. *Tasting the Dish: Rabbinic Rhetorics of Sexuality.* Brown Judaic Studies 303. Atlanta: Scholars Press, 1995.

Schaberg, Jane. *The Illegitimacy of Jesus: A Feminist Theological Interpretation of the Infancy Narratives.* San Francisco: Harper and Row, 1987.

———. "Infancy of Mary of Nazareth." In *Searching the Scriptures,* ed. Elisabeth Schüssler Fiorenza with the assistance of Shelley Matthews. 2 vols. New York: Crossroad, 1993–1994.

Scholes, Robert, and Robert Kellogg. *The Nature of Narrative.* New York: Oxford University Press, 1966.

Schottroff, Louise. "Das Magnificat und de alteste Tradition uber Jesus von Nazareth." *Evangelische Theologie* 38 (1978): 298–313.

Schubert, Paul. "The Structure and Significance of Luke 24." In *Neutestamentliche Studien für Rudolf Bultmann*. BZNW 21. Berlin: Alfred Topelmann, 1954.

Schwartz, Regina, ed. *The Book and the Text: The Bible and Literary Theory*. Oxford: Basil Blackwell, 1990.

Seboldt, Roland H. A. "Spiritual Marriage in the Early Church: A Suggested Interpretation of 1 Cor. 7. 36–38." *Concordia Theological Monthly* 30 (Feb. 1959): 103–19; (Mar. 1959): 176–89.

Seim, Turid Karlsen. *The Double Message: Patterns of Gender in Luke-Acts*. Nashville: Abingdon Press, 1994.

Shepherd, William H., Jr. *The Narrative Function of the Holy Spirit as a Character in Luke-Acts*. SBL Dissertation Series. Atlanta: Scholars Press, 1994.

Sissa, Giulia. *Greek Virginity*. Trans. Arthur Goldhammer. Cambridge, Mass.: Harvard University Press, 1990.

———. "Sexual Philosophies of Plato and Aristotle." In *A History of Women in the West*. Vol. 1: *From Ancient Goddesses to Christian Saints,* ed. Pauline Schmitt Pantel. Cambridge, Mass.: Belknap, 1992.

Smid, H. R. *Protevangelium Jacobi: A Commentary*. Apocrypha Novi Testamenti, vol. 1. Assen: Van Gorcum, 1965.

Söder, Rosa. *Die apokryphen Apostelgeschichten und die romanhafte Literatur der Antike*. Stuttgart: W. Kohlhammer Verlag, 1932; reprint, Darmstadt: Wissenschaftliche Buchgesellschaft, 1969.

Spencer, F. Scott. "Out of Mind, Out of Voice: Slave-Girls and Prophetic Daughters in Luke-Acts." *Biblical Interpretation* 7, no. 2 (1999): 133–55.

Spitta, F. "Die chronologischen Notizen und die Hymnen in Lc 1 u.2." *Zeitschrift für die Neutestamentliche Wissenschaft* 7 (1906): 281–317.

———. "Das Magnificat ein Psalm der Maria und nicht der Elisabeth." In *Theologische Anhandlungen, eine Festgabe zum 17 Mai 1902 für Heinrich Julius Holtzmann*. Tübingen: J. C. B. Mohr [Paul Siebeck], 1902.

Staples, Ariadne. *From Good Goddess to Vestal Virgins: Sex and Category in Roman Religion*. London: Routledge, 1998.

Sternberg, Meier. *The Poetics of Biblical Narrative: Ideological Literature and the Drama of Reading*. Bloomington: Indiana University Press, 1985.

Streeter, B. H. *The Four Gospels: A Study of Origins*. London, 1924.

Strelan, Rick. *Paul, Artemis, and the Jews in Ephesus*. Beihefte zur Zeitschrift für die neutestamentliche Wissenschaft und die Kunde der älteren Kirche. Herausgegeben von Erich Grässer, Band 80. Berlin: Walter de Gruyter, 1996.

Talbert, Charles H. *Literary Patterns, Theological Themes, and the Genre of Luke-Acts.* SBLMS 20. Missoula: Scholars Press, 1971.

———. "Prophecies of Future Greatness: The Contribution of Greco-Roman Biographies to an Understanding of Luke 1.5–4.15." In *The Divine Helmsman: Studies on God's Control of Human Events, presented to Lou H. Silberman,* ed. James L. Crenshaw and Samuel Sandmel. New York: KTAV Publishing House, 1980.

———. *Reading Luke.* New York: Crossroad, 1982.

Tannehill, Robert. "The Magnificat as Mary's Poem." *Journal of Biblical Literature* 93 (1974): 263–75.

———. *The Narrative Unity of Luke-Acts.* 2 vols. Philadelphia and Minneapolis: Fortress Press, 1986 and 1990.

Tapp, Ann Michele. "An Ideology of Expendability: Virgin Daughter Sacrifice in Genesis 19:1–11, Judges 11.30–39 and 19.22–26." In *Anti-Covenant: Counter-Reading Women's Lives in the Hebrew Bible,* ed. Mieke Bal. Sheffield: Almond Press, 1989.

Taylor, Vincent. *The Formation of the Gospel Tradition.* London, 1933.

Thomas, Christine M. "Stories without Texts and without Authors: The Problem of Fluidity in Ancient Novelistic Texts and Early Christian Literature." In *Ancient Fiction and Early Christian Narrative,* ed. Ronald F. Hock, J. Bradley Chance, and Judith Perkins. SBL Symposium Series 6. Atlanta: Society of Biblical Literature, 1998.

Tolbert, M. *Sowing the Gospel: Mark's World in Literary-Historical Perspective.* Minneapolis: Fortress Press, 1989.

Torrey, Charles Cutler. "Medina and Polis and Luke 1.39." *Harvard Theological Review* 17 (1924): 83–91.

———. "The Translations Made from the Original Aramaic Gospels." In *Studies in the History of Religions,* ed. Crawford Howell Toy, David Gordon Lyon, and George Foot Moore. London: Macmillan, 1912.

Trible, Phyllis. "Eve and Miriam: From the Margins to the Center." In *Feminist Approaches to the Bible,* ed. Hershel Shanks. Washington, D.C.: Biblical Archaeology Society, 1995.

Turner, N. "The Relationship of Luke 1 and 2 to Hebraic Sources and to the Rest of Luke and Acts." *New Testament Studies* 2 (1955–56): 100–109.

Tyson, Joseph B. "The Birth Narratives and the Beginning of Luke's Gospel." *Semeia* 52 (1990): 103–20.

Urbach, Ephraim E. *The Sages: Their Concepts and Beliefs.* Cambridge, Mass.: Harvard University Press, 1987.

van Stempvoort, P. A. "The Protevangelium Jacobi: The Sources of Its Theme and Style and Their Bearing on Its Date." In *Studia*

Evangelica 3, ed. F. Cross. TU 88. Berlin: Akademie-Verlag, 1959.

Vernant, Jean-Pierre. *Mortals and Immortals: Collected Essays.* Ed. Froma I. Zeitlin. Princeton, N.J.: Princeton University Press, 1991.

Vielhauer, Philipp. "Apokryphe Apostelgeschichten." In *Geschichte der urchristlichen Literatur.* New York: Walter de Gruyter, 1975.

———. "Das Benedictus des Zacharias (Lk 1.68–69)." *Zeitschrift für Theologie und Kirche* 49 (1952): 255ff.

———. "On the 'Paulinisms' of Acts." Trans. William C. Robinson, Jr. and Victor P. Furnish. In *Studies in Luke-Acts,* ed. Leander Keck and J. Louis Martyn. Philadephia: Fortress Press, 1966.

Vööbus, Authur. *Celibacy: A Requirement for Admission to Baptism in the Early Syrian Church.* Papers of the Estonian Theological Society in Exile 1. Stockholm: Etse, 1951.

Vorster, W. S. "The Annunciation of the Birth of Jesus in the Protevangelium of James." In *A South African Perspective on the New Testament,* ed. J. Petzer and P. Hartin. Leiden: E. J. Brill, 1986.

———. "The Protevangelium of James and Intertextuality." In *Text and Testimony: Essays on New Testament and Apocryphal Literature in Honour of A. F. J. Klijn,* ed. T. Baarda et al. Kampen: J. H. Kok, 1988.

Washington, Harold C. "Violence and the Construction of Gender in the Hebrew Bible: A New Historicist Approach." *Biblical Interpretation* 5, no. 4 (1997): 324–64.

Weaver, Mary Jo. *New Catholic Women: A Contemporary Challenge to Traditional Religious Authority.* San Francisco: Harper and Row, 1985.

Wegner, Judith Romney. *Chattel or Person? The Status of Women in the Mishnah.* Oxford: Oxford University Press, 1988.

Weiss, Bernhard. *Die Quellen der synoptischen Ueberlieferung.* Göttingen: Vanderhoech and Ruprecht, 1908.

Wilson, R. "Some Recent Studies in the Lucan Infancy Narratives." In *Studia Evangelica 3,* ed. F. Cross. TU 88. Berlin: Akademie-Verlag, 1959.

Wilson, Robert R. *Prophecy and Society in Ancient Israel.* Philadelphia: Fortress Press, 1980.

Wilson, S. G. *Luke and the Law.* SNTS Monograph Series 50. Cambridge: Cambridge University Press, 1983.

Winkler, John J., ed. *The Constraints of Desire.* New York: Routledge, 1990.

Winter, Paul. "Magnificat and Benedictus—Maccabean Psalms?" *Bulletin of the John Rylands Library of the University of Manchester* 37 (1954): 328–47.

———. "Some Observations on the Language in the Birth and Infancy

Stories of the Third Gospel." *New Testament Studies* 1 (1954–55): 111–21.

Witherington, Ben, III. *Women in the Earliest Churches.* New York: Cambridge University Press, 1991.

York, John O. *The Last Shall Be First: The Rhetoric of Reversal in Luke.* JSNT Supplement 46. Sheffield: Sheffield Academic Press, 1991.

Zeitlin, Froma I. "The Poetics of *Eros:* Nature, Art, and Imitation in Longus' *Daphnis and Chloe.*" In *Before Sexuality: The Construction of Erotic Experience in the Ancient Greek World,* ed. David M. Halperin et al. Princeton, N.J.: Princeton University Press, 1990.

Zervos, George T. "Prolegomena to a Critical Edition of the Genesis Marias [Protevangelium Jacobi]: The Greek Manuscripts." Ph.D. diss., Duke University, 1986.

Index

male gaze, 123
Marian tradition, 20
Mariology, 162
marital status, 25, 26
marriage, 35, 60; age of, 62, 71, 150;
deceased fathers and, 53; economics of, 44–50; honor and,
61; Jewish valuation of, 45–50;
puberty and, 50; rape and, 53,
54; rejection of, 104, 106; Roman valuation of, 44–45; sexual
desire in, 72
Martin, Dale, 33, 35, 182n24; on *hyperakmos,* 49–50; on sexuality
of prophecy, 37, 38–39
Mary (the Virgin): biography of, 3;
birth of, 141, 143–145; constructions of, 3, 4–8; as exemplar of faith, 120–124; Jesus'
ministry and, 135; as literary
figure, 4; as moral subject, 155–
156; as mother of Jesus, 10–11;
as object of praise, 125–126; as
parthenos, 16–19, 21, 142, 147,
155, 160, 163; as personification
of Israel, 136, 138, 140; portrayals in Luke-Acts, 10–20, 114–
120; portrayals in Protevangelium of James (PJ), 20–22,
141–164; praise of, 145–146,
160; pregnancy of, 16–17,
132, 134, 151–152, 153, 161,
206n44; as prophet, 14–15, 19,
128–132; as Pure Virgin of
the Lord, 148–150; as site of divine activity, 152–153; socio-
economic status of, 128, 134,
178n86; as symbol, 4, 12–13,
140; from virgin to mother,
133–136; virginity of, 1, 6, 119,
120; as witness, 136–140. *See
also* characterization of Mary;
sexual status of Mary
Masoretic Text, 16, 188n107
Matthew, Gospel of, 1, 153
medical literature, 25, 29–36, 148
Meeks, Wayne, 55, 187n102
menstruation, 147, 149, 181n16;
betulah designation and, 48;
health and, 33, 34, 35
Merenlahti, Petri, 4–5
messianism, 118
meter (mother), 132, 133, 159, 160;
Jesus' definition of, 137; virgin
transformed into, 134–136

midwives, 31, 157, 158
mimesis, 92, 95, 98, 167n16
Miscellanies (Clement of Alexandria), 71–72
Mishnah, 46, 47, 61, 117; on age of
marriage, 150; on assumption of
virginity, 47; on betrothed virgins, 52–53; on Mary's purity,
149; on place of minor daughters, 48–49; on rape, 50, 52;
temple cult in, 188n103
misogyny, 2
moisture, 34, 35, 39
Morgan, J. R., 76
Moses (biblical), 13, 36, 37, 68, 134
motherhood. *See meter* (mother)

naarah (girl, maiden), 53, 84,
188n107
naming, 121
nature, 51, 78, 88, 92, 93, 95
Nestorius, 10
New Historicism, 7
New Testament, 3, 16, 80, 171n36;
body metaphor in, 57–58; interpretation of, 7; Protevangelium
of James (PJ) and, 142
novels, ancient, 75–80, 194n5

Olyan, Saul, 148–149
On the Veiling of Virgins (Tertul-
lian), 70
Origen, 72, 173n49, 176n70
Orphism, 70
ovaries, 31
Ovid, 51, 54, 62

paganism, 36, 69, 133, 178n77; ascetic cults, 70; infancy narratives and, 18
paideia (instruction), 92–98
Parker, Robert, 68, 70
parthenia. See virginity
parthenos/parthenoi. See virgins
patriarchy, 48, 68
patristic writers, 10
Paul (apostle), 49, 57, 60–61,
104–108
Pausanias, 36, 38, 69
Pelikan, Jaroslav, 2
penis, 30, 31, 184n49
Perkins, Judith, 77
personality, 4, 5
Pervo, Richard I., 77, 80
Pharisees, 7

Mary F. Foskett is Assistant Professor of Religion at Wake Forest University.